Doctrine and Covenants

Who's WHO

ILLUSTRATED EDITION

Doctrine and Covenants

Who's WHO

ILLUSTRATED EDITION

A Comprehensive Guide to the People in the Doctrine and Covenants

Ed J. Pinegar · Richard J. Allen

Covenant Communications, Inc.

Front cover images (clockwise from top left): *The Angel Moroni Appearing to Joseph Smith* by Tom Lovell © Intellectual Reserve, Inc.; *Emma Hale Smith* image provided by Community of Christ Archives, Independence, Missouri. Used with permission.; *Organization of the Relief Society* by Nadine Barton © Intellectual Reserve, Inc.; *First Vision* © Greg Olsen Publishing Inc. For more information visit www.gregolsenart.com or call 208.888.2585.; *Joseph Smith, Sr.* by William Whitaker © Intellectual Reserves, Inc.; Courtesy of the The Museum of Church History and Art.; *Joseph and Hyrum Standing Near River* (Nauvoo in Background) by Theodore Gorka © Intellectual Reserve, Inc.; Parley P. Pratt. Courtesy of LDS Church Archives, Salt Lake City, Utah.; *Elijah Restoring the Melchizedek Priesthood* © Robert T. Barrett; *An Angel Shows the Gold Plates to Joseph Smith, Oliver Cowdery, and David Whitmer* © William L. Maughan.; Brigham Young. Courtesy of LDS Church Archives, Salt Lake City, Utah.; *Eight Witnesses Shown the Gold Plates* © Paul Mann; *Go Ye Into the Wilderness* by Robert T. Barrett © Intellectual Reserve, Inc.; *More than Friends* © Liz Lemon Swindle. Used with permission from Foundation Arts. For print information visit www.foundationarts.com or call 1.800.366.2781.; Martin Harris. Courtesy of LDS Church Archives, Salt Lake City, Utah.

Back cover and spine image: Joseph Smith and Orson Pratt © Robert T. Barrett.

Cover design copyrighted 2008 by Covenant Communications, Inc.

Published by Covenant Communications, Inc.
American Fork, Utah

Printed in the United States of America
First Printing: October 2008

15 14 13 12 11 10 09 08   10 9 8 7 6 5 4 3 2

ISBN 10: 1-59811-699-1
ISBN 13: 978-1-59811-699-1

PREFACE

Just as the Book of Mormon is "Another Testament of Jesus Christ," the Doctrine and Covenants is a modern, latter-day testament of Jesus Christ the Redeemer and the restoration of His covenants as promised by the prophets through the ages. The Doctrine and Covenants is therefore a dynamic chronicle of His dealings with mankind as the Architect of the Kingdom of God and the "author of eternal salvation unto all them that obey him" (Heb. 5:9). The pages of this scripture unfold the design of the Lord to sanctify His people through covenant practices and ordinances—line upon line and precept upon precept (D&C 98:12; 128:21; Isa. 29:10, 13; 2 Ne. 28:30)—and endow them with truth and light for the journey back home into His presence. In this sacred volume, His voice of loving kindness and compassionate warning calls together His people to follow the prophets in faith, worship in truth and valor, and assist tirelessly in the campaign to gather Israel's remnants from the four quarters of the earth in preparation for His millennial reign.

Reinforced throughout the Doctrine and Covenants are godly attributes all people are commanded to emulate to become "partakers of the divine nature" (2 Pet. 1:4) and rise to their potential as "children of the covenant" (3 Ne. 20:26). The Doctrine and Covenants testifies of the life and mission of the Holy One of Israel and manifests God's love in personal, moving, and inspiring ways through the miracle of the Atonement.

Doctrine and Covenants Who's Who examines the lives of all individuals referenced in the Doctrine and Covenants—not just the contemporaries of the Prophet Joseph Smith and his immediate successors, but also prophets of former times and ministrants of heaven who played a vital role in the Restoration of the gospel in the latter days. The Lord, in His wisdom, called elect individuals into the service of Zion in the last days as in the former days: "Unto whom I have committed the keys of my kingdom, and a dispensation of the gospel for the last times; and for the fulness of times, in the which I will gather together in one all things, both which are in heaven, and which are on earth" (D&C 27:13; compare Eph. 1:10). The Doctrine and Covenants is a guidebook for gathering all things into one. In its pages are gathered together the old and the new, former prophets and modern prophets, former Saints and latter-day Saints—all with the divine design to "bring to pass the immortality and eternal life of man" (Moses 1:39). In the pages of that sacred volume Adam, Abraham, Moses, Elijah, and Moroni are at home with Joseph Smith, Hyrum Smith, Heber C. Kimball, and Brigham Young. It is a blending together of many voices, many deeds of nobility and service, and many dispensations of time.

Some 238 entries are included in this *Who's Who* collection, of which 135 deal with contemporaries of the Prophet Joseph Smith, four with general authorities of the Church in more recent times, and most of the remainder with figures from former dispensations, many of whom played a key role in the unfolding of the Restoration. Also included is a detailed treatment of the mission of the Prophet Joseph Smith, plus a thorough analysis of the central figures of divinity as presented in the Doctrine and Covenants: Heavenly Father, His Son Jesus Christ, and the Holy Ghost.

It is instructive to consider the pattern of living of the contemporaries of Joseph Smith, all of whom were part of the fairly contained circle of participants in the extraordinary developments associated with the Restoration. How did they respond to the compelling evidence of divine manifestations taking place around them at the time? To what degree of obedience did they rise in supporting the Prophet Joseph Smith and the Kingdom of God in the latter days? The answers to these questions provide great lessons concerning the importance of embracing the covenants of salvation and exaltation and honoring what Nephi called the fundamental urgency to "press forward with a steadfastness in Christ, having a perfect brightness of hope, and a love of God and of all men" (2 Ne. 31:20).

By contrast, some of the case studies in the Doctrine and Covenants contain precisely what the Prophet Joseph Smith warned about from Liberty Jail:

> Behold, there are many called, but few are chosen. And why are they not chosen?
>
> Because their hearts are set so much upon the things of this world, and aspire to the honors of men, that they do not learn this one lesson—
>
> That the rights of the priesthood are inseparably connected with the powers of heaven, and that the powers of heaven cannot be controlled nor handled only upon the principles of righteousness. (D&C 121:34–36)

The Doctrine and Covenants describes the options that lie before each man, woman, and child and which choices will bring eternal joy and everlasting glory. Faith, charity, love, pure knowledge, and virtue will bring greater confidence in the presence of God and bring more truth and light into the lives of mankind: "The Holy Ghost shall be thy constant companion, and thy scepter an unchanging scepter of righteousness and truth; and thy dominion shall be an everlasting dominion, and without compulsory means it shall flow unto thee forever and ever" (D&C 121:46).

Through a careful and prayerful study of the Doctrine and Covenants, one can appreciate the extraordinary blessings the Lord has poured out upon the world in this, the dispensation of the fulness of times. The Kingdom of God is once again restored to the earth. A living prophet holds the keys of the priesthood and administers in all matters as the Lord's mouthpiece. As the Lord's representative upon the earth, the Prophet exhorts the Saints to preach the gospel to every nation, kindred, tongue, and people; counsels them to perform spiritual work for the dead; and entreats them to perfect themselves and prepare to perform their duties with valor. He asks that they stand in holy places for protection and enlightenment, gather often to partake of the sacrament and renew covenants, and make themselves instruments in the hand of the Lord in bringing souls unto Him. The Doctrine and Covenants is the book of revelations designated to teach these duties and responsibilities in the latter days and help prepare the honest in heart for the Second Coming.

The authors wish to thank those whose previous publications have provided historical facts and details concerning many of the personalities included in the Doctrine and Covenants; in particular, Lyndon W. Cook, *The Revelations of the Prophet Joseph Smith: A Historical and Biographical Commentary of the Doctrine and Covenants* (Salt Lake City: Deseret Book, 1985); Hoyt W. Brewster

Jr., *Doctrine and Covenants Encyclopedia* (Salt Lake City: Bookcraft, 1996); and Susan Easton Black, *Who's Who in the Doctrine & Covenants* (Salt Lake City: Bookcraft, 1997). The authors also express sincere appreciation for the support of the staff of Covenant Communications and their interest in producing this volume. Special thanks go to the managing editor, Kathryn Jenkins, and to her colleagues, editor Kat Gille, art director Margaret Weber, and graphic designer Heather Wiscombe, who worked tirelessly to bring this work to fruition. Gratitude is also extended to the artists and illustrators who have provided remarkable pictorial assets to enrich this volume and bring to life its contents. And finally, special thanks go to Pat Pinegar, wife of Ed Pinegar, and Carol Lynn Allen, wife of Richard Allen, for their support and encouragement.

The Authors

TABLE OF CONTENTS

ABBREVIATIONS

AGQ Joseph Fielding Smith, *Answers to Gospel Questions*, 5 vols. (Salt Lake City: Deseret Book, 1957, 1958, 1960, 1963, 1966)

APPP Parley P. Pratt, *Autobiography of Parley P. Pratt*, ed. by his son Parley P. Pratt (Salt Lake City: Deseret Book, 1985)

AQDC Richard O. Cowan, *Answers to Your Questions About the Doctrine and Covenants* (Salt Lake City: Deseret Book, 1996)

CHFT *Church History in the Fulness of Times*, rev. ed. (Salt Lake City: Corporation of the President of The Church of Jesus Christ of Latter-day Saints, 1993)

CHMR Joseph Fielding Smith, *Church History and Modern Revelation*, 4 vols. (Salt Lake City: Deseret Book, 1947–50)

DCC Hyrum M. Smith and Janne M. Sjodahl, *Doctrine and Covenants Commentary* (Salt Lake City: Deseret Book, 1978)

DCE Hoyt W. Brewster Jr., *Doctrine and Covenants Encyclopedia* (Salt Lake City: Bookcraft, 1996)

DCOMS Richard O. Cowan, *The Doctrine and Covenants: Our Modern Scripture* (Salt Lake City: Bookcraft, 1984)

DNTC Bruce R. McConkie, *Doctrinal New Testament Commentary*, 3 vols. (Salt Lake City: Bookcraft, 1973)

DS Joseph Fielding Smith, *Doctrines of Salvation*, 3 vols. (Salt Lake City: Bookcraft, 1954–56)

EM *Encyclopedia of Mormonism*, ed. Daniel H. Ludlow, 4 vols. (New York: Macmillan, 1992)

FAR Kent P. Jackson, *From Apostasy to Restoration* (Salt Lake City: Deseret Book, 1996)

HC Joseph Smith, *History of The Church of Jesus Christ of Latter-day Saints*, 7 vols., introduction and notes by B. H. Roberts (Salt Lake City: The Church of Jesus Christ of Latter-day Saints, 1932–51)

JD   *Journal of Discourses*, 26 vols. (London: Latter-day Saints' Book Depot, 1854–86)

JST   Joseph Smith Translation of the Bible

LDSBE   Andrew Jenson, *LDS Biographical Encyclopedia: A Compilation of Biographical Sketches of Prominent Men and Women in the Church of Jesus Christ of Latter-day Saints*, 4 vols. (Salt Lake City, 1901)

MA   John Taylor, *Mediation and Atonement* (Salt Lake City: Deseret News Company, 1882)

MD   Bruce R. McConkie, *Mormon Doctrine*, 2nd ed. (Salt Lake City: Bookcraft, 1966)

PPRG   Victor L. Ludlow, *Principles and Practices of the Restored Gospel* (Salt Lake City: Deseret Book, 1992)

RPJS   Lyndon W. Cook, *The Revelations of the Prophet Joseph Smith: A Historical and Biographical Commentary of the Doctrine and Covenants* (Salt Lake City: Deseret Book, 1985)

TPJS   Joseph Smith, *Teachings of the Prophet Joseph Smith* (Salt Lake City: Deseret Book, 1976)

WJS   Joseph Smith, *The Words of Joseph Smith: The Contemporary Accounts of the Nauvoo Discourses of the Prophet Joseph*, comp. Andrew F. Ehat and Lyndon W. Cook, 2nd ed. (Provo, UT: Grandin Book, 1996)

WWDC   Susan Easton Black, *Who's Who in the Doctrine & Covenants* (Salt Lake City: Bookcraft, 1997)

A

AARON

Aaron, older brother of Moses (see Ex. 7:7), assisted with the Exodus from Egypt and served as spokesman for Moses (Ex. 4:10–16, 37–31; 5:1–12). Aaron and his progeny served in the functions of the lesser or Aaronic Priesthood (Ex. 28:1–4). Aaron is mentioned twenty-seven times in the text of the Doctrine and Covenants. The word *Aaronic* occurs three times in the text of the Doctrine and Covenants (D&C 107:1, 6, 20) and once in Official Declaration—2. The Aaronic Priest-

hood was restored in the latter days under the hands of John the Baptist on May 15, 1829 (see D&C 13).

ABEL

Abel, son of Adam and Eve (see Gen. 4:4; Heb. 11:4), is mentioned twice in the text of the Doctrine and Covenants: once in connection with the descent of the priesthood lineage—"And from Enoch to Abel, who was slain by the conspiracy of his brother, who received the priesthood by the commandments of God, by the hand of his father Adam, who was the first man" (D&C 84:16)—and once again as one of the elect personages viewed by President Joseph F. Smith in his vision of the spirit realm: "Abel, the first martyr, was there, and his brother Seth, one of the mighty ones, who was in the express image of his father, Adam" (D&C 138:40).

ABRAHAM (SEE ALSO ELIAS)

Abraham—father of Isaac, grandfather of Jacob, and great-grandfather of Joseph—was the exemplary patriarch whose descendants

Aaron

1

carried forth the cause of the Abrahamic covenant to spread the blessings of the gospel of salvation and the priesthood of God to the world (Abr. 2:9–11). The Lord revealed to Joseph Smith details of a glorious future sacred meeting when all the faithful prophets of old would convene again, including "Joseph and Jacob, and Isaac, and Abraham, your fathers, by whom the promises remain" (D&C 27:10). The Lord declared the exaltation of Abraham, Isaac, and Jacob, who "because they did none other things than that which they were commanded, they have entered into their exaltation, according to the promises, and sit upon thrones, and are not angels but are gods" (D&C 132:37). Those who live up to the oath and covenant of the priesthood "become the sons of Moses and of Aaron and the seed of Abraham, and the church and kingdom, and the elect of God" (D&C 84:34).

On April 3, 1836, "Elias appeared, and committed the dispensation of the gospel of Abraham" (D&C 110:12). Thus the priesthood stewardship of the Abrahamic covenant was delegated to Joseph Smith in the dispensation of the fullness of times: "And as I said unto Abraham concerning the kindreds of the earth, even so I say unto my servant Joseph: In thee and in thy seed shall the kindred of the earth be blessed" (D&C 124:58). In terms of the ordinances of the new and everlasting covenant, the Lord has commanded: "Go ye, therefore, and do the works of Abraham; enter ye into my law and ye shall be saved" (D&C 132:32). Joseph Smith saw Father Abraham, "the father of the faithful" (D&C 138:41), among those manifested in his vision of the future world of glory (D&C 137:5). Abraham is mentioned in the text of the Doctrine and Covenants thirty-seven times.

ADAM

Adam (known as Michael in the premortal realm) is mentioned twenty-nine times in the Doctrine and Covenants (plus ten times as Michael). His presence is manifested in the events associated with the restoration of powers and truths in the latter days through the Prophet Joseph Smith:

> And the voice of Michael, the archangel; the voice of Gabriel, and of Raphael, and of divers angels, from Michael or Adam down to the present time, all declaring their dispensation, their rights, their keys, their honors, their majesty and glory, and the power of their priesthood. (D&C 128:21; see also D&C 128:18; 136:37)

Adam is also a participant in the Prophet Joseph Smith's remarkable vision of the celestial world of glory (see D&C 137:5) and in President Joseph F. Smith's vision of the work of salvation inaugurated by the Savior in the spiritual realm (see D&C 138:38, 40). Adam is depicted in various extraordinary settings yet to occur, including the future glorious meeting when all the faithful prophets of old shall convene again, including "Michael, or Adam, the father of all, the prince of all, the ancient of days" (D&C 27:11) and the gathering at Adam-ondi-Ahman where the Savior, at the dawning of His millennial reign, will receive back the keys dispensed to various prophets through the ages, beginning with Adam (see D&C 107:53, 54, 55, 56; 116:1; 117:8). In the capacity as Michael, the archangel, Adam plays a central role in the events associated with the final stages of the earth's history (see D&C 29:6; 88:112, 113, 115).

Adam

The Doctrine and Covenants also mentions Adam in the context of the first man on earth (see D&C 29:34, 36, 40, 42) and as a key figure in the sequence of events associated with the succession of priesthood lineage (see D&C 84:16; 107:41, 42, 44–48, 50). The following characterization of the commission given to Michael (Adam) provides a sense of his importance in the Lord's design for the salvation of mankind: "Who hath appointed Michael your prince, and established his feet, and set him upon high, and given unto him the keys of salvation under the counsel and direction of the Holy One, who is without beginning of days or end of life" (D&C 78:16).

AHMAN (SEE SON AHMAN)

ANCIENT OF DAYS (SEE ALSO ADAM)

This title was given to Adam (see D&C 116:1).

ANGEL ASCENDING FROM THE EAST (SEE ALSO ELIAS)

Section 77 of the Doctrine and Covenants provides inspired commentary on various passages written by John the Revelator, including the following reference: "And I saw another angel ascending from the east, having the seal of the living God: and he cried with a loud voice to the four angels, to whom it was given to hurt the earth and the sea" (Rev. 7:2). Latter-day scripture asks the question:

> Q. What are we to understand by the angel ascending from the east, Revelation 7th chapter and 2nd verse?
> A. We are to understand that the angel ascending from the east is he to whom is given the seal of the living God over the twelve tribes of Israel; wherefore, he crieth unto the four angels having the everlasting gospel, saying: Hurt not the earth, neither the sea, nor the trees, till we have sealed the servants of our God in their foreheads. And, if you will receive it, this is Elias which was to come to gather together the tribes of Israel and restore all things. (D&C 77:9)

Concerning this passage, President Joseph Fielding Smith observed that

> the restoration of the Gospel did not come through just one messenger, but there are several who came and bestowed their keys of authority and power. The name Elias is a title. This we have been taught by the Prophet Joseph Smith (*Teachings*, 335). Is it not possible, therefore, since so many ancient prophets had a hand in the restoration, that in speaking of the Elias who was to come and restore all things, do we not have a composite picture of several Eliases, rather than one single individual? The angel with the seal

directs the four angels holding the destiny of the world in their hands, not to hurt the earth until the servants of the Lord have been sealed. This could not be accomplished until the Gospel was restored and proclaimed to the nations of the earth. (CHMR, 2:71)

ANGELS

In a revelation given through the Prophet Joseph Smith at Nauvoo, February 9, 1843, the Lord declares that there are two kinds of beings in heaven: angels as resurrected personages with bodies of flesh and bones and the unembodied "spirits of just men made perfect" (D&C

Joseph, Nauvoo Temple

129:3). (For more details, see the entry entitled "Spirits of Just Men Made Perfect.")

APOLLOS

Apollos was an Alexandrian Jew and contemporary of the apostle Paul known for his eloquence and scriptural mastery (see Acts 18:24–19:1; 1 Cor. 1:12; 3:4–6, 22; 4:6; 16:12; Titus 3:13). In section 76 of the Doctrine and Covenants, concerning the degrees of glory, those in the telestial kingdom are characterized as having denied the testimony of the Savior, though they might verbally claim allegiance to Christ, John, Moses, Elias, Isaiah, Enoch, Paul, Apollos, or some other movement (see D&C 76:99).

ASHLEY, MAJOR N.

Major (a proper name rather than a military title) was born on March 3, 1798, in Sheffield, Berkshire County, Massachusetts. By 1831 he had been baptized a member of the Church and ordained to the office of high priest. He was called by revelation to serve as a missionary (see D&C 75:17). It is not known whether he served in this capacity. In July 1832 he was active as a tanner in Missouri. When the Saints were forced to leave Jackson Country, Missouri, Major denied the faith and lost his fellowship in the Church.

BABBITT, ALMON

Almon was born on October 1, 1812, at Cheshire, Berkshire County, Massachusetts. He participated in Zion's Camp, sent to bring relief to the suffering Saints in Missouri, and was ordained to the First Quorum of Seventy on February 28, 1835. However, his early membership in the Church was marred by charges of minimizing the essential role of the Book of Mormon, speaking ill of the Prophet Joseph Smith, and failing to live the Word of Wisdom. He was later rebuked for countering the Prophet's counsel to the Saints to gather to Nauvoo and for other conduct unbecoming of a priesthood holder. After such charges had been dealt with, Almon, a lawyer by training, was called on October 19, 1840, to be the president of the Kirtland Stake. On January 19, 1841, the Lord revealed through the Prophet Joseph Smith that "with my servant Almon Babbitt, there are many things with which I am not pleased; behold, he aspireth to establish his counsel instead of the counsel which I have ordained, even that of the Presidency of my Church; and he setteth up a golden calf for the worship of my people" (D&C 124:84). Failing to respond to this counsel, Almon was disfellowshipped in October 1841. On March 13, 1843, he was restored to fellowship and made presiding elder of the branch in Ramus, Illinois. He later refused to come to the Prophet's aid on the eve of the Martyrdom. After joining the Saints in the Salt Lake Valley, he was active in working toward statehood for the Territory of Utah. President Franklin Pierce appointed him secretary to the territory, but Almon, given his past behavior, was not universally trusted by Church leaders. While traveling from Washington, DC, to Salt Lake City, he was killed in Nebraska by Cheyenne Indians on September 7, 1856.

BAKER, JESSE

Jesse was born on January 23, 1778, at Charlestown, Washington County, Rhode Island. He joined the Church in Ohio and was ordained an elder by 1837. His migration to Missouri was short-lived, as persecution took its toll, forcing the Saints to seek refuge in Illinois. In the only reference to him in the Doctrine and Covenants, Jesse was appointed by revelation on January 19, 1841, to be a counselor to John Hicks in the presidency of the elders quorum (see D&C 124:137). Following the apostasy of John Hicks, Jesse continued to provide service in support of the work of the quorum until he was ordained a high priest in 1845. He died in Mills County, Iowa, on November 1, 1846.

BALDWIN, WHEELER

Born March 7, 1793, in Albany County, New York, Wheeler was baptized into the restored Church when thirty-seven years old. He was unable to fulfill his mission call (see D&C 52:31) because his appointed companion, William Carter, declined to go. Wheeler remained in Kirtland to strengthen the Saints, and he also served the Church for a time in Missouri. By 1853 he had denied his faith in the Church and eventually joined the Reorganized Church of Jesus Christ of Latter Day Saints. He passed away on May 11, 1887.

BASSET, HEMAN

Heman was born in 1814 in Guildhall, Essex County, Vermont. He was living in Kirtland in 1830 as a member of a communal organization on the Isaac Morley farm when he learned about the restored gospel. He was baptized in October 1830 and ordained an elder in the spring of 1831. The Prophet Joseph warned Heman to avoid the temptations of the devil, but the young man did not heed the counsel and therefore lost his intended calling as a missionary (see D&C 52:37). Heman passed away in 1876 in Philadelphia.

BENNETT, JOHN C.

Born on August 4, 1804, at Fairhaven, Bristol County, Massachusetts, John was a medical practitioner (of questionable credentials and values, as it turned out). He made the acquaintance of Joseph Smith in 1840, and the Prophet welcomed him into the Nauvoo community. Subsequently, John was elected mayor of Nauvoo and became major-general of the Nauvoo Legion and chancellor of the University of Nauvoo. In a revelation dated January 19, 1841, John was called to a special duty:

> Again, let my servant John C. Bennett help you in your labor in sending my word to the kings and people of the earth, and stand by you, even you my servant Joseph Smith, in the hour of affliction; and his reward shall not fail if he receive counsel.

John C. Bennett

And for his love he shall be great, for he shall be mine if he do this, saith the Lord. I have seen the work which he hath done, which I accept if he continue, and will crown him with blessings and great glory. (D&C 124:16–17)

But John did not receive this counsel with a willing heart. When his reputation of fraud and adultery caught up to him in Nauvoo, he resigned as mayor and was cut off from the Church. In mid-June 1842 he left Nauvoo and launched a bitter campaign of public denunciation against the Church in many cities throughout the country. The Prophet Joseph Smith continued to respond in a compassionate way, but John never returned to the faith. He died a pauper in Iowa on August 5, 1867.

The Lord extended to John C. Bennett great promises—based on his willingness to stand by the Prophet Joseph Smith and obey the counsel of the Lord. When he did not do so, he lost his covenant opportunity and dropped into obscurity.

BENSON, EZRA T.

Ezra was born on February 22, 1811, at Mendon, Worcester County, Massachusetts. He learned of the restored Church when he moved to Quincy, Illinois, in 1838. He and his wife were baptized on July 19, 1840. Soon thereafter, Ezra was ordained an elder and subsequently a high priest. Following his move to Nauvoo in 1841, he served the first of three missions for the Church. In 1846 he fled Nauvoo and encamped in the Iowa Territory with the Saints. It was during that time—on July 16, 1846—that he was appointed to the Quorum of the Twelve. On January 14, 1847, he was called by revela-

Ezra T. Benson

tion to organize a company for the trek west (see D&C 136:12). After the exodus he served in Zion as a colonizer, civil servant, and mission president in Great Britain. He passed away in Ogden on September 3, 1869. His great-grandson, Ezra Taft Benson, became the thirteenth President of the Church.

BENT, SAMUEL

Samuel, born on July 19, 1778, at Barre, Worcester County, Massachusetts, was baptized and ordained an elder by Jared Carter in January 1833 in Pontiac, Michigan. He was a devoted missionary and participant in Zion's Camp and the School of the Prophets, attended the dedication of the Kirtland Temple, and served on the Far West and Nauvoo high councils (see D&C 124:131–32). He was a colonel in the Nauvoo Legion and a captain in the 1846 exodus. Additionally, Samuel helped raise revenues for Church publications during the

Nauvoo period. He passed away on August 16, 1846, in the Iowa Territory.

BILLINGS, TITUS

Titus was born in March 1793 at Greenfield, Franklin County, Massachusetts. He was a stonemason and one of the first persons to be baptized in Kirtland. By revelation he was commanded to dispose of his land and journey to Missouri (see D&C 63:39). Obeying this directive, he moved to Zion, consecrated his holdings, and received an inheritance. In 1833 he was called as a counselor to Bishop Edward Partridge but was driven out of Jackson County by a mob before commencing his service. He moved to Clay County for a time and then to Far West, where he served as a counselor to Edward Partridge. Titus participated in the Battle of Crooked River and the flight that followed. His family joined him in Illinois before the mobs forced them to flee to Nauvoo and then onward to Iowa to join the westward migration.

Titus Billings

He died in Provo, Utah Territory, on February 6, 1866.

BOGGS, LILBURN W.

Lilburn Boggs is not mentioned in the text of the Doctrine and Covenants but is referred to in the introductory heading to section 124. This notorious political figure, born on December 14, 1792, in Lexington, Fayette County, Kentucky, rose in political prominence in the state of Missouri. He was a complicit and approving observer at many of the atrocities committed by the mobs against the Mormon settlers, including the destruction of W. W. Phelps's printing firm on July 20, 1833, and the tarring and feathering of Bishop Edward Partridge that same day. Lilburn Boggs became governor of the state of Missouri on September 30, 1836, and was reelected two years later. Using false accusations by the mobs, he issued the infamous extermination order against the Saints on October 27, 1838, authorizing the destruction or expulsion of the Mormons.

A year and a half following the end of his tenure, Boggs became the victim of an attempted assassination on May 6, 1842. The Prophet Joseph Smith and his associate Orrin Porter Rockwell were falsely accused of this crime. The Prophet was acquitted of the trumped-up charges in January 1843 when the Circuit Court of the United States for the District of Illinois determined that the allegation lacked foundation (*HC* 5:231, 244). Orrin Porter Rockwell was held in jail for nearly ten months but was finally released—as Joseph Smith had prophesied (see *HC* 5:305). Lilburn Boggs went on to become a United States senator from 1842 to 1846. He later settled in California, where he died on March 19, 1861.

Lilburn W. Boggs

Booth, Ezra

Ezra was born in Connecticut in 1792. By 1831 he had become a Methodist minister of some repute in Ohio. That same year he became convinced that the Book of Mormon was true and was baptized and ordained an elder—in part because of his being inspired while witnessing a healing performed by the Prophet Joseph Smith. In connection with the Fourth General Conference of the Church in June 1831, the Prophet Joseph blessed Ezra to be freed from the influence of an evil spirit. Ezra was called to travel to Missouri, preaching en route (D&C 52:23). He returned as an apostate and lost his fellowship in the Church on September 6, 1831.

The Lord had strong words for Ezra in a revelation dated September 11, 1831:

> Behold, I, the Lord, was angry with him who was my servant Ezra Booth, and also my servant Isaac Morley, for they kept not the law, neither the commandment;
>
> They sought evil in their hearts, and I, the Lord, withheld my Spirit. They condemned for evil that thing in which there was no evil; nevertheless I have forgiven my servant Isaac Morley. (D&C 64:15–16)

Ezra subsequently became the author of some of the earliest pieces of anti-Mormon literature—"a monument to his own shame" is how the Prophet Joseph characterized it (*HC* 1:217; see the introductory heading to section 71). Ezra participated in the tarring and feathering of Joseph in 1832. From that point on, nothing further is known about him.

Boynton, John F.

John was born on September 20, 1811, at Bradford, Essex County, Massachusetts. An intellectual man educated at Columbia in New York City and at medical school in St. Louis, he was baptized by the Prophet Joseph Smith, ordained an elder by the age of twenty-one, and sent on a mission to the eastern states and Canada. In February 1835 he was ordained a member of the Quorum of the Twelve Apostles. However, in 1837 he became embroiled in the troubling financial problems in Kirtland and cast blame on the Prophet Joseph Smith. Subsequently, he and fellow dissidents attempted unsuccessfully to seize control of the Kirtland Temple. Eventually, he was dismissed from the Quorum of the Twelve and in April 1838 excommunicated.

Thereafter he became a traveling lecturer on scientific themes, tried unsuccessfully to make his fortune in California, and subsequently settled in Syracuse, New York, where

John F. Boynton

he pursued an avid interest in genealogy. Among his patents were a fire extinguisher, a soda fountain, and various metallurgical processes. He passed away on October 20, 1890. John is not mentioned by name in the text of the Doctrine and Covenants, but is listed in the "Testimony of the Twelve Apostles to the Truth of the Book of Doctrine and Covenants."

BROTHER OF JARED

The brother of Jared is mentioned only once in the Doctrine and Covenants—in a revelation in June 1829 directed to the Three Witnesses prior to their viewing the plates containing the Book of Mormon record: "Behold, I say unto you, that you must rely upon my word, which if you do with full purpose of heart, you shall have a view of the plates, and also of the breastplate, the sword of Laban, the Urim and Thummim, which were given to the brother of Jared upon the mount, when he talked with the Lord face to face, and the miraculous directors which were given to Lehi while in the wilderness, on the borders of the Red Sea" (D&C 17:1). The brother of Jared was commended by the Lord for his extraordinary faith: "And the Lord said unto him . . . never has man come before me with such exceeding faith as thou hast" (Ether 3:9). So strong was his faith that he beheld the finger of the Lord when it was extended to touch the stones that had been prepared to illuminate the vessels constructed for the ocean voyage (see Ether 3:19–20).

The brother of Jared lived at the time of the Tower of Babel, some two millennia before the birth of the Savior. He was most likely a contemporary of Abraham and also of the very aged Noah (who passed away about this time). Just as Abraham was to be directed by the Lord to flee from his homeland in Ur of the Chaldees and settle in Palestine, the brother of Jared was directed somewhat earlier (with Jared and their two families) to leave their home and journey to the promised land. The brother of Jared is not identified by proper name in the Book of Mormon; however, the Prophet Joseph Smith indicated that his name was Mahonri Moriancumer (*Times & Seasons*, Vol. 2, No. 11, [April 1, 1841], 362; *Juvenile Instructor*, Vol. 27 [May 1, 1892], 282; see *EM*, 235).

BRUNSON, SEYMOUR

Seymour was born on September 18, 1799, at Orwell, Addison County, Vermont, and was baptized a member of the Church in January 1831 and ordained an elder. He was called by revelation to serve as a missionary (see D&C 75:33) and filled that assignment in Virginia, Ohio, and Kentucky. Seymour suffered great persecution by the mobs in Ohio and Missouri. Nevertheless, he assisted others, including

Parley P. Pratt and the Joseph Smith Sr. family. His final years were spent in Nauvoo, where he served on the high council, in the Nauvoo Legion, and as a bodyguard for the Prophet Joseph. He died on August 10, 1840, having remained faithful. On January 19, 1841, the Lord declared: "Seymour Brunson I have taken unto myself; no man taketh his priesthood, but another may be appointed unto the same priesthood in his stead" (D&C 124:132).

BURNETT, STEPHEN

Stephen, born in 1814, learned of the gospel in Ohio and joined the Church. Soon thereafter he was called by revelation on January 25, 1832, to serve as a missionary (see D&C 75:35). Apparently, this calling was not filled, because a second calling was issued by revelation in March 1832: "Verily, thus saith the Lord unto you my servant Stephen Burnett: Go ye, go ye into the world and preach the gospel to every creature that cometh under the sound of your voice" (D&C 80:1). Unfortunately, upon his return to Kirtland from this assignment, Stephen apostatized and denounced the Prophet and the Church. Details of his remaining years are unknown.

BURROUGHS, PHILIP

Philip was born in 1795 in New Hampshire. As a farmer in Fayette, Seneca County, New York, he was introduced to the gospel at the behest of his neighbor, John Whitmer, acting in fulfillment of the command of the Lord:

> Behold, I say unto you, my servant John, that thou shalt commence from this time forth to proclaim my gospel, as with the voice of a trump.
> And your labor shall be at your brother Philip Burroughs', and in that

region round about, yea, wherever you can be heard, until I command you to go from hence. (D&C 30:9–10)

Although Parley P. Pratt preached the gospel at the Burroughs' home in September 1830, it is not known whether Philip was converted to the gospel.

BUTTERFIELD, JOSIAH

Josiah was born on March 13, 1795, at Dunstable, Middlesex County, Massachusetts. He was baptized on October 1, 1833, and soon thereafter served a mission near his home community in Maine. By 1835 he had relocated to Kirtland, Ohio, where he helped build the temple. On April 6, 1837, he was called as one of the Presidents of the Seventy, a position he held for several years (see D&C 124:138). He labored in support of the poor in Missouri. Later, in Nauvoo, however, he was accused of a variety of illegal activities. Though acquitted and recognized again as one of the seven Presidents of the Seventy, he soon insulted the Prophet Joseph in unkindly ways (*HC* 5:316). He was excommunicated on October 7, 1844. He later rejoined the Church and received his endowment in the Nauvoo Temple. Nevertheless, Josiah declined to join the Saints in the trek to the Salt Lake Valley. He instead settled in northern California and joined the Reorganized Church of Jesus Christ of Latter Day Saints, though he claimed later that his testimony and faith in the restored Church was still strong. He passed away on March 3, 1871.

CAHOON, REYNOLDS

Reynolds was born on April 30, 1790, at Cambridge, Washington County, New York. A farmer and tanner near Kirtland, he was among the first converted by the missionaries who were sent to the Lamanites. He was baptized by Parley P. Pratt on October 12, 1830, and subsequently received a calling to travel to Missouri

Reynolds Cahoon

in companionship with Samuel H. Smith (see D&C 52:30; 61:35). Following this mission, Reynolds served the Church in Ohio as a member of the building committee (see D&C 94:14–15), a counselor to Bishop Newel K. Whitney, and then as a counselor in the stake presidency. He is also mentioned in one verse concerning Hyrum Smith (see D&C 75:32). Reynolds and his family were forced to flee persecution in Ohio and, via Missouri, came to live in Nauvoo where he continued to serve the Lord. After the Martyrdom of the Prophet, Reynolds joined the exodus to the Salt Lake Valley. He passed away in Cottonwood, Utah, on April 29, 1861.

CAINAN

Cainan, son of Enos and great-grandson of Adam and Eve (Gen. 5:9–14; Moses 6:17–19), is mentioned twice in the Doctrine and Covenants: once in connection with the descent of the priesthood lineage—"God called upon Cainan in the wilderness in the fortieth year of his age; and he met Adam in journeying to the place Shedolamak" (D&C 107:45)—and again as a participant in the assembly of elect individuals gathered by Adam to receive his benedictory blessing: "Three years previous to the death of Adam, he called Seth, Enos, Cainan, Mahalaleel, Jared, Enoch, and Methuselah, . . . into the valley of Adam-ondi-Ahman, and there bestowed upon them his last blessing" (see D&C 107:53).

CALEB

Caleb was a priesthood leader mentioned twice in the Doctrine and Covenants in connection with the lineage of the priesthood at the time of Moses, the latter having received the priesthood from his father-in-law Jethro, who "received it under the hand of Caleb; And Caleb received it under the hand of Elihu" (D&C 84:7–8). The Caleb in these references is not likely the same Caleb later sent by Moses (along with Joshua and others) to search out the land of Canaan (see Num. 13:6, 30; 14:6–38).

CARTER, GIDEON

Gideon, older brother of Jared, was born in 1798 at Benson, Rutland County, Vermont. After joining the Church, he preached the gospel in his capacity as a priest before being ordained an elder and receiving a mission call by revelation on January 25, 1832 (see D&C 75:34). Upon his return to Kirtland, he was active in various Church capacities, including serving on the high council. He then moved to Far West, Missouri. On October 25, 1838, he gave his life in the Battle of Crooked River.

CARTER, JARED

Jared was born on June 14, 1801, in Benson, Rutland County, Vermont. He was introduced to the Book of Mormon in January 1831 and immediately believed it was true. He was baptized by Hyrum Smith the following month. Jared and his family moved with the Colesville Saints to Ohio. He was ordained a priest in accordance with revelation dated June 7, 1831 (see D&C 52:38), and went on to become a successful missionary for a period of time. The following revelation calling him on a mission contains extraordinary promises:

> Verily I say unto you, that it is my will that my servant Jared Carter should go again into the eastern countries, from place to place, and from city to city, in the power of the ordination wherewith he has been ordained, proclaiming glad tidings of great joy, even the everlasting gospel.
>
> And I will send upon him the Comforter, which shall teach him the truth and the way whither he shall go;
>
> And inasmuch as he is faithful, I will crown him again with sheaves. (D&C 79:1–3)

Unfortunately, though he was called as a member of the building committee (see D&C 94:14–16) and high council in Kirtland (see D&C 102:3, 34), he became disaffected from the Church and was disfellowshipped in September 1844 for conspiracy against the Prophet Joseph. He died in July 1855 in DeKalb County, Illinois.

CARTER, JOHN S.

John was born in 1796 at Killingworth, Middlesex County, Connecticut, son of Gideon Carter (he was a brother of the Gideon Carter previously mentioned). He was baptized a member of the Church in 1832 and ordained an elder and a high priest that same year. Shortly thereafter he completed a mission in Vermont with his brother Jared. On February 17, 1834, he was called to serve on the newly organized Kirtland high council (see D&C 102:3, 34). This position was cut short by a further mission call to the East. He succumbed to cholera on June 26, 1834, while serving in Zion's Camp.

CARTER, SIMEON

Simeon, a brother to the three previous Carters, was born on June 7, 1794, in Killingworth, Middlesex County, Connecticut. Having been converted in 1830 through the work of Parley P. Pratt, he was baptized into the Church and ordained an elder. He was then ordained a high priest at the fourth conference of the Church in June of 1831. Soon thereafter he was called by revelation to journey to Missouri, doing missionary work along the way (see D&C 52:27). Following his return to Ohio, he was called on another mission (see D&C 75:30) and achieved admirable success. Thereafter, he settled in Missouri until mob action forced him to return to Kirtland. He served as a member of Zion's Camp. Simeon remained faithful to the Church throughout his life, serving a mission in England and emigrating with the Saints to the Salt Lake Valley. He died in Brigham City on February 3, 1869.

CARTER, WILLIAM

Information concerning William's birth and death is not known. He was baptized and ordained an elder by June 1831 and attended the fourth conference of the Church in that month. Following the conference, he was called on a mission by revelation—though he was blind (see D&C 52:31). He declined the call, but went on to help build the Kirtland Temple.

CEPHAS

Cephas is the Aramaic name given by the Savior to Simon when he was called as a disciple (see John 1:42; compare 1 Cor. 3:22; 9:5; 15:5; Gal. 2:9). The name means "stone" and is equivalent to the Greek *petros*. In section 76 of the Doctrine and Covenants, concerning the degrees of glory, those in the telestial kingdom are characterized as having denied the testimony of the Savior, though they might verbally claim allegiance to Christ, John, Moses, Elias, Isaiah, Enoch, Paul, Apollos, Cephas, or some other movement (see D&C 76:99; compare 1 Cor. 1:12).

COE, JOSEPH

Joseph was born on November 12, 1784, in Genoa, Cayuga County, New York. An early convert, he moved to Kirtland in time to participate in the Fourth General Conference of the Church held in June 1831. He was called shortly thereafter to serve a mission in Missouri (see D&C 55:6), where he was present at the dedication of Missouri as a land of inheritance. He was called as a member of the Kirtland high council (see D&C 102:3, 34). Joseph played various roles in the financial affairs of the Church, including contributing funds to purchase Egyptian mummies. He ended his affiliation with the Church in June 1837, alleging that Joseph Smith was a fallen prophet. Excommunicated in December 1838, Joseph passed away in Kirtland on October 17, 1854.

CHILDREN OF JUDAH (SEE JUDAH)

CHILDREN OF ZION

The Lord uses this term on six occasions in the text of the Doctrine and Covenants in reference to His people, as in the following example: "Pray earnestly that peradventure my servant Joseph Smith, Jun., may go with you, and preside in the midst of my people, and organize my kingdom upon the consecrated land, and establish the children of Zion upon the laws and commandments which have been and which shall be given unto you" (D&C 103:35; compare also 84:56, 58; 101:41, 81, 85).

COLESVILLE SAINTS

In section 37 of the Doctrine and Covenants, a revelation given to the Prophet Joseph Smith and Sidney Rigdon near Fayette, New York, December 1830 (see *HC* 1:139), the Lord instructs Joseph and Sidney to suspend their Bible translation activities for a season until they relocate to Ohio. They are to preach the gospel and strengthen the Church—especially in the community of Colesville, New York. Who were the Colesville Saints who garnered the favor of the Lord for their much faith and prayer? Concerning the community of Colesville, Hoyt Brewster provides the following account:

> The town of Colesville, New York, . . . was the home of Joseph Knight, Sr., a faithful man for whom Joseph Smith had labored in 1826. Knight's farm was located about twenty miles above what was known as the "Great Bend," . . . where the Susquehanna River makes a dip into Pennsylvania and then hooks back up into New York (C[omprehensive] H[istory of the] C[hurch] 1:85). It is located about one hundred miles south of Fayette. . . .

It was here that the "first miracle" of the Church took place, when an evil spirit was cast out of Newel Knight. This was also the location where the Prophet Joseph suffered his first arrest, following the organization of the Church. He was charged with being a "disorderly person by preaching the Book of Mormon" (CHC 1:201–10). About sixty Saints from this location went en masse to Ohio, where they settled at Thompson, sixteen miles northeast of Kirtland. However, they soon moved to Jackson County, Missouri, settling about twelve miles outside of Independence, in an area that is now part of Kansas City. (*DCE*, 90)

COLTRIN, ZEBEDEE

Zebedee was born on September 7, 1804, at Ovid, Seneca County, New York. His family settled in Ohio where, in January 1831, he

Zebedee Coltrin

15

learned of the Church through the missionary work of Solomon Hancock and was baptized immediately. In June1831 he was called by revelation on a mission to Missouri (see D&C 52:29). He was blessed to receive several visionary manifestations during his lifetime. In Nauvoo he supported himself as a merchant and served several additional missions for the Church. In 1847 he journeyed to the Salt Lake Valley and later served yet another mission for the Church in Iowa and Wisconsin. President John Taylor ordained him a patriarch on May 31, 1873. Zebedee passed away on July 2, 1887, in Spanish Fork, Utah.

COPLEY, LEMAN

Leman, born in 1781 in Connecticut, was a member of the Shakers (the United Society of Believers in Christ's Second Coming). In 1831 he became a convert of the restored Church. The Prophet Joseph Smith discerned that Leman's conversion was somewhat frail and sought counsel from the Lord, who directed that Leman, Sidney Rigdon, and Parley P. Pratt preach the gospel to the Shakers (see D&C 49:1, 4). The Lord gave a conditional promise that

> Leman shall be ordained unto this work, that he may reason with them [the Shakers], not according to that which he has received of them, but according to that which shall be taught him by you my servants; and by so doing I will bless him, otherwise he shall not prosper. (D&C 49:4)

The three fulfilled the commission by going to the small Shaker settlement in North Union, Ohio, where they presented the doctrines of the gospel, including a reading of the new rev-

elation (section 49). The Shakers rejected the message. Leman's subsequent years were characterized by instability in his Church service and relationships. He is mentioned in the introductory heading to section 54 as one who dishonored his pledge to assist those gathering to Ohio from the East. Eventually Leman's apostasy was complete and he took up other religious affiliations. He died a wealthy landowner in Ohio in December 1862.

CORRILL, JOHN

John was born on September 17, 1794, in Bone, Worcester County, Massachusetts. He heard the gospel from missionaries passing through Harpersville, Ohio, where he was. He was baptized in January 1831 and became an elder. In May 1831 the Lord included John as one of those called to "go forth among the churches and strengthen them by the word of exhortation" (D&C 50:37). John was called in June 1831 to join many of the priesthood leaders in journeying to Missouri (see D&C 52:7). He served in various capacities, including second counselor to Bishop Edward Partridge, and even offered himself to the mobs in Missouri as a ransom for the Church. After being expelled from Missouri, he continued to serve faithfully in the Kingdom. However, he fell into apostasy beginning in 1838 and betrayed the Prophet Joseph by testifying falsely against him in court hearings. On March 17, 1839, he was excommunicated.

COVILL, JAMES

Details of James's birth and death are not known. It is known that he was a Baptist minister and that the Lord spoke to him in a remarkable revelation given through the Prophet Joseph on January 5, 1831. The Lord tells James,

"I have looked upon thy works and I know thee" (D&C 39:7). He then gives him extraordinary promises in connection with the calling to preach the gospel to the people in Ohio:

> But, behold, the days of thy deliverance are come, if thou wilt hearken to my voice, which saith unto thee: Arise and be baptized, and wash away your sins, calling on my name, and you shall receive my Spirit, and a blessing so great as you never have known.
>
> And if thou do this, I have prepared thee for a greater work. Thou shalt preach the fulness of my gospel, which I have sent forth in these last days, the covenant which I have sent forth to recover my people, which are of the house of Israel.
>
> And it shall come to pass that power shall rest upon thee; thou shalt have great faith, and I will be with thee and go before thy face. (D&C 39:10–12)

James Covill

Whether James was baptized into the Church is not a matter of record. The revelation given through the Prophet Joseph Smith in January 1831 describes how James received the Lord's promises and what he then did:

> Behold, verily I say unto you, that the heart of my servant James Covill was right before me, for he covenanted with me that he would obey my word.
>
> And he received the word with gladness, but straightway Satan tempted him; and the fear of persecution and the cares of the world caused him to reject the word.
>
> Wherefore he broke my covenant, and it remaineth with me to do with him as seemeth me good. Amen. (D&C 40:1–3)

COWDERY, OLIVER

Oliver was born October 3, 1806, in Wells, Rutland County, Vermont. Having heard of the work of the Prophet Joseph Smith, he came to meet him at Harmony, Pennsylvania, on April 5, 1829, and started two days later to serve as scribe in the translation of the Book of Mormon. With Joseph, he received the Aaronic Priesthood under the hands of John the Baptist on May 15, 1929, and the Melchizedek Priesthood shortly thereafter from Peter, James, and John. Oliver was thus the second elder of the Church. He was ordained an assistant to the President of the Church on December 5, 1834 (*HC* 2:176). With Joseph, he beheld the Lord Jesus Christ in the Kirtland Temple on April 3, 1836, and there received sacred priesthood keys from Elijah, Elias, and Moses.

Oliver Cowdery, with Joseph Smith

Oliver Cowdery is mentioned in the text of the Doctrine and Covenants thirty-eight times. Four revelations were given to the Prophet Joseph Smith and Oliver Cowdery jointly (sections 6, 7, 24, 110). Three revelations were given specifically to Oliver Cowdery through the Prophet Joseph Smith (sections 8, 9, 28), and four were given to Oliver and one or more others through the Prophet Joseph Smith (sections 17, 18, 23, 26). It was upon the heads of Joseph and Oliver that John the Baptist restored the Aaronic Priesthood (see section 13). Joseph and Oliver were both sustained as presiding officers on the occasion of the formal organization of the Church (see section 21). Oliver was

a witness with Joseph of the appearance of the Savior and three heavenly ministrants who restored essential priesthood keys in the Kirtland Temple on April 3, 1836 (see section 110). He also drafted the text of the statement on governments and laws that became section 134. Clearly, Oliver played a leading role in the epic history of the restored Church.

The words given to Oliver by the Lord teach great lessons concerning the intimate operation of personal revelation:

> Verily, verily, I say unto you, if you desire a further witness, cast your mind upon the night that you cried unto me

in your heart, that you might know concerning the truth of these things.

Did I not speak peace to your mind concerning the matter? What greater witness can you have than from God?

And now, behold, you have received a witness; for if I have told you things which no man knoweth have you not received a witness? (D&C 6:22–24)

When Oliver desired to translate from ancient records, just as Joseph was doing, the Lord granted his request—but Oliver found that the process was not as easy as he had imagined. Again, the Lord taught him more specifics concerning the process of personal revelation:

Yea, behold, I will tell you in your mind and in your heart, by the Holy Ghost, which shall come upon you and which shall dwell in your heart.

Now, behold, this is the spirit of revelation; . . .

Remember that without faith you can do nothing; therefore ask in faith. (D&C 8:2–3, 10)

When Oliver once more fell short in his attempt to translate, the Lord, in compassion, removed from him this assignment and gave him counsel that applies to all who seek guidance through the Spirit:

Behold, you have not understood; you have supposed that I would give it unto you, when you took no thought save it was to ask me.

But, behold, I say unto you, that you must study it out in your mind;

then you must ask me if it be right, and if it is right I will cause that your bosom shall burn within you; therefore, you shall feel that it is right.

But if it be not right you shall have no such feelings, but you shall have a stupor of thought that shall cause you to forget the thing which is wrong; therefore, you cannot write that which is sacred save it be given you from me. (D&C 9:7–9)

Oliver was then commanded to continue as scribe for the Prophet in bringing forth the Book of Mormon. Through the miracle of revelation, the translation process was completed in less than three months (beginning April 7, 1829; see JS—H 1:67) and the publication of the volume was completed in March 1830. In a footnote at the conclusion of the Joseph Smith—History, Oliver described these events as "days never to be forgotten—to sit under the sound of a voice dictated by the inspiration of heaven, awakened the utmost gratitude of this bosom! Day after day I continued, uninterrupted, to write from his mouth, as he translated with the Urim and Thummim, or, as the Nephites would have said, 'Interpreters,' the history or record called 'The Book of Mormon.'"

Together with David Whitmer and Martin Harris, Oliver was one of the three witnesses who could confirm the truth of the Book of Mormon. Thereafter, Oliver continued his service as "second elder" (D&C 20:3) in building the Kingdom of God—but with an increasing tendency to forget that Joseph Smith was the only one chosen of the Lord to hold all the keys of leadership.

On one occasion, Oliver tried to correct Joseph concerning a passage from a revelation enumerating the qualities of those preparing for baptism: "and truly manifest by their works that they have received of the Spirit of Christ unto the remission of their sins" (D&C 20:37). Oliver stated in a letter to the Prophet: "I command you in the name of God to erase these words, that no priestcraft be amongst us!" (*HC* 1:105). A few days later the Prophet visited Oliver and the Whitmer family, some of whom were siding with Oliver, and convinced them by reason and the authority of the scriptures to acknowledge and correct their mistake.

Unfortunately, Oliver failed to make this lesson a governing principle in his life. In April 1830 the Lord warned Oliver to "beware of pride, lest thou shouldst enter into temptation" (D&C 23:1). The Lord was more specific in his warnings to Oliver in September 1830:

Behold, I say unto thee, Oliver, that it shall be given unto thee that thou shalt be heard by the church in all things whatsoever thou shalt teach them by the Comforter, concerning the revelations and commandments which I have given.

But, behold, verily, verily, I say unto thee, no one shall be appointed to receive commandments and revelations in this church excepting my servant Joseph Smith, Jun., for he receiveth them even as Moses. . . .

And if thou art led at any time by the Comforter to speak or teach, or at all times by the way of commandment unto the church, thou mayest do it.

But thou shalt not write by way of commandment, but by wisdom;

And thou shalt not command him who is at thy head, and at the head of the church. (D&C 28:1–2, 4–6)

Pride continued to fester in Oliver's soul until on April 7, 1838, various charges were drawn against him, including that of impugning the character of the Prophet Joseph Smith. He was excommunicated in Far West on April 12, 1838. Subsequently, on January 19, 1841, Hyrum Smith, in becoming patriarch to the Church by revelation, received the office and calling that Oliver had once occupied, "a prophet, and a seer, and a revelator unto my church, as well as my servant Joseph . . . and be crowned with the same blessing, and glory, and honor, and priesthood, and gifts of the priesthood, that once were put upon him that was my servant Oliver Cowdery" (D&C 124:94–95).

Originally a school teacher, Oliver turned to law following his excommunication, but he suffered from ill health and financial difficulties. Over a decade after his excommunication, Oliver Cowdery petitioned for fellowship once again and was rebaptized in November 1848. His poor health precluded his joining the Saints in the Salt Lake Valley. To his credit, Oliver was forever true to his testimony of the Book of Mormon, dying on March 3, 1850, at Richmond, Ray County, Missouri.

COWDERY, WARREN A.

Warren was born in October 1788 at Poultney, Rutland County, Vermont. He became a successful farmer and medical practitioner in Freedom, New York. Introduced to the Book of Mormon by his younger brother Oliver, he joined the Church in 1831 and was called on November 25, 1834, as a "presiding high priest" in his community (D&C 106:1). At that time, the Lord gave mighty warnings and promises to Warren:

[B]lessed is my servant Warren, for I will have mercy on him; and, notwithstanding the vanity of his heart, I will lift him up inasmuch as he will humble himself before me.

And I will give him grace and assurance wherewith he may stand; and if he continue to be a faithful witness and a light unto the church I have prepared a crown for him in the mansions of my Father. Even so. Amen. (D&C 106:7–8)

Unfortunately, Warren vacillated from time to time in his devotion to the cause of Zion. He was censured for a prideful repudiation of the Twelve Apostles but repented in moving to Kirtland in 1836. He served in various capacities as a scribe, recorder, editor, and agent for the Church and was also a member of the Kirtland high council. He left the Church after 1838, disaffected with Church leaders. He never returned to the Church and died in Kirtland on February 23, 1851.

CUTLER, ALPHEUS

Alpheus was born on February 20, 1784, at Plainfield, Sullivan County, New Hampshire. He joined the Church on January 20, 1833, following the miraculous healing of his infirm daughter by priesthood holders. After moving to Kirtland, Alpheus attended the School of the Prophets, assisted with the construction of the temple, and served on the high council. Persecution forced him to leave Ohio for Missouri and from there to Nauvoo. He returned to Missouri to lay the cornerstone of the temple in Far West on April 24, 1839. In Nauvoo he served on the high council (see D&C 124:131–32) and later assisted with the exodus to Iowa. Thereafter, Alpheus chose apostasy, claiming to be the successor to Joseph Smith

Alpheus Cutler

and forming a church of his own—the Cutlerites. During his later years of ill health, he confirmed that he was aware of his errors and renewed his witness of the mission of Joseph Smith and Brigham Young. He died on August 10, 1864, in Manti, Iowa.

DAVID

David, celebrated king of Judah whose life is presented in the books of 1 Samuel and 2 Samuel, is mentioned four times in the Doctrine and Covenants, once in the dedicatory prayer for the Kirtland Temple—"And the yoke of bondage may begin to be broken off from the house of David" (D&C 109:63); and three times in connection with the doctrine of plural marriage (see D&C 132:1, 38, 39). In connection with the latter, the Lord declares: "David's wives and concubines were given unto him of me, by the hand of Nathan, my servant, and others of the prophets who had the keys of this power; and in none of these things did he sin against me save in the case of Uriah and his wife; and, therefore he hath fallen from his exaltation, and received his portion; and he shall not inherit them out of the world, for I gave them unto another, saith the Lord" (D&C 132:39).

In his office as king of Judah, David excelled with valor and leadership. It was only in his moral lapse regarding Bathsheba and Uriah that David relinquished his opportunity for exaltation.

DAVIES, AMOS

Amos was born on September 20, 1813, at Hopkinton, Rockingham County, New Hampshire. When the Saints arrived in Commerce, Illinois, Amos was active there as a merchant, postmaster, and landowner. He joined the Church in April 1840. In a revelation dated January 19, 1841, he was called to be a stockholder in the planned Nauvoo House:

And again, verily I say unto you, let my servant Amos Davies pay stock into the hands of those whom I have appointed to build a house for boarding, even the Nauvoo House.

This let him do if he will have an interest; and let him hearken unto the counsel of my servant Joseph, . . .

And when he shall prove himself faithful in all things that shall be entrusted unto his care, yea, even a few things, he shall be made ruler over many;

Let him therefore abase himself that he may be exalted. Even so. Amen. (D&C 124:112–14)

Soon thereafter Amos was ordained an elder and made a first lieutenant in the Nauvoo Legion. Meanwhile, he was the subject of several court proceedings, including slander against the Prophet Joseph Smith. To his credit, he declined to join forces against the Prophet on the eve of the Martyrdom. After the exodus from Nauvoo in 1846, Amos showed kindness and generosity to the Saints encamped in the Iowa Territory. After excursions to California and Michigan, he returned to Illinois, where he died on March 22, 1872.

DANIEL

Daniel, one of the Lord's great prophets of the Old Testament (see the Book of Daniel) and a younger contemporary of Lehi and Nephi, is alluded to in the Doctrine and Covenants in connection with his prophecy about the coming forth of the Kingdom of God in the last days as "the stone" that was "cut out of the mountain without hands" and rolled forth until it "became a great mountain, and filled the whole earth" (Dan. 2:45, 35). The Doctrine and Covenants states, concerning the Restoration of the gospel:

> The keys of the kingdom of God are committed unto man on the earth, and from thence shall the gospel roll forth unto the ends of the earth, as the stone which is cut out of the mountain without hands shall roll forth, until it has filled the whole earth. (D&C 65:2)

Daniel is mentioned by name in the Doctrine and Covenants once concerning his prophecy of the return of Adam in the last days to convene with his people at Adam-ondi-Ahman

(see D&C 116:1; compare Dan. 7:13–14) and once in connection with the elect prophets witnessed by President Joseph F. Smith in his vision of the work of salvation in the spirit world, including "Daniel, who foresaw and foretold the establishment of the kingdom of God in the latter days, never again to be destroyed nor given to other people" (D&C 138:44).

DODDS, ASA

Asa, born in 1793 in New York, joined the Church in the early 1830s and accompanied Orson Pratt on the first leg of Orson's missionary journey from Ohio to Missouri. In January 1832, Asa was called by revelation to serve as a missionary (see D&C 75:15). Although he was ordained a high priest by Hyrum Smith shortly after receiving the mission call, the historical record does not confirm whether the mission call was fulfilled. Few details of Asa's subsequent life are known.

DORT, DAVID

On January 6, 1793, David was born at Surry, Cheshire County, New Hampshire. He married Mary Mack, the cousin of Joseph Smith (daughter of the brother of Joseph's mother), and, after Mary's death, Fanny Mack (her sister). It was Joseph's mother, Lucy Mack Smith, who arranged for David, then in Michigan, to learn of the restored gospel. David was baptized in 1831. He subsequently participated in Zion's Camp and then moved to Kirtland. He served, in turn, on the Kirtland and Far West high councils. On January 19, 1841, he was called to serve on the Nauvoo high council (see D&C 124:131–32). He passed away shortly thereafter on March 10, 1841.

EAMES, RUGGLES

Ruggles joined the Church in Medina, Ohio, and was thereafter ordained a priest. He was called in January 1832 by revelation to serve a mission (see D&C 75:35), although it is not known whether he accepted and fulfilled that commission. He withdrew his Church membership in 1832 and faded from the history of the Restoration.

EIGHT WITNESSES

The "Testimony of the Eight Witnesses" to the Book of Mormon is given in the Introduction to that sacred volume. These witnesses include Christian Whitmer, Jacob Whitmer, Peter

Eight Witnesses

Whitmer Jr., John Whitmer, Hiram Page, Joseph Smith Sr., Hyrum Smith, and Samuel H. Smith. All of these with the exception of Christian Whitmer and Jacob Whitmer (who are not mentioned in the Doctrine and Covenants) have individual entries in the current volume.

ELIAS (SEE ALSO ANGEL ASCENDING FROM THE EAST)

Elias is both an individual prophet and a title. Along with other heavenly ministrants coming to restore their several keys, Elias the individual appeared to Joseph Smith and Oliver Cowdery in the Kirtland Temple on April 3, 1836, "and committed the dispensation of the gospel of Abraham, saying that in us and our seed all generations after us should be blessed" (D&C 110:12). President Joseph Fielding Smith taught that Elias, in this extraordinary appearance, was Noah, also known as the Angel Gabriel (see *AGQ* 3:339–41). Elder Bruce R. McConkie says in this context only the following: "We have no information, at this time, as to the mortal life or ministry of

Elias. Apparently he lived in the days of Abraham, but whether he was Abraham, or Melchizedek, or some other prophet, we do not know" (*MD*, 220). It is of interest that the ancient prophet Noah may have still been alive, in his very senior years, during the time of Abraham (see Gen. 9:28–29). Elias also appeared on the Mount of Transfiguration with Moses in the act of restoring priesthood keys (see D&C 138:45; Matt. 17:3).

The title Elias implies a forerunner, such as John the Baptist, who, in the authority of the Aaronic Priesthood, prepared the way in "the spirit of Elias" (D&C 27:7; compare Matt. 17:11–13) for the Savior in the meridian of time. Elias as a title also can refer to all the heavenly messengers who came to restore keys and authorities in the dispensation of the fulness of times leading up to the Second Coming. Elder Bruce R. McConkie explains:

> Since it is apparent that no one messenger has carried the whole burden of the restoration, but rather that each has come with a specific endowment from on high, it becomes clear that Elias is a composite personage. The expression must be understood to be a name and a title for those whose mission it was to commit keys and powers to men in this final dispensation. (*Doctrines of Salvation*, vol. 1, 170–74.) (*MD*, 221)

The title Elias can also refer to the Savior Jesus Christ, as John the Baptist confirmed: "He it is of whom I bear record. He is that prophet, even Elias, who, coming after me, is preferred before me, whose shoe's latchet I am not worthy to unloose, or whose place I am not able to fill; for he shall baptize, not only with water, but with fire,

and with the Holy Ghost" (JST John 1:28). In the Doctrine and Covenants, the term "Elias" is used seven times in its various meanings (D&C 27:6, 7; 76:100; 77:9, 14; 110:12; and 138:45).

ELIHU

Elihu is a priesthood leader mentioned in the Doctrine and Covenants in connection with the lineage of the priesthood prior to the time of Moses: "And Caleb received it under the hand of Elihu; and Elihu under the hand of Jeremy" (D&C 84:8–9). More details concerning the life and character of Elihu are not known.

ELIJAH

Elijah is one in a long line of extraordinary prophets of the Lord. His influence was felt among the Israelites and non-Israelites of his day (see 1 Kings 17–2 Kings 2; 2 Chr. 21:12–15), was called forth again on the Mount of Transfiguration (Matt. 17:1–11), and touches countless lives today through the restored keys of the sealing power of the priesthood placed in his charge (D&C 110:13–16). The prophet Elijah occupies a central position in the design of God as the one holding the "keys of the power of turning the hearts of the fathers to the children, and the hearts of the children to the fathers, that the whole earth may not be smitten with a curse" (D&C 27:9). It was this prophet whom God sent on April 3, 1836, to the Kirtland Temple to restore these sacred keys to Joseph Smith as an essential priesthood power in the dispensation of the fullness of times (see D&C 110:14–16; compare also Mal. 4:5–6; 3 Ne. 25:5).

Through Elijah the sealing powers were restored, by which is typically understood the work of temples. But the mission of Elijah accomplished more than that, as the Prophet

Joseph Smith emphasized: "Elijah was the last prophet that held the keys of this priesthood, and who will, before the last dispensation, restore the authority and delive[r] the Keys of this priesthood in order that all the ordinances may be attended to in righteousness" (*WJS*, 43).

Thus the keys of Elijah do *more* than validate and empower the redemptive work for the dead. Scholar Kent Jackson confirms that "they seal and validate *all* ordinances of the priesthood so that ordinances performed on earth are binding in heaven as well. . . . In the latter days, this transmittal of keys was an indispensable step in the process of the Restoration" (*FAR*, 223).

ENOCH

Enoch was the great high priest, seventh from Adam, who, along with his righteous city of Zion, was translated, as the Savior said, "into mine own bosom" (D&C 38:4). The biblical account offers few details of the life and ministry of Enoch (see Gen. 5:18–24; Luke 3:37; Heb. 11:5; Jude 1:14); however, modern-day revelation provides an additional recounting of Enoch's extraordinary accomplishments (especially Moses 6 and 7). The text of the Doctrine and Covenants mentions Enoch eleven times. Among these references, the greatness of Enoch is confirmed in the passage that speaks of those who inherit the celestial realm of glory as "priests of the Most High, after the order of Melchizedek, which was after the order of Enoch, which was after the order of the Only Begotten Son" (D&C 76:57). Such celestial beings are spoken of as those who "have come to an innumerable company of angels, to the general assembly and church of Enoch, and of the Firstborn" (D&C 76:67). Enoch was a key figure in the continuity of the priesthood lineage, being ordained at age twenty-five by Adam

Enoch

(see D&C 107:48). Enoch was present, with many other noble and great high priests, at the event where Adam pronounced his benedictory blessing on his posterity (see D&C 107:53). The details of "these things were all written in the book of Enoch, and are to be testified of in due time" (D&C 107:57). Enoch will return at the Second Coming (D&C 133:54) and be "in the presence of the Lamb" (D&C 133:55) among all of the elect prophets of God.

ENOS

Enos, son of Seth and grandson of Adam and Eve (Gen. 4:26; 5:6–11; Luke 3:38; Moses 6:13–18) is mentioned in connection with the descent of the priesthood lineage—"Enos was ordained at the age of one hundred and thirty-four years and four months, by the hand of Adam" (D&C 107:44)—and again as a participant in the assembly of elect individuals gathered together "three years previous to the death of Adam, [when Adam] called Seth, Enos, Cainan, Mahalaleel, Jared, Enoch, and Methuselah, who were all high priests, with the residue of his posterity who were righteous, into the valley of Adam-ondi-Ahman, and there bestowed upon them his last blessing" (D&C 107:53).

EPHRAIM

Ephraim, the second son (after Manasseh) of the patriarch Joseph (Gen. 41:52; 46:20), is mentioned six times in the Doctrine and Covenants. He is referred to in connection with the Book of Mormon—the "stick of Ephraim" (D&C 27:5)—and in the well-known passage:

> Wherefore, be not weary in well-doing, for ye are laying the foundation of a great work. And out of small things proceedeth that which is great.
>
> Behold, the Lord requireth the heart and a willing mind; and the willing and obedient shall eat the good of the land of Zion in these last days.
>
> And the rebellious shall be cut off out of the land of Zion, and shall be sent away, and shall not inherit the land.
>
> For, verily I say that the rebellious are not of the blood of Ephraim, wherefore they shall be plucked out. (D&C 64:33–36)

Ephraim is also mentioned in connection with the "rod" that should come forth "out of the stem of Jesse" (see Isa. 11:1): "Behold, thus saith the Lord: It [the rod] is a servant in the hands of Christ, who is partly a descendant of Jesse as well as of Ephraim, or of the house of Joseph, on whom there is laid much power" (D&C 113:4). The term *rod* very likely refers to the Prophet Joseph Smith. Ephraim is also mentioned three times in connection with the return of the Ten Tribes and the glorious blessings to be poured out upon Israel at that time—and especially upon Ephraim, who holds the birthright (1 Chr. 5:1–2; Jer. 31:9) and serves in a leadership capacity to further the cause of the Abrahamic covenant in bringing the message of the restored gospel of Jesus Christ to the world (see D&C 133:30–34).

ESAIAS

Esaias is the Greek form of the name Isaiah (see Luke 4:17; Acts 8:30). In section 76 of the Doctrine and Covenants, concerning the degrees of glory, those in the telestial kingdom are characterized as having denied the testimony

Jacob blessing Ephraim and Manasseh

of the Savior, though they might verbally claim allegiance to Christ, John, Moses, Elias, Esaias, Isaiah, Enoch, Paul, Apollos, Cephas, or some other movement (see D&C 76:100).

The name Esaias is also used in connection with the ancient prophet of that name who lived during the time of Abraham and was a key figure in the descent of the priesthood lineage:

> And Gad [received the priesthood] under the hand of Esaias;
> And Esaias received it under the hand of God.
> Esaias also lived in the days of Abraham, and was blessed of him. (D&C 84:11–13)

EVE

Eve, wife of Adam (see Gen. 2:21–22; 3:20; Moses 4:26; 1 Ne. 5:11), is mentioned only once in the Doctrine and Covenants text in connection with the vision of President Joseph F. Smith concerning the work of salvation in the spirit world:

> Among the great and mighty ones who were assembled in this vast congregation of the righteous were Father Adam, the Ancient of Days and father of all,
> And our glorious Mother Eve, with many of her faithful daughters

Adam and Eve

who had lived through the ages and worshiped the true and living God. (D&C 138:38–39)

EZEKIEL

Ezekiel, one of the Lord's great prophets of the Old Testament, and a younger contemporary of Lehi, prophesied during the period 592 to 570 BC. Among his visionary messages is the prophecy of the coming together of the scriptural records of Judah and Joseph (see Ezek. 37:15–17)—an event accomplished through the coming forth and publication of the Book of Mormon. Ezekiel is mentioned twice in the Doctrine and Covenants, in the first instance as follows:

> And the great and abominable church, which is the whore of all the earth, shall be cast down by devouring fire, according as it is spoken by the mouth of Ezekiel the prophet, who spoke of these things, which have not come to pass but surely must, as I live, for abominations shall not reign. (D&C 29:21; compare Ezek. 38:22)

In addition, Ezekiel is noted as one of the noble and elect prophets witnessed by President Joseph F. Smith in his vision of the work of salvation in the spirit realm:

> Moreover, Ezekiel, who was shown in vision the great valley of dry bones, which were to be clothed upon with flesh, to come forth again in the resurrection of the dead, living souls. (D&C 138:43; compare Ezek. 37:1–14)

Ezekiel

FATHER IN HEAVEN (SEE ALSO JESUS CHRIST; HOLY GHOST)

The word *Father*, referring to Heavenly Father, occurs 140 times in the text of the Doctrine and Covenants, among which are four occurrences of the term *God the Father* (D&C 21:1; 88:19; 107:19; 138:14). The word *God* itself (which can have reference to the Father or the Son, or both, depending on the usage) occurs 516 times.

Among the most memorable references to our Father in Heaven in the Doctrine and Covenants are these: "For ye know that there is no unrighteousness in them [the revelations], and that which is righteous cometh down from above, from the Father of lights" (D&C 67:9).

Concerning the oath and covenant of the priesthood, there is this well-known passage:

And also all they who receive this priesthood receive me, saith the Lord;

For he that receiveth my servants receiveth me;

And he that receiveth me receiveth my Father;

And he that receiveth my Father receiveth my Father's kingdom; therefore all that my Father hath shall be given unto him. (D&C 84:35–38)

Furthermore, the following passage illustrates the inseparable relationship between the Father and the Son:

Verily, thus saith the Lord: It shall come to pass that every soul who forsaketh his sins and cometh unto me, and calleth on my name, and obeyeth my voice, and keepeth my commandments, shall see my face and know that I am;

And that I am the true light that lighteth every man that cometh into the world;

And that I am in the Father, and the Father in me, and the Father and I are one—

The Father because he gave me of his fulness, and the Son because I was in the world and made flesh my tabernacle, and dwelt among the sons of men.

I was in the world and received of my Father, and the works of him were plainly manifest. (D&C 93:1–5; compare John 19:30; John 17:22; 1 Jn. 5:7; Mosiah 15:4; 3 Ne. 11:27, 36; 20:35; 28:10; Morm. 7:7)

Heavenly Father is the one to whom we pray in the name of the Son (see the sacramental prayers—D&C 20:77, 79). He is the benevolent and ever-loving Father of our Spirits. He is the source of truth and light, the pattern for all holiness and perfection. The Savior declared during His intercessory prayer: "And this is life eternal, that they might know thee the only true God, and Jesus Christ, whom thou hast sent" (John 17:3). And the Savior admonished the Saints in ancient America: "Therefore I would that ye should be perfect even as I, or your Father who is in heaven is perfect" (3 Ne. 12:48). He then assured the Saints in the latter days, concerning Deity: "Which Father, Son, and Holy Ghost are one God, infinite and eternal, without end. Amen" (D&C 20:28).

FOSTER, JAMES

James was born on April 1, 1775, in Morgan County, Indiana. In 1834, approximately a year following his conversion and baptism, he joined Zion's Camp (see *HC* 2:88). The Prophet Joseph Smith blessed him and nurtured him as he recovered from illness during the trek. In 1837 he was called to serve as one of the seven Presidents of the Seventy (an appointment confirmed in D&C 124:138). As such, he assisted the poor in their migration to Missouri but later abandoned the group to attend to his own safety and failed to join the Saints in Nauvoo. He passed away on December 21, 1841.

FOSTER, ROBERT D.

Robert was born on March 14, 1811, at Braunston, Northampton County, England. He attained considerable prominence in Church circles as a regent of the University of Nauvoo, surgeon-general of the Nauvoo Legion, and member of the Agricultural and Manufacturing Association. He was not without his faults, as the revelation dated January 19, 1841, made clear:

And again, verily I say unto you, if my servant Robert D. Foster will obey my voice, let him build a house for my servant Joseph, according to the contract which he has made with him, as the door shall be open to him from time to time.

And let him repent of all his folly, and clothe himself with charity; and cease to do evil, and lay aside all his hard speeches;

And pay stock also into the hands of the quorum of the Nauvoo House, for himself and for his generation after him, from generation to generation;

And hearken unto the counsel of my servants Joseph, and Hyrum, and William Law, and unto the authorities which I have called to lay the foundation of Zion; and it shall be well with him forever and ever. Even so. Amen. (D&C 124:115–118)

Regretfully, Robert did not fully heed that counsel but instead cultivated opposition to the Prophet with such defiance that charges were brought against him before the high council in April 1844. He was excommunicated from the Church for immorality and apostasy and court-martialed by the Nauvoo Legion for unbecoming conduct. Robert joined forces with apostates bent on destroying the Prophet. He also co-authored the anti-Mormon newspaper the *Nauvoo Expositor*, the destruction of which by the Nauvoo city council led directly to the martyrdom of the Prophet Joseph Smith. Robert appeared at one point to oppose the murder of the Prophet—but the campaign was too far advanced and the martyrdom, to which Robert was an accessory, took place. The details of Robert's death are not known.

FOUR AND TWENTY ELDERS

Section 77 of the Doctrine and Covenants provides inspired commentary on various passages written by John the Revelator, including the following reference: "The four and twenty elders fall down before him that sat on the throne, and worship him that liveth for ever and ever, and cast their crowns before the throne, saying, Thou art worthy, O Lord, to receive glory and honour and power: for thou hast created all things, and for thy pleasure they are and were created" (Rev. 4:10–11). Latter-day scripture asks:

> Q. What are we to understand by the four and twenty elders, spoken of by John?
> A. We are to understand that these elders whom John saw, were elders who had been faithful in the work of the ministry and were dead; who belonged to the seven churches, and were then in the paradise of God. (D&C 77:5)

President Joseph Fielding Smith comments: "It will be recalled that the forepart of John's Revelation contains a charge to the seven churches, or branches of the Church, in Asia Minor. [Rev. 1–3.] We may judge from what is written that these seven branches were all that were considered worthy of a standing in the Church at that time, indicating that the apostasy had at that day become extensive, and each of these branches received a deserved rebuke" (*CHMR*, 2:69).

FOUR ANGELS

From the Doctrine and Covenants comes the following text concerning the four angels mentioned at one point by John the Revelator:

> Q. What are we to understand by the four angels, spoken of in the 7th chapter and 1st verse of Revelation?
> A. We are to understand that they are four angels sent forth from God, to whom is given power over the four parts of the earth, to save life and to destroy; these are they who have the everlasting gospel to commit to every nation, kindred, tongue, and people; having power to shut up the heavens, to seal up unto life, or to cast down to the regions of darkness. (D&C 77:8)

President Joseph Fielding Smith provides this commentary: "These angels have been given power over the four parts of the earth and they have the power of committing the everlasting Gospel to the peoples of the earth. The fulness of the Gospel was not restored by any one messenger sent from the presence of the Lord. All the ancient prophets who held keys and came and restored them, had a hand in this great work of restoration. There are, we learn from this revelation, four angels unto whom the power has been given, to shut up the heavens, to open them and with power unto life and also death and destruction. These are now at work in the earth on their sacred mission" (*CHMR*, 2:70–71).

FULLER, EDSON

Edson, who was born in 1809 in New York, was living in Ohio as a carpenter when he became a member of the Church. He was baptized in 1831 and that same year in June, in connection with the fourth conference of the Church, was called on a mission to Missouri (see D&C 52:28). Apparently he did not obey but remained in Ohio as a preacher, cultivating a somewhat eccentric and non-edifying delivery style. He eventually was cut off from the Church and later moved to Michigan.

FULLMER, DAVID

David was born on July 7, 1803, at Chillisquaque, Northumberland County, Pennsylvania. He was baptized in Richland, Ohio, on September 16, 1836. After being ordained an elder, he joined the Saints in Missouri but soon retreated to Illinois because of mob violence. In Nauvoo he served on the city council and the high council (see D&C 124:132). Again, persecution terminated his stay, and he left for Iowa, where he presided over a group of Saints encamped at a location known as Garden Grove. Charges of misconduct within the branch brought David before a high council, but the charges were dropped and fellowship restored to all within the branch. He journeyed to the Salt Lake Valley in 1848 as part of the Willard Richards company. His civic accomplishments included drafting a constitution for the planned State of Deseret, serving as chief judge of the county court, and serving in the territorial legislature. Church assignments included acting president of the Salt Lake Stake (while the stake president was serving a mission in England) and, beginning in 1870, patriarch. He passed away on October 21, 1879.

GABRIEL (SEE ALSO ELIAS)

Gabriel is mentioned once in the Doctrine and Covenants, in connection with the manifestations of various divine messengers during the foundation period of the Restoration:

> And again, the voice of God in the chamber of old Father Whitmer, in Fayette, Seneca county, and at sundry times, and in divers places through all the travels and tribulations of this Church of Jesus Christ of Latter-day Saints! And the voice of Michael, the archangel; the voice of Gabriel, and of Raphael, and of divers angels, from Michael or Adam down to the present time, all declaring their dispensation, their rights, their keys, their honors, their majesty and glory, and the power of their priesthood; giving line upon line, precept upon precept; here a little, and there a little; giving us consolation by holding forth that which is to come, confirming our hope! (D&C 128:21)

The Elias appearing to Joseph Smith and Oliver Cowdery in the Kirtland Temple on April 3, 1836 (see D&C 110:12), was identified by President Joseph Fielding Smith as Noah, also known as Gabriel. Elder Bruce R. Mc-Conkie says in this context only the following: "We have no information, at this time, as to the mortal life or ministry of Elias. Apparently he lived in the days of Abraham, but whether he was Abraham, or Melchizedek, or some other prophet, we do not know" (*MD*, 220).

GAD

Gad was a priesthood leader mentioned in connection with the priesthood lineage prior to the time of Moses:

> And Jeremy [received the priesthood] under the hand of Gad;
> And Gad under the hand of Esaias;
> And Esaias received it under the hand of God. (D&C 84:10–12)

No additional details concerning the life and character of Gad are known. This individual is not to be confused with Gad who was one of the sons of Jacob (see Gen. 30:11) nor the prophet Gad who was the mentor of David (see 1 Sam. 22:5; 2 Sam. 24:11–19; 1 Chron. 21:9–19).

GALLAND, ISAAC

Isaac was born on May 15, 1792, in Somerset County, Pennsylvania. He was an ambitious medical practitioner and land dealer of mixed repute. Having become acquainted with the Prophet Joseph Smith, Isaac cultivated an interest in the restored Church and was baptized by the Prophet on July 3, 1839, and ordained an elder on that same occasion. It was Isaac Galland who encouraged the Prophet to settle in Commerce, Illinois, later renamed Nauvoo. Isaac was later appointed land agent for the Church (see D&C 124:78–79); however, his dealings proved unsatisfactory and he slipped into apostasy. He thereafter was in Iowa. He

Isaac Galland

died on September 27, 1858, leaving a legacy of writings on frontier history and other themes.

GAUSE, JESSE

Jesse is not mentioned in the text of the Doctrine and Covenants but is referred to in the current introduction to section 81. He was born in 1784 or 1785 in East Marlborough, Chester County, Pennsylvania. He was affiliated with the Quakers and later the Shakers, having settled in the Shaker community of North Union, Ohio, about fifteen miles from Kirtland. On March 8, 1832, the Prophet Joseph Smith chose and ordained Jesse Gause and Sidney Rigdon as his counselors (see the *Kirtland Revelation Book*, 10, as cited by Robert J. Woodford in "Jesse Gause, Counselor to the Prophet," *BYU Studies* 15 (Spring 1975); referenced in *WWDC*, 101). The appointment of Jesse Gause as counselor is confirmed in the introduction to section 81. However, Jesse did not live up to the high calling afforded him, and his position was transferred to Frederick G. Williams. Jesse did journey to Missouri in April 1832 with the Prophet Joseph and several other priesthood leaders; he also commenced a mission for the Church in 1832, but his whereabouts thereafter are not recorded. According to the introduction to section 81, he was excommunicated from the Church.

GENTILES

In general, the word *Gentiles* (meaning "nations") refers to those people who are not of the House of Israel. Gentiles can also refer to nations that do not yet have the gospel, even though there may be those of Israelite lineage among them (see Bible Dictionary, 679). It is in this latter sense that the term is used in the

Doctrine and Covenants. The Restoration is to take place among the Gentiles (beginning in America): "And it shall come to pass that there shall be a great work in the land, even among the Gentiles, for their folly and their abominations shall be made manifest in the eyes of all people" (D&C 35:7). The Lord defines the audience to which the Book of Mormon is to be proclaimed: "Which is my word to the Gentile, that soon it may go to the Jew, of whom the Lamanites are a remnant, that they may believe the gospel, and look not for a Messiah to come who has already come" (D&C 19:27). The "times of the Gentiles" is in fact the age of the Restoration:

> And when the times of the Gentiles is come in, a light shall break forth among them that sit in darkness, and it shall be the fulness of my gospel;
>
> But they receive it not; for they perceive not the light, and they turn their hearts from me because of the precepts of men.
>
> And in that generation shall the times of the Gentiles be fulfilled. (D&C 45:28–30)

The Saints of the Restoration are, in fact, identified with the Gentiles. They come from among the Gentile populace, as the Prophet Joseph Smith indicated in his inspired dedicatory prayer for the Kirtland Temple: "Now these words, O Lord, we have spoken before thee, concerning the revelations and commandments which thou hast given unto us, who are identified with the Gentiles" (D&C 109:60). Elder Bruce R. McConkie explains the dual character of the Saints in the latter days:

> Members of the Church in general are both of Israel and of the Gentiles. Indeed, the gospel has come forth in the last days in the times of the Gentiles and, in large measure, will not go to the Jews until the Gentile fulness comes in. (D&C 45:28–30.)
>
> Having in mind the principle that Gentiles are adopted into the lineage of Israel when they accept the gospel, and that those who fail to believe the truths of salvation (no matter what their lineage) lose any preferential status they may have had, it is not inappropriate in our day to speak of members of the Church as Israelites and unbelievers as Gentiles. (*MD*, 311)

GILBERT, ALGERNON SIDNEY

Sidney was born on December 28, 1789, at New Haven, New Haven County, Connecticut. He became a merchant and real property entrepreneur in Ohio, establishing in due time a partnership with Newel K. Whitney to operate a store in Kirtland. During this time he and Newel became members of the restored Church. The Lord reached out to Sidney in a personal revelation delivered through the Prophet Joseph Smith in June 1831:

> Behold, I say unto you, my servant Sidney Gilbert, that I have heard your prayers; and you have called upon me that it should be made known unto you, of the Lord your God, concerning your calling and election in the church, which I, the Lord, have raised up in these last days.
>
> Behold, I, the Lord, who was crucified for the sins of the world, give

unto you a commandment that you shall forsake the world.

Take upon you mine ordination, even that of an elder, to preach faith and repentance and remission of sins, according to my word, and the reception of the Holy Spirit by the laying on of hands;

And also to be an agent unto this church in the place which shall be appointed by the bishop, according to commandments which shall be given hereafter.

And again, verily I say unto you, you shall take your journey with my servants Joseph Smith, Jun., and Sidney Rigdon.

Behold, these are the first ordinances which you shall receive; and the residue shall be made known in a time to come, according to your labor in my vineyard.

And again, I would that ye should learn that he only is saved who endureth unto the end. Even so. Amen. (D&C 53:1–7)

Following his ordination, Sidney traveled with the Prophet Joseph Smith to Independence, Missouri, where he served as a land agent for the Church and opened a grocery and dry goods store in obedience to revelation (see D&C 57:6, 8–10). Although he felt inadequate and self-conscious as a speaker, he did personally make and preserve valuable handwritten copies of many of the early revelations. Sidney subsequently raised eyebrows through insinuations against leaders in Kirtland, and the Lord called Sidney and several others to repentance in March 1833 (see D&C 90:35). Mob action partially destroyed Sidney's store in Independence in 1833, forcing him to move to another location to continue his generous support of the Saints with goods and services. He also opened his home to members of Zion's Camp, a number of whom were suffering from cholera. Several died while in Sidney's home, and he also contracted the disease and passed away on June 29, 1834.

GOULD, JOHN

John was born in Ontario, Canada. While serving as a Baptist minister in New York in 1831, he was converted to the restored gospel and brought a large segment of his congregation into the Church. In 1833 he and Orson Hyde were sent by the Prophet Joseph Smith to Missouri to give counsel and assistance to the beleaguered Saints there. The Lord subsequently gave assurances to the Prophet that these agents would be protected (see D&C 100:14); they returned from their assignment unharmed. John helped the Prophet recruit participants for Zion's Camp in 1834 and was also active in doing missionary work. He later became for a time one of the seven Presidents of the Seventy. He passed away in Iowa on May 9, 1851.

GRANGER, OLIVER

Oliver was born on February 7, 1794, at Phelps, Ontario County, New York. A sheriff and militia officer in New York, he obtained a copy of the Book of Mormon in 1830 and became converted. He was baptized and ordained an elder by Brigham Young and Brigham's brother Joseph. Oliver moved to Kirtland in 1833, where he served on the high council and worked on the temple before mob violence forced him to leave and go to Missouri. On July 8, 1838, Oliver was called by revelation to help settle the financial affairs of the Church—a mission he performed with distinction, earning him the respect and appreciation of the Prophet and the eternal commendation of the Savior:

> And again, I say unto you, I remember my servant Oliver Granger; behold, verily I say unto him that his name shall be had in sacred remembrance from generation to generation, forever and ever, saith the Lord.
>
> Therefore, let him contend earnestly for the redemption of the First Presidency of my Church, saith the Lord; and when he falls he shall rise again, for his sacrifice shall be more sacred unto me than his increase, saith the Lord.
>
> Therefore, let him come up hither speedily, unto the land of Zion; and in the due time he shall be made a merchant unto my name, saith the Lord, for the benefit of my people.
>
> Therefore let no man despise my servant Oliver Granger, but let the blessings of my people be on him forever and ever. (D&C 117:12–15)

Oliver continued his service for the Church as a land agent in Illinois and Iowa before passing away on August 25, 1841.

GRIFFIN, SELAH J.

Born on March 17, 1799, at Redding, Fairfield County, Connecticut, Selah took up the blacksmith trade in Kirtland, where he became a member of the Church and was ordained an elder on June 6, 1831, by Joseph Smith. The next day he was called by revelation to journey to Missouri (see D&C 52:32; 56:5, 6). After settling in Missouri, he and his family suffered intense persecution from the mobs, which drove them from their home in 1833. He was ordained a seventy in Kirtland in 1836 and then returned to Missouri until the extermination order forced his expulsion once again. Having lost everything, he concluded that the price for his Church service was too high and separated himself from the mainstream Saints before their exodus to the West.

GROVER, THOMAS

Thomas was born on July 22, 1807, at Whitehall, Washington County, New York. After hearing the Prophet Joseph Smith preach, he was baptized in September 1834 by Warren A. Cowdery and then moved to Kirtland, Ohio, donating the resources from the sale of his farm to support the erection of the Kirtland Temple. He served as a member of the high councils in Kirtland, Far West, and Nauvoo (see D&C 124:132) and continued such service on high councils in the West following the exodus. During his Nauvoo days he also served in the Nauvoo Legion and acted as a personal bodyguard to the Prophet Joseph. In the Salt Lake Valley, Thomas prospered financially and remained active in Church and civic affairs. He died on February 20, 1886, generous and faithful to the end.

HAGAR

Hagar was an Egyptian handmaiden to Sarah and was also later the mother of Abraham's son Ishmael (see Gen. 16:1–16; 21:9–21; 25:12; Gal. 4:24–25). Hagar is mentioned three times in the Doctrine in Covenants, each time in connection with the principle of plural marriage (D&C 132:34, 65).

HANCOCK, LEVI W.

Levi, born on April 7, 1803, in Springfield, Hampden County, Massachusetts, became an accomplished carpenter in Ohio by age nineteen. Upon learning of the Book of Mormon, he investigated the restored gospel and was baptized on November 10, 1830, by Parley P. Pratt. He was called by revelation in June 1831 to journey to Missouri (see D&C 52:29). Upon his return from Missouri, he found that claimants had falsely appropriated all his holdings, forcing him to start afresh with his profession. He was called by the Prophet Joseph to participate in Zion's Camp, which he willingly did. In February 1835 he was called as one of the seven Presidents of the Seventy (see D&C 124:138), an office he held with honor for the next forty-seven years. He served in the Mormon Battalion and earned the respect of his associates. Upon his discharge from the Battalion in 1847 he joined the Saints in the Rockies, settling in Payson and then Manti, and was eventually ordained

Levi W. Hancock

a patriarch. He died in Washington County on June 10, 1882.

HANCOCK, SOLOMON

Solomon was born August 1793 in Springfield, Hampden County, Massachusetts. He was a Methodist with a keen musical talent. In Ohio he heard of the restored gospel from Parley P. Pratt and was baptized into the Church. In June 1831 he was called on a mission through revelation (see D&C 52:27) and helped organize branches of the Church in several states. He

Various Elders are called on missions.

then moved to Missouri, where he came under mob violence and, at one point, protected 120 women and children for ten days from suffering and death. He served on the high council in Clay County, Missouri, and then left on a second mission to the East, during which time his wife passed away. Later, as a resident of Far West, he remarried and stood firmly in support of the Prophet and the Church. After being driven from Missouri, he fled to Illinois where he and his brothers, Levi and Joseph, worked tirelessly to feed and assist refugees. Ultimately, he fled to Nauvoo after his community was burned by the mobs. His dream was to go West with the Saints, but his health failed him before he could prepare to go, and he passed away on December 2, 1847, near Council Bluffs, Iowa.

HARRIS, EMER

Emer, older brother of Martin Harris, was born on May 29, 1781. Through the instrumentality of the Book of Mormon, Emer became converted and was baptized on February 10, 1831, by Hyrum Smith. He moved to Ohio where he was ordained a high priest on October 25, 1831, by the Prophet Joseph Smith and served for a time as his scribe. He was called on a mission by revelation in January 1832 (see D&C 75:30) and experienced much success in working as a companion with his brother Martin. Following his mission he helped with the construction of the Kirtland Temple. With his family he subsequently moved to Missouri in 1838 where they endured great persecution with their fellow Saints. Later, in Nauvoo, Emer assisted with the construction of the Nauvoo Temple, including building the circular staircase. He emigrated west in 1850 and served as a patriarch among the Saints in Utah. He passed away in Logan on November 28, 1869.

Martin Harris, with Joseph Smith

HARRIS, GEORGE W.

George was born on April 1, 1780, in Berkshire County, Massachusetts. He was baptized by Orson Pratt in the fall of 1834 in Terre Haute, Indiana. He later moved to Far West, Missouri, where he was called on March 3, 1836, to serve on the high council. George labored diligently in the fight against mob violence in Missouri. In Nauvoo he was called to serve on the high council (see D&C 124:132) and was active in civic affairs. As an alderman and president pro tem of the city council, he signed the document declaring the *Nauvoo Expositor* "a public nuisance." It was that action by the city council that led directly to the martyrdom of the Prophet on June 27, 1844. Following the exodus from Nauvoo,

George served as a bishop and later a member of the high council in Council Bluffs, Iowa. He declined the opportunity to continue with the Saints in the westward exodus and passed away in 1857.

HARRIS, MARTIN

Martin was born in 1783 at Easttown, Saratoga County, New York. By trade he was a farmer in Palmyra during the early part of the Restoration. Having become intrigued with the mission of the young Prophet Joseph Smith, he delivered transcribed characters to scholar Charles Anthon in New York City, who confirmed their authenticity but withdrew his testimony when he learned that the original source could not be accessed (see JS—H 1:61–65; compare Isaiah's prophecy concerning this event as recorded in Isa. 29:11). Martin served as scribe for the translation of the early part of the record in 1828 (the Book of Lehi) but was responsible for the loss of the first 116 pages of the manuscript. Having repented, Martin became one of the three witnesses to the Book of Mormon in June 1829 (see sections 5 and 17). He mortgaged his farmland to finance the publication of the Book of Mormon, which appeared in March of 1830. On April 6, 1830, he was baptized by Oliver Cowdery. In 1832 he served a mission for the Church in New York and later participated in Zion's Camp. He was one of the three appointed to choose the members of the Quorum of the Twelve Apostles in 1835 and served on the high council in Kirtland (see D&C 102:3, 34). Soon thereafter he became estranged from the Church through his own prideful lapses. Brigham Young later assisted him to move to Utah. Though never excommunicated, he was rebaptized on September 17, 1870, and he reconfirmed his testimony just before he died on July 10, 1875, at Clarkston, Cache Valley, Utah.

Martin is mentioned by name twelve times in the text of the Doctrine and Covenants and seven additional times in the overviews to sections 3, 5, 10, 17, 19. Sections 5 and 19 were revealed specifically to Martin Harris through the Prophet Joseph Smith; section 17 was revealed to Martin Harris, Oliver Cowdery, and David Whitmer—the three witnesses of the Book of Mormon—through the Prophet Joseph Smith. From the beginning of Martin's involvement with the restored gospel and, specifically in response to his desire to have a witness of its authenticity (see D&C 5:1), the Lord made very clear His design for involving Martin in the cause of Zion as a witness to the truth:

Behold, I say unto him [Martin Harris], he exalts himself and does not humble himself sufficiently before me; but if he will bow down before me, and humble himself in mighty prayer and faith, in the sincerity of his heart, then will I grant unto him a view of the things which he desires to see.

And then he shall say unto the people of this generation: Behold, I have seen the things which the Lord hath shown unto Joseph Smith, Jun., and I know of a surety that they are true, for I have seen them, for they have been shown unto me by the power of God and not of man.

And I the Lord command him, my servant Martin Harris, that he shall say no more unto them concerning these things, except he shall say: I have seen them, and they have been shown unto me by the power of God; and these are the words which he shall say.

But if he deny this he will break the covenant which he has before covenanted with me, and behold, he is condemned.

And now, except he humble himself and acknowledge unto me the things that he has done which are wrong, and covenant with me that he will keep my commandments, and exercise faith in me, behold, I say unto him, he shall have no such views, for I will grant unto him no views of the things of which I have spoken. (D&C 5:24–28)

The Lord explained to Joseph Smith the dangers lying along the forward pathway and specifically foresaw "that if my servant Martin

Harris humbleth not himself and receive a witness from my hand, that he will fall into transgression" (D&C 5:32). This warning was based on past history when Martin prevailed upon the Prophet to share with him the initial 116 pages of the Book of Mormon translation and then lost that material, following which the Prophet received divine censure.

Martin was privileged to be one of the three witnesses of the Book of Mormon (see section 17) and contribute revenues for its publication—but not without the direct warning of the Lord: "And again, I command thee that thou shalt not covet thine own property, but impart it freely to the printing of the Book of Mormon, which contains the truth and the word of God" (D&C 19:26). Martin went on to labor in Missouri for the cause of the Church (see D&C 52:24; 58:35, 38), to serve with other leaders as "stewards over the revelations and commandments" (D&C 70:3, meaning the forthcoming publication of the revelations given to that time in 1831), and to participate in the United Order (see D&C 82:11; 104:26). It was Martin to whom the Lord communicated some of the most inspiring scriptural truths about the Atonement:

> For behold, I, God, have suffered these things for all, that they might not suffer if they would repent;
> But if they would not repent they must suffer even as I;
> Which suffering caused myself, even God, the greatest of all, to tremble because of pain, and to bleed at every pore, and to suffer both body and spirit—and would that I might not drink the bitter cup, and shrink—
> Nevertheless, glory be to the Father, and I partook and finished my preparations unto the children of men.

Wherefore, I command you again to repent, lest I humble you with my almighty power; and that you confess your sins, lest you suffer these punishments of which I have spoken, of which in the smallest, yea, even in the least degree you have tasted at the time I withdrew my Spirit. (D&C 19:16–20)

Martin Harris

Section 19 contains words of counsel given to Martin Harris but applicable to all Latter-day Saints: "Learn of me, and listen to my words; walk in the meekness of my Spirit, and you shall have peace in me" (D&C 19:23). It took Martin many years to recover his peace, but eventually he did return to the fold of the Lord before he passed away in Clarkston, Utah—with a copy of the Book of Mormon in his right hand and a copy of the Doctrine and Covenants in his left (see *WWBM*, 127).

HAWS, PETER

Peter was born on February 17, 1795, in Young Township, Leeds County, Ontario, Canada. After joining the Church in Canada, he moved to Nauvoo and became a prominent landholder known for his generosity to the poverty-stricken Saints flowing in from Missouri. He was appointed by revelation to assist with the building of the Nauvoo House (see D&C 124:62, 70). In 1843 he went on a mission to help raise funds for this project and also for the Nauvoo Temple. He remained faithful and service-minded in the Church until his post-Nauvoo years in Iowa when he developed disaffection toward the leaders of the Church. He became entangled with apostate Lyman Wight in Texas and was later cut off from the Church for speaking against Brigham Young and the Twelve. He later moved to Nevada and then California, where he died in 1862.

HEATHENS

The Doctrine and Covenants refers to the heathen nations on three occasions. The first indicates that they shall be redeemed after the day of the Gentiles and after the Jews shall have recognized Jesus as their Savior upon His Second Coming: "And then shall the heathen nations be redeemed, and they that knew no law shall have part in the first resurrection; and it shall be tolerable for them" (D&C 45:54). The second comes in reference to the work of the Lord's missionaries among the Gentiles—particularly when a household rejects the gospel message: "And it shall be more tolerable for the heathen in the day of judgment, than for that house; therefore, gird up your loins and be faithful, and ye shall overcome all things, and be lifted up at the last day" (D&C 75:22). The third instance comes in special instruc-

tions to members of the First Presidency concerning their duty to proclaim the gospel of Jesus Christ first to the Gentiles and then to the Jews:

> And then cometh the day when the arm of the Lord shall be revealed in power in convincing the nations, the heathen nations, the house of Joseph, of the gospel of their salvation.
>
> For it shall come to pass in that day, that every man shall hear the fulness of the gospel in his own tongue, and in his own language, through those who are ordained unto this power, by the administration of the Comforter, shed forth upon them for the revelation of Jesus Christ. (D&C 90:10–11)

According to Elder Bruce R. McConkie,

> The heathens are those who do not even profess a knowledge of the true God as record is borne of him in the scriptures. They worship idols or other gods that are entirely false as distinguished from so-called Christian peoples who attempt to worship the Lord, but who have totally false concepts of the nature and kind of being that he is. (*MD*, 347)

The references to the heathen nations in the Doctrine and Covenants and elsewhere in the scriptures confirm the universal love of God for all of His children. Nephi expresses this aptly: "And he remembereth the heathen; and all are alike unto God, both Jew and Gentile" (2 Ne. 26:33).

HERRIMAN, HENRY

Henry was born on June 9, 1804, at Rowley, Essex County, Massachusetts. He joined the Church in 1832 and moved to Kirtland the following year to be with the Saints. He joined Zion's Camp in support of the cause of the oppressed members in Missouri. In January 1838 he was called as one of the seven Presidents of the Seventy (see D&C 124:138) and assisted the Saints in their ongoing though ill-fated migration to Zion. During the Nauvoo period he served two missions for the Church and then joined the Heber C. Kimball company as a captain in 1848 for the trek westward. Henry responded to the call of Church leaders to expand his efforts for enhancing the work of the seventies, plus he served an additional mission, this time in England. He spent his remaining years in the St. George area, passing away on May 17, 1891, having served as a General Authority for more than fifty-three years.

HICKS, JOHN A.

John was born in 1810 in New York. His early years in the Church were marked by controversy over his tendency to speak ill of others. His repentance seemed to have been confirmed through his appointment as president over the elders' quorum in Nauvoo on January 19, 1841 (see D&C 124:137). However, he was not sustained in the general conference that was convened in April 1841 (his quorum having objected to his divisive and dissembling character), and his membership in the Church was suspended in October of that same year. John thereupon became allied with apostates of the Church and joined with the Carthage mob. Details of the death of John Hicks are not known.

HIGBEE, ELIAS

Elias was born on October 23, 1795, at Galloway, Gloucester County, New Jersey. He joined the Church in Ohio and moved his family to Missouri, where he held various Church positions and also was elected judge in Caldwell County (see *WWBM*, 134). As judge he issued an order for the sheriff to call out the militia to disperse the mobs acting against the Saints. The Battle of Crooked River ensued. In March 1838 he asked the Prophet Joseph Smith to explain certain passages in Isaiah (see D&C 113:7; with explanations following in verses 8–10). Having been forced by the mobs to leave Missouri, Elias moved to Illinois and continued his ecclesiastical and civic duties—among other things accompanying the Prophet to Washington, DC, on the unfruitful mission to seek redress from President Martin Van Buren for the atrocities

Joseph at the Nauvoo Temple

committed against the Saints. In Nauvoo, Elias, who had earned the friendship and respect of the Prophet Joseph, served on the temple committee—but not without some chastening from the Prophet on occasion. Elias died on June 7, 1843. The Prophet eulogized him in appreciative and laudatory terms.

HOLY APOSTLES

A term that refers to Christ's apostles at the time of His earthly ministry. See the entry entitled "Twelve Apostles in the Meridian of Time)."

HOLY GHOST (SEE ALSO FATHER IN HEAVEN; JESUS CHRIST)

The Holy Ghost is the third member of the Godhead. He is that personage "which beareth record of the Father and of the Son; which Father, Son, and Holy Ghost are one God, infinite and eternal, without end" (D&C 20:27–28; see also D&C 1:39; 42:17). Unlike the Father and the Son, who have glorified bodies of flesh and bones, "the Holy Ghost has not a body of flesh and bones, but is a personage of Spirit. Were it not so, the Holy Ghost could not dwell in us" (D&C 130:22).

The Holy Ghost is involved at every stage of the unfolding of the Father's plan of salvation. He is intimately connected with the instruction and enlightenment of the children of God through the ages, beginning with Adam, who, in his later years, "stood up in the midst of the congregation; and, notwithstanding he was bowed down with age, being full of the Holy Ghost, predicted whatsoever should befall his posterity unto the latest generation" (D&C 107:56). When the Savior was baptized, "the heavens were opened, and the Holy Ghost descended upon him in the form of a dove, and sat upon him, and there came a voice out of heaven saying: This is my beloved Son" (D&C 93:15). In the ultimate endowment of glory in the various mansions of the Father, the Holy Ghost will be the administering representative of the Godhead for the telestial realm: "These are they [of the telestial glory] who receive not of his [Christ's] fulness in the eternal world, but of the Holy Spirit through the ministration of the terrestrial" (D&C 76:86).

The text of the Doctrine and Covenants includes 220 references to the Holy Ghost (including the many related terms, such as Spirit, my Spirit, Comforter, Holy Spirit, Spirit of truth, his Spirit, Spirit of God, Spirit of the Lord, Spirit of Christ, and thy Spirit). The equivalence of such appellations is confirmed in various passages where two or more of these synonyms are used together: the Holy Ghost is the Comforter (D&C 35:19; 39:6), the Holy Ghost is the Holy Spirit (D&C 121:26), the Holy Ghost is both the Spirit and the Comforter (D&C 36:2), the Spirit is the Comforter (D&C 50:14), the Comforter is the Spirit of truth (D&C 50:17), the Comforter is "my Spirit" (D&C 124:97), the Comforter is both the Holy Ghost as well as "my Spirit" (D&C 36:2), the Spirit is the Spirit of Jesus Christ (D&C 84:45), the Spirit is the Spirit of truth (D&C 93:23), and the Spirit of truth is, in fact, Jesus Christ (D&C 93:26).

The Doctrine and Covenants is an extraordinary archive of doctrines and explanations concerning the operation and ministry of the Holy Ghost. In general, there are seven broad categories of administration concerning the work of the Holy Ghost: (1) the agent of the power and voice of the Word, Jesus Christ; (2) the confirming central figure involved with the ordinances of salvation, i.e., baptism by water and by fire; (3) the spiritual guide for the gathering of the Saints through missionary work; (4) the key to personal revelation; (5) the inspirational force to guide the organizational work of the Church and Kingdom of God; (6) the ongoing source of peace and comfort for the Saints as they endure to the end; and (7) the Holy Spirit of Promise who places the seal of divine approval on the ordinances leading to eternal life and exaltation for the faithful and obedient.

1. The Holy Ghost as the Agent for the Voice of the Word, Jesus Christ. It is the Word, even Jesus Christ, who renews the sacred covenants and promises of old on behalf of mankind in this last dispensation of time: "Wherefore, I say unto you that I have sent unto you mine everlasting covenant, even that which was from the beginning" (D&C 49:9). In doing so, He acts through the Spirit to impart the saving truths of heaven: "Verily, verily, I say unto you, I who speak even by the voice of my Spirit, even Alpha and Omega, your Lord and your God" (D&C 75:1; compare D&C 29:30). The Lord speaks to the world once again through His chosen prophet, who receives the word through the Comforter: "For, behold, I will bless all those who labor in my vineyard with a mighty blessing, and they shall believe on his [the prophet's] words, which are given him through me by the Comforter, which manifesteth that Jesus was crucified by sinful men for the sins of the world, yea, for the remission of sins unto the contrite heart" (D&C 21:9; see also D&C 90:14). When the Lord speaks, the Spirit confirms: "I, the Lord, have spoken it, and the Spirit beareth record" (D&C 59:24). It is a celestial partnership of redemption and spiritual communion involving two members of the Godhead, acting by the will of the Father.

The process by which the Lord extends the word of God unto mortals through the Spirit is of universal scope: "And the Spirit giveth light to every man that cometh into the world; and the Spirit enlighteneth every man through the world, that hearkeneth to the voice of the Spirit" (D&C 84:46). The Spirit and the name of Christ are inseparably bound: "And again, I say unto you, all things must be done in the name of Christ, whatsoever you do in the Spirit" (D&C 46:31). The Holy Ghost is therefore of supreme importance in sustaining, promulgating, confirming, and maintaining the words of truth, "even as they are in mine own bosom, to the salvation of mine own elect" (D&C 35:20).

2. The Holy Ghost as the Confirming Figure Central to the Ordinances of Salvation. The gospel of eternal salvation originates with, and emanates from, the Father; it is empowered and administered by the Son; and it is sustained and confirmed as a pathway to sanctification by the Holy Ghost. The process is as follows: "And this is my gospel—repentance and baptism by water, and then cometh the baptism of fire and the Holy Ghost, even the Comforter, which showeth all things, and teacheth the peaceable things of the kingdom" (D&C 39:6).

The Holy Ghost serves a pivotal role in the process of applying gospel principles. Like the Father and the Son, He is invoked in the baptismal prayer (see D&C 20:73) and in the confirmation prayer where the gift of the Holy Ghost is bestowed (see D&C 20:41). Every baptismal covenant, to be complete, involves both water and fire as cleansing elements: "And behold, whosoever believeth on my words, them will I visit with the manifestation of my Spirit; and they shall be born of me, even of water and of the Spirit" (D&C 5:16; see also D&C 20:37). The Holy Ghost may visit an individual, but not tarry (see D&C 130:23). It is the gift of the Holy Ghost that enables an individual who faithfully endures to the end to have the constant companionship of this member of the Godhead (see D&C 121:46). The sacramental prayers are reminders of the need to renew and strengthen covenants perpetually in order to have the Lord's Spirit (see D&C 20:77, 79). So important is this doctrine that the Holy Ghost is also active in the realm of the spirits, as President Joseph F. Smith learned in his remarkable vision: "These were taught faith in God, repentance from sin, vicarious baptism for the remission of sins, the gift of the Holy Ghost by the laying on of hands" (D&C 138:33).

3. The Holy Ghost as the Spiritual Guide for the Gathering of the Saints through Missionary Work. Consider the role of the Holy Ghost in gathering the elect from among the peoples of the earth through the ministry of those called into service as missionaries. The Spirit tells them where to go in their ministry (see D&C 31:11; 75:27; 79:2), what to say (see D&C 28:1, 4; 36:2; 42:6; 43:15; 50:14, 17; 52:9; 68:3; 97:1), and what to do (see D&C 46:7). So important is the companionship of the Holy Ghost in this work that missionaries simply cannot succeed on their own: "And the Spirit shall be given unto you by the prayer of faith; and if ye receive not the Spirit ye shall not teach" (D&C 42:14; see also 68:1; 71:1; 109:38). On the other hand, if the Spirit directs the teaching, then the agents of the Lord will know immediately what to say: "For it shall be given you in the very hour, yea, in the very moment, what ye shall say" (D&C 100:6).

The agenda for teaching is clear: "And let them journey from thence preaching the word by the way, saying none other things than that which the prophets and apostles have written, and that which is taught them by the Comforter through the prayer of faith" (D&C 52:9).

The apostolic commission to bear witness of the Savior to all nations depends upon the power of the Holy Spirit: "For the preparation wherewith I design to prepare mine apostles to prune my vineyard for the last time, that I may bring to pass my strange act, that I may pour out my Spirit upon all flesh" (D&C 95:4; compare 112:21–22). Teaching by the Spirit constitutes prophecy: "Wherefore, lift up your voice and spare not, for the Lord God hath spoken; therefore prophesy, and it shall be given by the power of the Holy Ghost" (D&C 34:10; compare Alma 17:2–3). Remarkably, those who preach with the Spirit deliver the words of scripture:

> And whatsoever they shall speak when moved upon by the Holy Ghost shall be scripture, shall be the will of the Lord, shall be the mind of the Lord, shall be the word of the Lord, shall be the voice of the Lord, and the power of God unto salvation. (D&C 68:4)

Those who hear such words with open minds and hearts will receive confirmation through the Spirit that the words are true (see D&C 100:8). The Holy Ghost will join the missionary companionship, along with the Lord Jesus Christ and His angels: "And whoso receiveth you, there I will be also, for I will go before your face. I will be on your right hand and on your left, and my Spirit shall be in your hearts, and mine angels round about you, to bear you up" (D&C 84:88).

4. The Holy Ghost as the Key to Personal Revelation. The Lord counseled Hyrum Smith concerning the blessing of enlightenment through the Spirit:

And now, verily, verily, I say unto thee, put your trust in that Spirit which leadeth to do good—yea, to do justly, to walk humbly, to judge righteously; and this is my Spirit.

Verily, verily, I say unto you, I will impart unto you of my Spirit, which shall enlighten your mind, which shall fill your soul with joy. (D&C 11:12–13)

This blessing of enlightenment, given through the visitation of the Holy Ghost, is extended to all who will prayerfully seek it: "God shall give unto you knowledge by his Holy Spirit, yea, by the unspeakable gift of the Holy Ghost, that has not been revealed since the world was until now" (D&C 121:26). The Lord shares that portion of knowledge and truth that is "expedient" for the individual to know concerning his or her salvation (D&C 18:18; see also D&C 75:10). Thus the sacred experience of receiving personal revelation is a universal opportunity: "And it shall come to pass that he that asketh in Spirit shall receive in Spirit" (D&C 46:28).

Oliver Cowdery learned intimate details concerning the purpose of personal revelation that are of great benefit to all the honest of heart:

Behold, thou knowest that thou hast inquired of me and I did enlighten thy mind; and now I tell thee these things that thou mayest know that thou hast been enlightened by the Spirit of truth;

Yea, I tell thee, that thou mayest know that there is none else save God that knowest thy thoughts and the intents of thy heart.

I tell thee these things as a witness unto thee—that the words or the work which thou hast been writing are true. . . .

Verily, verily, I say unto you, if you desire a further witness, cast your mind upon the night that you cried unto me in your heart, that you might know concerning the truth of these things.

Did I not speak peace to your mind concerning the matter? What greater witness can you have than from God?

And now, behold, you have received a witness; for if I have told you things which no man knoweth have you not received a witness? (D&C 6:15–17, 22–24)

Subsequently, the Lord instructed Oliver how the Spirit would interact with him in giving him revelation to sustain and advance his ministry: "Yea, behold, I will tell you in your mind and in your heart, by the Holy Ghost, which shall come upon you and which shall dwell in your heart. Now, behold, this is the spirit of revelation; behold, this is the spirit by which Moses brought the children of Israel through the Red Sea on dry ground" (D&C 8:2–3). When Oliver failed to be productive in translating from the ancient records according to this counsel, the Lord gave further instruction on the operation of the Holy Ghost:

Behold, you have not understood; you have supposed that I would give it unto you, when you took no thought save it was to ask me.

But, behold, I say unto you, that you must study it out in your mind;

then you must ask me if it be right, and if it is right I will cause that your bosom shall burn within you; therefore, you shall feel that it is right.

But if it be not right you shall have no such feelings, but you shall have a stupor of thought that shall cause you to forget the thing which is wrong; therefore, you cannot write that which is sacred save it be given you from me. (D&C 9:7–9)

The power of the Holy Ghost to impart eternal truth and divine knowledge to the pure in heart is central to all spiritual progression and unique in its ability to reveal "the works of the Lord, and the mysteries of his kingdom" (D&C 76:114). The sublime experience of Joseph Smith and Sidney Rigdon in beholding the visions of the degrees of glory (section 76) illustrates how the Spirit transforms sight in miraculous ways: "By the power of the Spirit our eyes were opened and our understandings were enlightened, so as to see and understand the things of God" (D&C 76:12).

5. The Holy Ghost as the Inspirational Force to Guide the Organizational Work of the Church and Kingdom of God. The chosen prophet of God is "inspired of the Holy Ghost to lay the foundation [of the Church], and to build it up unto the most holy faith" (D&C 21:2). Concurrently, priesthood holders are blessed of the Spirit to rise to their potential according to the oath and covenant of the priesthood: "For whoso is faithful unto the obtaining these two priesthoods of which I have spoken, and the magnifying their calling, are sanctified by the Spirit unto the renewing of their bodies. They become the sons of Moses and of Aaron and the seed of Abraham, and the church and kingdom, and the elect of God"

(D&C 84:33–34). Each worthy brother called to the priesthood is to be "ordained by the power of the Holy Ghost, which is in the one who ordains him" (D&C 20:60). Furthermore, the leader of the Church and Kingdom is "enabled to discern by the Spirit" (D&C 63:41) how to organize the Saints of Zion (see also D&C 72:24). Meetings are to be conducted as directed by the Holy Ghost (see D&C 46:2; compare also D&C 20:45; 44:2).

In addition, gifts are imparted through the blessing of the Spirit to help nurture and advance the cause of the Lord: "For all have not every gift given unto them; for there are many gifts, and to every man is given a gift by the Spirit of God. To some is given one, and to some is given another, that all may be profited thereby" (D&C 46:11–12).

Additional blessings of the Spirit enable a servant of God to "expound scriptures, and to exhort the church" (D&C 25:7)—even so far as "reproving betimes [i.e., without delay] with sharpness, when moved upon by the Holy Ghost; and then showing forth afterwards an increase of love toward him whom thou hast reproved, lest he esteem thee to be his enemy" (D&C 121:43). Those who are in tune with the Spirit are to strengthen others: "And if any man among you be strong in the Spirit, let him take with him that is weak, that he may be edified in all meekness, that he may become strong also" (D&C 84:106). The operation of the Spirit allows the Lord and His servants to "reason together, that ye may understand" (D&C 50:10). In addition, the Spirit guides the preparation of materials to preserve the history of the Church and promote its influence (see D&C 18:2; 124:4–5; 24:5; 47:4; 57:13; 58:50; 104:81). Clearly, the Holy Ghost exerts an all-encompassing influence for good upon the Lord's Church.

6. The Holy Ghost as the Ongoing Source of Peace and Comfort for the Saints as They Endure to the End. One of the tender and memorable passages from the Doctrine and Covenants reads: "Learn of me, and listen to my words; walk in the meekness of my Spirit, and you shall have peace in me" (D&C 19:23). The principle is that the Holy Ghost brings peace into the lives of those who are humble and obedient. The promise is that "you shall receive my Spirit, the Holy Ghost, even the Comforter, which shall teach you the peaceable things of the kingdom" (D&C 36:2; compare D&C 112:22). Such blessings flow into the lives of the prayerful: "Pray always, and I will pour out my Spirit upon you, and great shall be your blessing—yea, even more than if you should obtain treasures of earth and corruptibleness to the extent thereof" (D&C 19:38). Direction and guidance "shall be signalized unto you by the peace and power of my Spirit, that shall flow unto you" (D&C 111:8). Those who endure to the end in obedience are assured that "the Holy Ghost shall be thy constant companion, and thy scepter an unchanging scepter of righteousness and truth; and thy dominion shall be an everlasting dominion, and without compulsory means it shall flow unto thee forever and ever" (D&C 121:46).

7. The Holy Ghost as the Holy Spirit of Promise Who Places the Seal of Divine Approval on the Ordinances Leading to Eternal Life and Exaltation. The Doctrine and Covenants makes clear that all ordinances and covenants entered into by those striving for perfection in Christ are to be sealed (that is, ratified and confirmed) by the Holy Ghost in order to be efficacious beyond mortal life. The Holy Ghost, acting in this capacity, is referred to as the "Holy Spirit of Promise":

And verily I say unto you, that the conditions of this law are these: All covenants, contracts, bonds, obligations, oaths, vows, performances, connections, associations, or expectations, that are not made and entered into and sealed by the Holy Spirit of promise, of him who is anointed, both as well for time and for all eternity, and that too most holy, by revelation and commandment through the medium of mine anointed, whom I have appointed on the earth to hold this power (and I have appointed unto my servant Joseph to hold this power in the last days, and there is never but one on the earth at a time on whom this power and the keys of this priesthood are conferred), are of no efficacy, virtue, or force in and after the resurrection from the dead; for all contracts that are not made unto this end have an end when men are dead (D&C 132:7; compare also D&C 132: 18, 19, 26).

Those who keep the commandments of faith, repentance, baptism, and receiving the gift of the Holy Ghost by the laying on of hands by one in authority are then in a position to receive the ratifying blessing from the Holy Ghost that ensures that their obedience is recognized in heaven as well as on earth. These are they "who overcome by faith, and are sealed by the Holy Spirit of promise, which the Father sheds forth upon all those who are just and true. They are they who are the church of the Firstborn. They are they into whose hands the Father has given all things" (D&C 76:53–55). An individual can obtain all things only through strict covenant obedience whereby he honors sacred obligations in order to enjoy the promised blessings: "Wherefore, he is possessor of all things; for all things are subject unto him, both in heaven and on the earth, the life and the light, the Spirit and the power, sent forth by the will of the Father through Jesus Christ, his Son. But no man is possessor of all things except he be purified and cleansed from all sin" (D&C 50:27–28).

The ultimate destination of man is to return to the celestial realm and live in the presence of the Father and the Son forever. No one looking forward to the next life can hope to behold again the face of the Lord without receiving a great blessing granted through the Spirit, as confirmed in the case of Hyrum Smith. When he was called in 1841 to be Patriarch of the Church and also given a position as a deputy President next to his brother Joseph, the Lord declared: "First, I give unto you Hyrum Smith to be a patriarch unto you, to hold the sealing blessings of my church, even the Holy Spirit of promise, whereby ye are sealed up unto the day of redemption, that ye may not fall notwithstanding the hour of temptation that may come upon you" (D&C 124:124). This kind of sealing blessing provided by the Holy Spirit of Promise assured Hyrum of a celestial destiny. In effect, he had demonstrated his abiding loyalty to the Lord to such an extent and degree that he could look forward with confidence to a heavenly reward of the highest stature. This is further explained when Jesus made known to His Saints the revelation referred to as the "Olive Leaf":

Wherefore, I now send upon you another Comforter, even upon you my friends, that it may abide in your hearts, even the Holy Spirit of promise; which other Comforter is the same that I promised unto my disciples, as is recorded in the testimony of John.

This Comforter is the promise which I give unto you of eternal life, even the glory of the celestial kingdom;

Which glory is that of the church of the Firstborn, even of God, the holiest of all, through Jesus Christ his Son—

He that ascended up on high, as also he descended below all things, in that he comprehended all things, that he might be in all and through all things, the light of truth;

Which truth shineth. This is the light of Christ. (D&C 88:3–7)

The highest level of blessing granted through the Holy Spirit of Promise is to have one's calling and election made sure through the "more sure word of prophecy" (2 Pet. 1:19), which "means a man's knowing that he is sealed up unto eternal life, by revelation and the spirit of prophecy, through the power of the Holy Priesthood" (D&C 131:5). An individual of such a noble and righteous character could look forward with assurance that he or she would be able to see the face of the Lord in joy and glory (see D&C 101:38). Having the transcendent experience of being ministered to in person by the Lord Jesus Christ would constitute receiving what the Prophet Joseph Smith referred to as "the other Comforter"—namely, Jesus Christ Himself (see *TPJS*, 149–51). Thus, the Holy Ghost is the Comforter of first resort—the Holy Spirit of Promise—and the Lord Jesus Christ is the ultimate Comforter, "*the* other Comforter," whose presence is reserved for those who endure to the end in perfect harmony with the principles of the new and everlasting covenant—meaning all ordinances and

Kirtland Temple

covenants designated by the Lord as essential for salvation and exaltation in the celestial realm. (For additional details on this principle, see *MD*, 109–10, 361–62.)

So important is the role of the Holy Ghost in this eternal process that the only transgression that would place an individual outside the grasp of redemption from the second death (separation from God) is to commit blasphemy against the Holy Ghost: "Having denied the Holy Spirit after having received it, and having denied the Only Begotten Son of the Father, having crucified him unto themselves and put him to an open shame" (D&C 76:35; see also D&C 132:27).

HUMPHREY, SOLOMON

Solomon was born on September 23, 1775, at Canton, Hartford County, Connecticut. He was touched by the truth of the Book of Mormon and joined the Church, moving then to Kirtland to be among the Saints. In June 1831 he and a companion were called on a mission by revelation: "And again, I say unto you, let my servants Joseph Wakefield and Solomon Humphrey take their journey into the eastern lands; Let them labor with their families, declaring none other things than the prophets and apostles, that which they have seen and heard and most assuredly believe, that the prophecies may be fulfilled" (D&C 52:35–36). This was the first of several such opportunities for Solomon to share the gospel and bring people into the fold of Christ. He helped build the Kirtland Temple and participated in Zion's Camp. When the camp was disbanded, Solomon remained in Missouri, where he accepted a call for yet another mission. Death intervened, however, and he passed away in September 1834, having endured faithfully.

HUNTINGTON, WILLIAM

William was born on March 28, 1784, at New Grantham, Cheshire County, New Hampshire. In 1833 he encountered the Book of Mormon and became converted, moving to Kirtland in 1836. After becoming impoverished, he moved to Missouri, where persecution by mobs forced him to flee to Illinois. In Nauvoo he served on the high council (see D&C 124:132) and assisted in laying the first stone of the Nauvoo Temple. It was William who helped bury the bodies of the martyred Joseph and Hyrum. He continued his work on the Nauvoo Temple until the last stone was laid. In 1846 he left Nauvoo and presided over one of the Iowa encampments until his death on August 19, 1846.

HYDE, ORSON

Orson was born on January 8, 1805, at Oxford, New Haven County, Connecticut. An orphan in his youth, he moved to Ohio as a teenager and eventually got a job at the Gilbert and Whitney store in Kirtland. He became convinced of the truthfulness of the Book of Mormon and was baptized by Sidney Rigdon on October 30, 1831. He was called by revelation to preach the restored gospel (see D&C 68:1, 7) and subsequently went on a mission with Samuel Smith (see D&C 75:13). His memory was extraordinary and served him well as an instructor in the School of the Prophets. He knew the Bible by heart in English, German, and Hebrew. As a clerk for the First Presidency, he recorded many of the early revelations and historical minutes of the Church. After participating in Zion's Camp (see D&C 103:40), he returned to Kirtland and received a call to the Council of the Twelve Apostles in 1835. Thereafter he served a mission in Great Britain

Orson Hyde

with Heber C. Kimball. In 1838 Orson brought cause against the Prophet Joseph. Orson consequently lost his fellowship in the Church later that year. After repenting, he was reinstated and was promised that he would be called upon to dedicate the Holy Land—a commission he fulfilled on October 24, 1841. Following the martyrdom, he moved with the Saints to the Salt Lake Valley in 1852 and served with distinction in public office and as a member of the Quorum of the Twelve. He passed away on November 28, 1878.

Orson Hyde is referred to in the text of the Doctrine and Covenants concerning his call as a missionary (D&C 68:1, 7; 75:13), his safety while in Missouri (D&C 100:14), his position as a member of the high council in Kirtland (D&C 102:3, 34; also as clerk), his call to participate in Zion's Camp (D&C 103:40), and his call as a member of the Quorum of the Twelve (D&C 124:129). He is also listed in the Introduction to the Doctrine and Covenants as among those proclaiming the "Testimony of the Twelve Apostles to the Truth of the Book of Doctrine and Covenants." In addition, he is mentioned in the current introductory headings to sections 68 and 102. It is in conjunction with section 68 that the Lord gives an extraordinary promise to Orson Hyde and his associates Luke S. Johnson, Lyman E. Johnson, and William E. McLellin—and by extension to "all the faithful elders of my church" (D&C 68:7):

> And, behold, and lo, this is an ensample unto all those who were ordained unto this priesthood, whose mission is appointed unto them to go forth—
>
> And this is the ensample unto them, that they shall speak as they are moved upon by the Holy Ghost.
>
> And whatsoever they shall speak when moved upon by the Holy Ghost shall be scripture, shall be the will of the Lord, shall be the mind of the Lord, shall be the word of the Lord, shall be the voice of the Lord, and the power of God unto salvation. (D&C 68:2–4)

ISAAC

Isaac was the son of Abraham and Sarah and the heir of the covenant promises of the Lord (see Gen. 15:1–6; 17:15–19; 18:9–15; 21:1–8). Abraham's willingness to sacrifice Isaac by command of the Lord (see Gen. 22; D&C 132:36) was the supreme manifestation of this father's ultimate faith and devotion to God—and a symbol of the Father's sacrifice of His Only Begotten Son for all mankind. The Lord revealed to Joseph Smith details of a future glorious sacrament meeting when all the faithful prophets of old would convene again, including "Joseph and Jacob, and Isaac, and Abraham, your fathers, by whom the promises remain" (D&C 27:10). Moreover, the Lord declared the exaltation of Abraham, Isaac, and Jacob, who "because they did none other things than that which they were commanded, they have entered into their exaltation, according to the promises, and sit upon thrones, and are not angels but are gods" (D&C 132:37). Other references to Isaac deal with the Lord's law of war (D&C 98:32–33), the doctrine of plural marriage (D&C 132:1), the glorious congregation of the elect of God at the Second Coming (D&C 133:55), the identity of the Lord as "the God of your fathers, the God of Abraham and of Isaac and of Jacob" (D&C

Isaac

136:21), and the presence of Isaac (D&C 138:41) among "the great and might ones who were assembled" in the "congregation of the righteous" (D&C 138:38) in the vision granted to President Joseph F. Smith concerning the work of salvation in the spirit realm.

ISAIAH

Isaiah was the great prophet of the Lord in Jerusalem in the time frame 740 BC to 701 BC—and the most quoted of all the prophets in holy writ. Isaiah is mentioned six times in the Doctrine and Covenants: four times in connection with interpretations given of passages in Isaiah 11 and 52 (see D&C 113), once in connection with President Joseph F. Smith's vision of the spirit realm (see D&C 138:42), and once in section 76, concerning the degrees of glory. In this latter case, those in the telestial kingdom are characterized as having denied the testimony of the Savior, though they might verbally claim allegiance to Christ, John, Moses, Elias, Esaias, Isaiah, Enoch, Paul, Apollos, Cephas, or some other movement (see D&C 76:100).

Isaiah

ISHMAELITES

The Ishmaelites (see D&C 3:18) were the progeny of Ishmael, who accompanied Lehi and his family on their journey to the Promised Land. In the eventual separation of the family into two streams of descendants—one embracing the righteous manner of life of Nephi and his followers, and the other embracing the rebellion of Laman and Lemuel and their followers—the Ishmaelites blended in with the latter and were absorbed as part of that segment of the population in the Book of Mormon.

JACOB (SEE ALSO SONS OF JACOB)

Jacob, son of Isaac, grandson of Abraham, and father of Joseph, was one of the leading patriarchs whose descendants carried forth the work of the Abrahamic covenant to spread the blessings of the gospel of salvation and the priesthood of God to the world (Abr. 2:9–11). The Lord revealed to Joseph Smith details of a future glorious meeting when all the faithful prophets of old would convene again, including "Joseph and Jacob, and Isaac, and Abraham, your fathers, by whom the promises remain" (D&C 27:10). The Lord declared the exaltation of Abraham, Isaac, and Jacob, who "did none other things than that which they were commanded; and because they did none other things than that which they were commanded, they have entered into their exaltation, according to the promises, and sit upon thrones, and are not angels but are gods" (D&C 132:37). Jacob is mentioned in the text of the Doctrine and Covenants fifteen times, among which are various references to the house of Jacob.

JACOBITES

The Jacobites, mentioned in the Doctrine and Covenants as among those to receive the restored gospel (see D&C 3:17), were descendants of Jacob, a younger brother of Nephi. They constituted one of the divisions of the Nephite people (see Jacob 1:13–14).

JAMES

James (English equivalent of the Hebrew name Jacob), son of Zebedee, was one of the original Twelve Apostles called by the Lord during His mortal ministry (Matt. 4:21; Mark 1:19–20; Luke 5:10). He belonged to the inner circle of three leading Apostles (Peter, James, and John). All three were with the Savior on the Mount of Transfiguration (see Matt. 17: 1–13) and at Gethsemane (see Matt. 26:36–37; Mark 14:32–33; Luke 22:39). James participated with Peter and John in the latter-day restoration of the Melchizedek Priesthood, most likely in late May 1829 (see D&C 27:12–13; 128:20), following the restoration of the Aaronic Priesthood under the hands of John the Baptist on May 15, 1829 (see D&C 13).

James is mentioned by name three times in the text of the Doctrine and Covenants: first, in connection with the ministry of John the Beloved who was granted his desire to remain on earth until the Second Coming: "And I will make thee [Peter] to minister for him [John] and for thy brother James; and unto you three I will give this power and the keys of this ministry until I come" (D&C 7:7); second, in connection with the future assembly of elect priesthood leaders who will partake of the sacrament with the Savior: "And also with Peter, and James, and John, whom I have sent unto you, by whom I have ordained you and confirmed you to be apostles, and especial witnesses of my name, and bear the keys of your ministry and of the same things which I revealed unto them" (D&C 27:12); and, third, in Joseph Smith's summation of the restoration of the priesthood authority and keys: "The voice of Peter, James, and John in the wilderness between Harmony, Susquehanna county, and Colesville, Broome county, on the Susquehanna river, declaring themselves as possessing the keys of the kingdom, and of the dispensation of the fulness of times!" (D&C 128:20).

JAMES, GEORGE

George was born in 1797 in Massachusetts. He moved to Ohio where he learned of the restored gospel and joined the Church in 1831. In June 1831 the Lord instructed the Prophet Joseph Smith to arrange for George to be ordained a priest (see D&C 52:38). He was also later ordained an elder but failed to engage himself fully in the work of the ministry and finally withdrew from fellowship. He died in November 1864 in his hometown of Brownshelm, Ohio.

JAQUES, VIENNA

Vienna Jaques (also spelled Jacques) was born on June 10, 1787, in Beverly, Essex County, Massachusetts. The Book of Mormon so moved her that she journeyed alone to Kirtland to meet with and be instructed by the Prophet Joseph Smith. Following her baptism, she returned again to the Boston area, shared the gospel with her family, and then came back to Kirtland with her valuables, including $1,400 in savings. On March 8, 1833, she was instructed of the Lord to consecrate her wealth to the Church and then journey to Missouri to receive a promised inheritance (see D&C 90:28–31). This she did; however, the mounting persecution there forced her to abandon her holdings and flee to northern Missouri, where she used her nursing skills to relieve the suffering of the Saints. Eventually she crossed

Vienna Jaques

the plains to the Salt Lake Valley, driving her own wagon. Faithful and self-reliant to the end, she passed away at ninety-six on February 7, 1884.

JARED

The ancient patriarch Jared, son of Mahalaleel and father of Enoch (Moses 6:20–21), is mentioned twice in the Doctrine and Covenants: once in connection with the descent of the priesthood lineage—"Jared was two hundred years old when he was ordained under the hand of Adam, who also blessed him" (D&C 107:47)—and again when Adam "called Seth, Enos, Cainan, Mahalaleel, Jared, Enoch, and Methuselah, who were all high priests, with the residue of his posterity who were righteous, into the valley of Adam-ondi-Ahman, and there bestowed upon them his last blessing" (D&C 107:53).

JEREMY

Jeremy was a priesthood leader mentioned in the Doctrine and Covenants in connection with the lineage of the priesthood prior to the time of Moses: "And Elihu [received the priesthood] under the hand of Jeremy; And Jeremy under the hand of Gad" (D&C 84:9–10). No other details are known.

JESSE (SEE ALSO EPHRAIM; JOSEPH)

Jesse, father of David, and therefore in the direct line of descent leading to Christ (see Ruth 4:17, 22; 1 Chr. 2:5–12; Matt. 1:5–6) is mentioned five times in the Doctrine and Covenants, all in connection with interpretations given in section 113 for certain passages from Isaiah. For example, "Who is the Stem of Jesse spoken of in the 1st, 2d, 3d, 4th, and 5th verses of the 11th chapter of Isaiah? Verily thus saith the Lord: It is Christ" (D&C 113:1–2).

JESUS CHRIST

The presentation of the person and mission of the Lord Jesus Christ in the Doctrine and Covenants—much of it given directly in His own words—testifies to the world "that the holy scriptures are true, and that God does inspire men and call them to his holy work in this age and generation, as well as in generations of old; thereby showing that he is the same God yesterday, today, and forever" (D&C 20:11–12). The Doctrine and Covenants is thus a testament of the mercy and condescension of the Only Begotten Son in once again communicating to mortals the will of the Father.

The Doctrine and Covenants provides a rich and abundant source of saving truths concerning the Lord Jesus Christ, His divine qualities, His sacred mission, and His design and purpose in bringing forth the Restoration in the latter days. He is the Son of God, the Only Begotten of the Father, with whom He is one; He is the Lord God and the Word (among many other names); He is a person of transcendent glory. His qualities include being of eternal scope ("Alpha and Omega, the beginning and the end"), infinite, omnipotent, omniscient, unchanging, of unlimited perspective, full of grace, and the light and the life of the world. He is the Creator, the Redeemer, the atoning Lamb of God, the Finisher of the will of the Father, the Advocate before the Father, the Savior, and the font of mercy and forgiveness. His purpose in bringing about the Restoration in the latter days is to enable the obedient to become sons and daughters of

The First Vision

God, to receive the riches of eternity, and to have the blessings of salvation and exaltation.

The Lord is the Author of the Doctrine and Covenants, according to the will of the Father, with Joseph Smith the curator of the revealed word of heaven and the spokesperson for Jesus Christ in the dispensation of the ful-

ness of times. The words of the Savior in the sections of the Doctrine and Covenants establish the divine framework for latter-day communication from heaven. The Savior presents Himself in specific dimensions of His nature and His mission, as in the following example:

I AM Alpha and Omega, Christ the Lord; yea, even I am he, the beginning and the end, the Redeemer of the world.

I, having accomplished and finished the will of him whose I am, even the Father, concerning me—having done this that I might subdue all things unto myself—

Retaining all power, even to the destroying of Satan and his works at the end of the world, and the last great day of judgment, which I shall pass upon the inhabitants thereof, judging every man according to his works and the deeds which he hath done.

And surely every man must repent or suffer, for I, God, am endless. . . .

Learn of me, and listen to my words; walk in the meekness of my Spirit, and you shall have peace in me.

I am Jesus Christ; I came by the will of the Father, and I do his will. (D&C 19:1–4, 23–24)

The Savior's presence in the pages of this sacred scripture is pervasive, the term *Jesus Christ* occurring seventy-eight times in the text (with "I am Jesus Christ" occurring eleven times and "Christ" forty-four times). In addition, the term *Savior* occurs nineteen times, *Jehovah* six times, the *Son* (meaning the Son of God) seventy-eight times, and *Redeemer* twenty-two times. The Lord Jesus Christ is understandably the foremost personality in the Doctrine and Covenants. The following chart can serve as a compass for navigating through this material:

1. Who is Jesus Christ?

• **Son of God.** The Doctrine and Covenants confirms that Jesus Christ is the Son of God and the Savior of the world: "Hearken, O ye elders of my church, who have assembled yourselves together in my name, even Jesus Christ the Son of the living God, the Savior of the world; inasmuch as ye believe on my name and keep my commandments" (D&C 42:1). The expression "Son of God" is used nineteen times throughout the pages of the Doctrine and Covenants, in many cases as part of the direct witness of the Savior Himself, saying "I am Jesus Christ, the Son of God" (or a variant; see D&C 10:57; 11:28; 36:8; 45:52; 52:44). The blessing of sonship, in turn, is promised to the faithful in the fold of Christ—those who are justified and sanctified through the Atonement and through personal covenant obedience, thus becoming the sons and daughters of God: "I am Jesus Christ, the Son of God, who was crucified for the sins of the world, even as many as will believe on my name, that they may become the sons of God, even one in me as I am one in the Father, as the Father is one in me, that we may be one" (D&C 35:2). The Lord confirmed this truth to the wife of the Prophet Joseph: "Hearken unto the voice of the Lord your God, while I speak unto you, Emma Smith, my daughter; for verily I say unto you, all those who receive my gospel are sons and daughters in my kingdom" (D&C 25:1).

• **One with the Father.** Jesus is one with the Father—and Father, Son, and Holy Ghost are one. The Holy Ghost "beareth record of the Father and of the Son; which Father, Son, and Holy Ghost are one God, infinite and eternal, without end" (D&C 20:27–28). The Doctrine and Covenants is a testament to that divine oneness manifested by the Savior: "I am Jesus Christ, the Son of God, . . . even as many as will believe on my name, that they may become the sons of God, even one in me as I am one in the Father, as the Father is one in me, that we may be one" (D&C 35:2). Furthermore: "And the Father and I are one. I am in the Father and the Father in me; and inasmuch as ye have received me, ye are in me and I in you" (D&C 50:43; see also John 17:22; 1 John 5:7; Mosiah 15:4; 3 Ne. 11:27, 36). In Deity is the supreme example of unity of purpose and oneness of mission.

• **Lord God.** Jesus Christ is God, even the "Lord God" who is referenced thirty-six times in the text of the Doctrine and Covenants in such an example as this: "BEHOLD, and hearken, O ye elders of my church, saith the Lord your God, even Jesus Christ, your advocate, who knoweth the weakness of man and how to succor them who are tempted" (D&C 62:1). Jesus Christ does the will of the Father in all things (see D&C 19:24; 3 Ne. 11:11) and therefore commands with supreme authority that all repent and sanctify themselves: "That I may testify unto your Father, and your God, and my God, that you are clean from the blood of this wicked generation" (D&C 88:75). Thus the Father is the God of Jesus Christ and our God as well—and Jesus is our God, being "Christ the Lord; yea, . . . the beginning and the end, the Redeemer of the world" (D&C 19:1).

• **The Word.** Jesus Christ is the Word (D&C 93:8; John 1:1). As the Word, "the words of salvation are in him, . . . he carries the Father's word to all men; . . . he is the executive and administrator who does the will of the Father; . . .

the Father speaks and his word is executed by the Son (*MD*, 844).

• **A Multitude of Names.** Jesus Christ is known in the Doctrine and Covenants by a variety of names and designations: "Son of God" (D&C 6:21), the "light and the life of the world" (D&C 12:9), "the glorious Majesty on high" (D&C 20:16), the "unchangeable God, the framer of heaven and earth" (D&C 20:17), the "Only Begotten Son" (D&C 20:21), the "Redeemer, the Great I AM" (D&C 29:1), "the Lord God, the Mighty One of Israel" (D&C 36:1), " Alpha and Omega, the beginning and the end" (D&C 38:1), "the living God" (D&C 50:1), "the good shepherd, and the stone of Israel" (D&C 50:44), "the Lord of the whole earth" (D&C 55:1), "Christ the Lamb" (D&C 76:85), "Lamb of God" (D&C 88:106), the "Word" (D&C 93:8), "Jehovah" (D&C 109:34, 42, 56, 68; 110:3), and other appellations occurring in variant forms.

• **Person of Glory.** The Savior is a person of glory. The Doctrine and Covenants provides compelling evidence of this in Joseph Smith's and Oliver Cowdery's vision in the Kirtland Temple on April 3, 1836:

> The veil was taken from our minds, and the eyes of our understanding were opened.
> We saw the Lord standing upon the breastwork of the pulpit, before us; and under his feet was a paved work of pure gold, in color like amber.
> His eyes were as a flame of fire; the hair of his head was white like the pure snow; his countenance shone above the brightness of the sun; and

his voice was as the sound of the rushing of great waters, even the voice of Jehovah, saying:

I am the first and the last; I am he who liveth, I am he who was slain; I am your advocate with the Father.

Behold, your sins are forgiven you; you are clean before me; therefore, lift up your heads and rejoice. (D&C 110:1–5)

The promise of this same hallowed experience is extended to the faithful: "When the Savior shall appear we shall see him as he is. We shall see that he is a man like ourselves" (D&C 130:1).

2. What are the Qualities of Jesus Christ?

• **Of eternal scope: Alpha and Omega.** The Savior identifies Himself in terms of "Alpha and Omega" thirteen times in the text of the Doctrine and Covenants (as well as four times in Revelation—Rev. 1:8, 11; 21:6; 22:13—and once in the Book of Mormon—3 Ne. 9:18). Alpha and omega are the first and last letters of the Greek alphabet. When the Savior characterizes Himself as Alpha and Omega—the first and the last—He identifies the all-encompassing scope of His mission and calling. The expression "alpha and omega" constitutes what is known as a "merism"—a stylistic device in which an entire range of objects, events, deeds, etc., is implied through mentioning only parts of that range (from the Greek word *meros*, meaning "part"). Thus the first verse of the Old Testament states that God created "the heaven and the earth," implying that He created all things, including all living things. Everyday speech uses merisms such as "searching high and low," implying a comprehensive and complete search.

"Alpha and Omega" (together with "the beginning and the end") is the most elevated and sublime example of this kind of rhetorical device.

One might wonder why the frequency of the expression Alpha and Omega is particularly high in the Doctrine and Covenants, compared with the other standard works? Could it be that the Savior is speaking at the end of the long sequence of dispensations and wishes now to remind His listeners that the Second Coming is nigh—when the grand cycle of time is about to end and a new cycle of everlasting service is about to begin?

• **Infinite.** The Lord Jesus Christ is of infinite existence. He refers to Himself as "the beginning and the end, the Redeemer of the world" (D&C 19:1; compare D&C 38:1) and "the first and the last" (D&C 110:4). He is "the same God yesterday, today, and forever" (D&C 20:12). He is "from all eternity to all eternity, the Great I AM, even Jesus Christ" (D&C 39:1). He "has all power" and is "from everlasting to everlasting" (D&C 61:1). He is unchanging in His devotion to the plan of salvation: "From eternity to eternity he is the same, and his years never fail" (D&C 76:4).

• **Omnipotent.** The Savior is all-powerful, even to the overcoming of all fear: "Fear not, little children, for you are mine, and I have overcome the world, and you are of them that my Father hath given me; and none of them that my Father hath given me shall be lost" (D&C 50:41–42). Said He: "Behold, and hearken unto the voice of him who has all power, who is from everlasting to everlasting, even Alpha and Omega, the beginning and the end" (D&C 61:1).

In the words of John, "he received all power, both in heaven and on earth, and the glory of the Father was with him, for he dwelt in him" (D&C 93:17).

• **Omniscient.** The Lord Jesus Christ is all-knowing, as He Himself confirms: "Thus saith the Lord your God, even Jesus Christ, the Great I AM, . . . the same which knoweth all things, for all things are present before mine eyes" (D&C 38:1–2). As the omniscient Lord, He has the capacity to bestow infinite wisdom upon His faithful and obedient servants:

> And to them will I reveal all mysteries, yea, all the hidden mysteries of my kingdom from days of old, and for ages to come, will I make known unto them the good pleasure of my will concerning all things pertaining to my kingdom.
>
> Yea, even the wonders of eternity shall they know, and things to come will I show them, even the things of many generations.
>
> And their wisdom shall be great, and their understanding reach to heaven; and before them the wisdom of the wise shall perish, and the understanding of the prudent shall come to naught.
>
> For by my Spirit will I enlighten them, and by my power will I make known unto them the secrets of my will—yea, even those things which eye has not seen, nor ear heard, nor yet entered into the heart of man. (D&C 76:7–10)

• **Unchanging.** The Lord is perpetually the eternal One, the unchanging One. In fact, *Jehovah*—a name for Jesus Christ used five times in the Doctrine and Covenants (D&C 109:34, 42, 56, 68; 110:3)—means "Unchangeable One," "The Eternal I Am." He is therefore "the same God yesterday, today, and forever. . . . infinite and eternal, from everlasting to everlasting the same unchangeable God." (D&C 20:12, 17). His invitation to all is thus grounded in His eternal Godhood: "Listen to the voice of the Lord your God, even Alpha and Omega, the beginning and the end, whose course is one eternal round, the same today as yesterday, and forever" (D&C 35:1).

• **Unlimited Perspective.** The Lord Almighty has the capacity of infinite vision and perspective, "for verily the voice of the Lord is unto all men, and there is none to escape; and there is no eye that shall not see, neither ear that shall not hear, neither heart that shall not be penetrated (D&C 1:2). He sees all, from the premortal sphere to the ending of time and beyond: "Thus saith the Lord your God, even Jesus Christ, the Great I AM, Alpha and Omega, the beginning and the end, the same which looked upon the wide expanse of eternity, and all the seraphic hosts of heaven, before the world was made; The same which knoweth all things, for all things are present before mine eyes" (D&C 38:1–2).

• **Full of Grace.** The Son is full of grace and truth, having become, through obedience to the Father, the Redeemer of mankind: "And being made perfect, he became the author of eternal salvation unto all them that obey him" (Heb. 5:9). This process of fulfilling His mission of atoning sacrifice with perfection was described by John: "And I, John, saw that he received not of the fulness at the first, but received grace for grace; And he received not of the fulness at first, but continued from grace to grace, until he received a fulness; And thus he was called the Son of God, because he received not of the fulness at the first" (D&C 93:12–14). The word *grace* is used in the Doctrine and Covenants sometimes as an attribute of the Savior (D&C 17:8; 18:31; 21:1; 84:99; 93:11; 109:44), sometimes as an attribute of the Father (D&C 66:12; 76:94; 109:10), sometimes as an attribute of "God" (D&C 84:102; 88:133; 102:4), and sometimes as an attribute of both Father and Son (see D&C 138:14). In all things, the grace of the Lord Jesus Christ is "sufficient" for His obedient followers (D&C 17:8; 18:31; compare 2 Cor. 12:9; Ether 12:26–27; Moro. 10:32) to receive the miracle of rebirth on the pathway to salvation and exaltation.

• **Light and Life of the World.** The Savior is, by His own pronouncement, "the light and life of the world" (D&C 39:2; 45:7). He is the essence of all that is light in a world of darkness and shadows. It is the "light of Christ" (D&C 88:7) that sustains the operation of the universe and quickens one's understanding (D&C 88:11). This is "the light which is in all things, which giveth life to all things, which is the law by which all things are governed, even the power of God who sitteth upon his throne, who is in the bosom of eternity, who is in the midst of all things" (D&C 88:13). Said Jesus Christ: "I am the true light that lighteth every man that cometh into the world" (D&C 93:2; compare also Moro. 7:16). The standard works are the archives of eternal light. The word *light* appears 509 times in the scriptures—almost half of these references (235) in the Doctrine and Covenants. Jesus bestows this gift of light and life through mercy and compassion on all who

will receive it: "Ye who are quickened by a portion of the celestial glory shall then receive of the same, even a fulness" (D&C 88:29).

3. What is the Mission of Jesus Christ?

• **Creator.** The Savior testifies in the Doctrine and Covenants that He is the Creator: "I am the same which spake, and the world was made, and all things came by me" (D&C 38:3) and "by whom all things were made which live, and move, and have a being" (D&C 45:1). The Doctrine and Covenants also declares:

> By these things [the revelations of God] we know that there is a God in heaven, who is infinite and eternal, from everlasting to everlasting the same unchangeable God, the framer of heaven and earth, and all things which are in them;
> And that he created man, male and female, after his own image and in his own likeness, created he them. (D&C 20:17–18; compare also other references concerning the process of the Creation: D&C 14:9; 76:24; 77:2, 12; 88:20)

It is by virtue of the divine Creation that the Lord commands the nations of the world to heed His word: "And again, the Lord shall utter his voice out of heaven, saying: Hearken, O ye nations of the earth, and hear the words of that God who made you" (D&C 43:23). The testimony of John gives additional confirmation of the role of the Lord as Creator:

> Therefore, in the beginning the Word was, for he was the Word, even the messenger of salvation—

The light and the Redeemer of the world; the Spirit of truth, who came into the world, because the world was made by him, and in him was the life of men and the light of men.

The worlds were made by him; men were made by him; all things were made by him, and through him, and of him. (D&C 93:8–10; compare John 1:1–5)

• **Redeemer.** The office of the Son of God is that of Redeemer, even "the light and the Redeemer of the world; the Spirit of truth, who came into the world, because the world was made by him, and in him was the life of men and the light of men" (D&C 93:9). This sacred office is confirmed by the witness of the Savior Himself:

I am Alpha and Omega, Christ the Lord; yea, even I am he, the beginning and the end, the Redeemer of the world.

I, having accomplished and finished the will of him whose I am, even the Father, concerning me—having done this that I might subdue all things unto myself—

Retaining all power, even to the destroying of Satan and his works at the end of the world, and the last great day of judgment, which I shall pass upon the inhabitants thereof, judging every man according to his works and the deeds which he hath done.

And surely every man must repent or suffer, for I, God, am endless. (D&C 19:1–4)

The promise of the Redeemer to His children is all-encompassing:

Fear not, little children, for you are mine, and I have overcome the world, and you are of them that my Father hath given me;

And none of them that my Father hath given me shall be lost.

And the Father and I are one. I am in the Father and the Father in me; and inasmuch as ye have received me, ye are in me and I in you.

Wherefore, I am in your midst, and I am the good shepherd, and the stone of Israel. He that buildeth upon this rock shall never fall.

And the day cometh that you shall hear my voice and see me, and know that I am.

Watch, therefore, that ye may be ready. Even so. Amen. (D&C 50:41–46)

• **Atoning Lamb of God.** The Atonement is the transcendent gift of the Only Begotten Son, who acted according to the will of the Father in giving an infinite measure of His mercy and love on behalf of all mankind. The Savior does not use the word *Atonement* in characterizing Himself in the first person to those receiving the words of latter-day revelation. However, He does describe the act of the Atonement in significant detail in the Doctrine and Covenants. Section 19, in particular, presents a poignant account of the Savior's sacrificial ordeal:

Therefore I command you to repent—repent, lest I smite you by the rod of my mouth, and by my wrath, and by my anger, and your sufferings be sore—how sore you know not, how exquisite you know not, yea, how hard to bear you know not.

For behold, I, God, have suffered these things for all, that they might not suffer if they would repent;

But if they would not repent they must suffer even as I;

Which suffering caused myself, even God, the greatest of all, to tremble because of pain, and to bleed at every pore, and to suffer both body and spirit—and would that I might not drink the bitter cup, and shrink—

Nevertheless, glory be to the Father, and I partook and finished my preparations unto the children of men. (D&C 19:15–19)

As the Redeemer and "the author and the finisher of [the] faith" (Moro. 6:4), Jesus Christ can say: "Listen to the voice of Jesus Christ, your Redeemer, the Great I AM, whose arm of mercy hath atoned for your sins; Who will gather his people even as a hen gathereth her chickens under her wings, even as many as will hearken to my voice and humble themselves before me, and call upon me in mighty prayer" (D&C 29:1–2). Moreover, He proclaims: "I am the same which have taken the Zion of Enoch into mine own bosom; and verily, I say, even as many as have believed in my name, for I am Christ, and in mine own name, by the virtue of the blood which I have spilt, have I pleaded before the Father for them" (D&C 38:4). Thus, "Jesus Christ the Son of the living God, the Savior of the world" (D&C 42:1), is "he who was crucified for the sins of the world" (D&C 54:1). "I am he who liveth," He declared. "I am he who was slain" (D&C 110:4).

There are three passages in the Doctrine and Covenants where the significance of the Savior's descent and resulting triumph are mentioned in the third person: first, "little children are sancti-fied through the atonement of Jesus Christ" (D&C 74:7); second, the inhabitants of the celestial kingdom are those "who are just men made perfect through Jesus the mediator of the new covenant, who wrought out this perfect atonement through the shedding of his own blood" (D&C 76:69); and third, the reference to the Redeemer by President Joseph F. Smith in his vision of the work being carried on in the spirit realm: "That through his atonement, and

Jesus Christ, with Mary Magdalene

by obedience to the principles of the gospel, mankind might be saved" (D&C 138:4; verse 2 in that section also refers to the "atoning sacrifice"). The essence and spirit of the Atonement are evident throughout the pages of the Doctrine and Covenants, even though the use of the word *Atonement* and its variants is sparse. In contrast, the Book of Mormon speaks some three dozen times of the Atonement or its variants.

• **Finisher of the Will of the Father.** The Savior pronounced this glorious summation of His commission as "one sent down from on high" (D&C 65:1), saying: "I AM Alpha and Omega, Christ the Lord; yea, even I am he, the beginning and the end, the Redeemer of the world. I, having accomplished and finished the will of him whose I am, even the Father, concerning me— . . . Learn of me, and listen to my words; walk in the meekness of my Spirit, and you shall have peace in me. I am Jesus Christ; I came by the will of the Father, and I do his will" (D&C 19:1–2, 23–24). As the Finisher of the Will of the Father, Jesus Christ is ordained of the Father as the Redeemer of the world, for the term *Messiah* or *Christ* means "anointed"—divinely commissioned, authorized, and foreordained for His sacred mission. Having been ordained and anointed by the Father, the Savior, in turn, calls and ordains others as His agents to bring about the establishment of Zion:

> The Lord spake unto Joseph Smith, Jun., saying: Hearken unto me, saith the Lord your God, who are ordained unto the high priesthood of my church, who have assembled yourselves together;
>
> And listen to the counsel of him who has ordained you from on high, who shall speak in your ears the words of wisdom, that salvation may be unto you in that thing which you have presented before me, saith the Lord God. (D&C 78:1–2)

• **Advocate.** An advocate, by definition, is one who is called to testify before an authorized tribunal on behalf of an individual or cause. When the Savior identifies Himself as an Advocate in the Doctrine and Covenants, He defines His role before the Father as the Defender of those who follow in the pathway of righteousness in honor and obedience to the commandments. The role of advocacy is empowered through the Atonement. Having fulfilled the will of the Father and given His life for mankind, Jesus can say: "Lift up your hearts and be glad, for I am in your midst, and am your advocate with the Father; and it is his good will to give you the kingdom" (D&C 29:5). Those called into service in the Kingdom of God need not fear because "I myself will go with them and be in their midst; and I am their advocate with the Father, and nothing shall prevail against them" (D&C 32:3). As Advocate, the Savior pleads for those in His care: "and in mine own name, by the virtue of the blood which I have spilt, have I pleaded before the Father for them" (D&C 38:4). The Doctrine and Covenants relates the Savior's pleadings before His Father:

> Father, behold the sufferings and death of him who did no sin, in whom thou wast well pleased; behold the blood of thy Son which was shed, the blood of him whom thou gavest that thyself might be glorified;
>
> Wherefore, Father, spare these my brethren that believe on my name, that they may come unto me and have everlasting life. (D&C 45:4–5)

By virtue of the Savior's mortal ministry, He knows and understands the role of Advocate: "Behold, and hearken, O ye elders of my church, saith the Lord your God, even Jesus Christ, your advocate, who knoweth the weakness of man and how to succor them who are tempted" (D&C 62:1; compare Alma 34:14–16). He prepares His mortal clients for the hour of their appearance before the Father:

And I give unto you, who are the first laborers in this last kingdom, a commandment that you assemble yourselves together, and organize yourselves, and prepare yourselves, and sanctify yourselves; yea, purify your hearts, and cleanse your hands and your feet before me, that I may make you clean;

That I may testify unto your Father, and your God, and my God, that you are clean from the blood of this wicked generation; that I may fulfil this promise, this great and last promise, which I have made unto you, when I will. (D&C 88:74–75)

Upon the appearance of the Savior in vision before Joseph Smith and Oliver Cowdery in the Kirtland Temple on April 3, 1836, He confirmed again His sacred role as Advocate:

I am the first and the last; I am he who liveth, I am he who was slain; I am your advocate with the Father. Behold, your sins are forgiven you; you are clean before me; therefore, lift up your heads and rejoice. Let the hearts of your brethren rejoice, and let the hearts of all my people rejoice, who have, with their might, built this house to my name. (D&C 110:4–6)

• **Savior.** Jesus Christ is the only name whereby man can be saved. It is only through His authority and power, and the principles and ordinances of His priesthood, that the plan of happiness and salvation has efficacy. Consider the following passage recounting the power of the name of Jesus Christ:

And as many as repent and are baptized in my name, which is Jesus Christ, and endure to the end, the same shall be saved.

Behold, Jesus Christ is the name which is given of the Father, and there is none other name given whereby man can be saved;

Wherefore, all men must take upon them the name which is given of the Father, for in that name shall they be called at the last day;

Wherefore, if they know not the name by which they are called, they cannot have place in the kingdom of my Father. . . .

And I, Jesus Christ, your Lord and your God, have spoken it. (D&C 18:22–25, 33; compare 2 Ne. 25:20; 31:21; Mosiah 3:17; 5:8; Acts 4:12)

• **Font of Mercy and Forgiveness.** The Lord God is "full of mercy" (D&C 84:102). That is one of His everlasting hallmarks—and one of the central themes of the Doctrine and Covenants:

Behold, and hearken unto the voice of him who has all power, who is from everlasting to everlasting, even Alpha and Omega, the beginning and the end.

Behold, verily thus saith the Lord unto you, O ye elders of my church, who are assembled upon this spot, whose sins are now forgiven you, for I, the Lord, forgive sins, and am merciful unto those who confess their sins with humble hearts. (D&C 61:1–2)

The mercy of the Lord is manifested in myriad ways: the power to translate the Book of

Mormon (D&C 1:29); the power of the Atonement: "Listen to the voice of Jesus Christ, your Redeemer, the Great I AM, whose arm of mercy hath atoned for your sins" (D&C 29:1); the continual emanation of truth from above "by the voice of mercy all the day long" (D&C 43:25); the blessings for those "who have kept the covenant and observed the commandment, for they shall obtain mercy" (D&C 54:6); the blessings for the meek and humble (see D&C 97:2; 106:7); the solace and protection for the faithful in the day of wrath (see D&C 101:9); and the manifestations of the divine in the House of the Lord (see D&C 110:7).

The dedicatory prayer of the Kirtland Temple given by the Prophet Joseph Smith on March 27, 1836, invokes the Lord's mercy seven times: for those who keep the covenants, for those repenting from sins, for the wicked mobs who have persecuted the Saints, for the nations of the earth and their rulers, for the children of Jacob, for the Prophet's wife and children, and for their immediate "connections," or associates (see D&C 109:1, 34, 50, 54, 62, 69, 70). In his concluding words, the Prophet supplicates: "O Lord God Almighty, hear us in these our petitions, and answer us from heaven, thy holy habitation, where thou sittest enthroned, with glory, honor, power, majesty, might, dominion, truth, justice, judgment, mercy, and an infinity of fulness, from everlasting to everlasting" (D&C 109:77).

In a promise prefacing the visions of glory seen by the Prophet Joseph Smith and Sidney Rigdon on February 16, 1832, the Lord declared:

> I, the Lord, am merciful and gracious unto those who fear me, and delight to honor those who serve me in righteousness and in truth unto the end.

> Great shall be their reward and eternal shall be their glory. (D&C 76:5–6; compare various other scriptures using the word *merciful:* D&C 3:10; 38:14; 50:16; 70:18; 101:92; 109:53)

4. What is the Purpose of Jesus Christ in Bringing about the Restoration?

What was the design behind the Restoration? Why did the Father and Son appear to the boy Joseph Smith? Why did the Only Begotten of the Father open the extraordinary dialogue with His circle of believers who became agents for renewing the covenants and promises of old in a world hungering and thirsting for light? There is no better answer than that given by Jesus Christ Himself in the pages of the Doctrine and Covenants:

> Listen to the voice of the Lord your God, even Alpha and Omega, the beginning and the end, whose course is one eternal round, the same today as yesterday, and forever. I am Jesus Christ, the Son of God, who was crucified for the sins of the world, even as many as will believe on my name, that they may become the sons of God, even one in me as I am one in the Father, as the Father is one in me, that we may be one. (D&C 35:1–2)

The heritage, promise, and opportunity of belonging to the family of God—this constitutes the shield of protection and the fortress of security for the Saints on the eve of the Second Coming:

> Wherefore, I the Lord, knowing the calamity which should come upon

the inhabitants of the earth, called upon my servant Joseph Smith, Jun., and spake unto him from heaven, and gave him commandments;

And also gave commandments to others, that they should proclaim these things unto the world; and all this that it might be fulfilled, which was written by the prophets—

The weak things of the world shall come forth and break down the mighty and strong ones, that man should not counsel his fellow man, neither trust in the arm of flesh—

But that every man might speak in the name of God the Lord, even the Savior of the world. (D&C 1:17–20)

• **The Sons and Daughters of God.** The Restoration was inaugurated as a supreme blessing for the faithful children of God, allowing them to rise to the fulfillment of their potential as participants in the eternal family of heaven: "But to as many as received me [in the meridian of time], gave I power to become my sons; and even so will I give unto as many as will receive me, power to become my sons" (D&C 39:4). As the Restorer of covenant blessings, the Lord speaks with "the voice of mercy all the day long, and by the voice of glory and honor and the riches of eternal life" (D&C 43:25), saying:

I have sent mine everlasting covenant into the world, to be a light to the world, and to be a standard for my people, and for the Gentiles to seek to it, and to be a messenger before my face to prepare the way before me.

Wherefore, come ye unto it, and with him that cometh I will reason as with men in days of old, and I will show unto you my strong reasoning.

Wherefore, hearken ye together and let me show unto you even my wisdom. (D&C 45:9–11)

• **The Riches of Eternity.** The Saints are commanded to "give ear to the voice of the living God; and attend to the words of wisdom which shall be given unto you" (D&C 50:1) in order to "grow in grace and in the knowledge of the truth" (D&C 50:40). To that end, He empowers His servants to minister with authority and with the restored keys of priesthood power (see D&C 65:2). With His all-seeing eye He views the destiny of His children and prepares to pour blessings without measure upon their heads: "Behold and lo, mine eyes are upon you, and the heavens and the earth are in mine hands, and the riches of eternity are mine to give" (D&C 67:2). Nothing can stop the advance of His program because

His purposes fail not, neither are there any who can stay his hand. . . .

For thus saith the Lord—I, the Lord, am merciful and gracious unto those who fear me, and delight to honor those who serve me in righteousness and in truth unto the end.

Great shall be their reward and eternal shall be their glory. (D&C 76:3, 5–6)

• **Salvation and Exaltation.** The Savior calls upon His flock to "listen to the counsel of him who has ordained you from on high, who shall speak in your ears the words of wisdom, that salvation may be unto you in that thing which you have presented before me, saith the Lord God" (D&C 78:2). The purpose of the Restoration is to bring again Zion, to redeem Israel, to gather all things in one, to clothe the earth with the glory of her God, and to establish a celestial place where God "stands in the midst of his people" in "glory, and honor, and power, and might . . . Forever and ever" (D&C 84:101–102). The promise to the faithful is clear:

> Verily, thus saith the Lord: It shall come to pass that every soul who forsaketh his sins and cometh unto me, and calleth on my name, and obeyeth my voice, and keepeth my commandments, shall see my face and know that I am;
>
> And that I am the true light that lighteth every man that cometh into the world;
>
> And that I am in the Father, and the Father in me, and the Father and I are one. (D&C 93:1–3)

The Savior comforts His flock with the promise that their prayers will be heard and answered: "Therefore, he giveth this promise unto you, with an immutable covenant that they shall be fulfilled; and all things wherewith you have been afflicted shall work together for your good, and to my name's glory, saith the Lord" (D&C 98:3). Through the Restoration, the promises of the Abrahamic covenant are again activated among the Saints. They shall carry out the ministry of bearing the gospel and the priesthood to the four quarters of the world and enjoy the blessings of eternal lives through the perpetuation of the family unit in the hereafter:

> This promise is yours also, because ye are of Abraham, and the promise was made unto Abraham; and by this law is the continuation of the works of my Father, wherein he glorifieth himself.
>
> Go ye, therefore, and do the works of Abraham; enter ye into my law and ye shall be saved. (D&C 132:31–32)

There is a miracle awaiting the discerning reader of the Doctrine and Covenants, in that the recorded words of the Savior reveal the nature of the relationship that He seeks with His children. That relationship is meant to be personal and real. As the First Vision burst upon the world in 1820, the truth of this relationship was confirmed once again. In the words of the young Prophet: "When the light rested upon me I saw two Personages, whose brightness and glory defy all description, standing above me in the air. One of them spake unto me, calling me by name and said, pointing to the other—*This is My Beloved Son. Hear Him!*" (JS—H 1:17). To be called by name by Deity is to know that a relationship of a divine nature is personal. This same mutual friendship of the Shepherd and His sheep is repeated again and again in the Doctrine and Covenants: "Behold, thou art Oliver. . . . Behold, I am Jesus Christ" (D&C 6:20, 21). "Behold thou art Hyrum. . . . Behold, I am Jesus Christ" (D&C 11:23, 28). "Behold, I am Jesus Christ. . . . And behold, thou art David" (D&C 14:9, 11). It is a miracle to contemplate that the Savior—the Creator, the Redeemer, the Only Begotten of the Father—calls each man, woman, and child individually by name and seeks to cultivate a personal relationship. It is a measure of His generosity that He shares ownership of the Church with each member. It is both the Church of Jesus Christ and the Church of Jesus Christ of Latter-day Saints (see D&C 115:4). "He numbereth his sheep, and they know him; and there shall be one fold and one shepherd; and he shall feed his sheep, and in him they shall find pasture" (1 Ne. 22:25).

Beginning with Adam, the Lord sanctioned and directed a one-on-one relationship with His children: "And thou art after the order of him who was without beginning of days or end of years, from all eternity to all eternity. Behold, thou art one in me, a son of God; and thus may all become my sons. Amen" (Moses 6:67–68).

The "I am . . . thou art" pattern is one of the most inspiring and yet humbling doctrines of the gospel. It applies not just to the prophets but to everyone: "Behold, I speak unto all who have good desires, and have thrust in their sickle to reap" (D&C 11:27).

JETHRO

Jethro, prince of Midian and father-in-law of Moses (see Ex. 3:1; 4:18; 18:1–12), is mentioned in the Doctrine and Covenants concerning priesthood lineage:

> And the sons of Moses, according to the Holy Priesthood which he [Moses] received under the hand of his father-in-law, Jethro;
> And Jethro received it under the hand of Caleb. (D&C 84:6–7)

JEWS (SEE ALSO JUDAH)

The term *Jews*, in the most specific sense, refers to people of the lineage of Judah, son of Jacob. In a broader sense the term can be applied to those, over the generations, who were citizens of Jerusalem, even though they were not of Jewish lineage (as in 2 Ne. 30:4). Thus,

Lehi and Ishmael were part of the Jewish community in their day, although Lehi was by lineage from the tribe of Joseph through Manasseh, son of Joseph (see Alma 10:3), while Ishmael and his posterity derived from the tribe of Ephraim, son of Joseph (see *JD* 23:184–85). The text of the Doctrine and Covenants contains nineteen references to "Jews" and three to the word *Jew*—most of the references applying to the specific meaning of the term, i.e., of the lineage of Judah.

The most frequent usage of the term *Jews* in the Doctrine and Covenants comes in passages distinguishing the flow of gospel truth—i.e., first to the Gentiles, and then to the Jews (see D&C 20:9; 21:12; 90:9; 107:33, 34, 35, 97; 112:4; 133:8). However, in one passage concerning the Book of Mormon, the word *Jew* is used in the broader sense of the term: "Which is my word to the Gentile, that soon it may go to the Jew, of whom the Lamanites are a remnant, that they may believe the gospel, and look not for a Messiah to come who has already come" (D&C 19:27; compare 57:4). In this usage, the Lamanites are identified as a branch of the Jews. Such is the case in regard to Lehi and his posterity being of Jewish citizenship (though of the lineage of Joseph). In a more direct sense, the Mulekites—as colonists to the New World who were later integrated into the Nephite generations under the leadership of Mosiah I—introduced the direct blood lineage of Judah into Book of Mormon demographics, since Mulek was the surviving son of Zedekiah, king of Judah (see Hel. 8:21; Omni 1:12–16). Thus, the Lamanites of the latter days could be thought of as Jewish in two senses: through the Jewish citizenship of Lehi and, in part, through the blood lineage of Mulek blended in with the Josephite lineage of Lehi and his descendants.

JOHN THE BAPTIST

John was the forerunner of the Messiah. The son of Zacharias and Elizabeth, he embodied the continuation of the lineage of the Aaronic Priesthood from the days of Moses and Aaron down to the time of the Savior's mortal ministry (see D&C 84:27). He was the one chosen to baptize the Savior (John 1:29–34; Matt. 3:13–17) and of whom the Savior said, "Among those that are born of women there is not a greater prophet than John the Baptist: but he that is least in the kingdom of God is greater than he" (Luke 7:28).

There are seven references to the name John in the text of the Doctrine Covenants that unequivocally apply to John the Baptist (D&C 27:7 [twice], 8; 35:4; 76:100; 84:27; 133:55). John is mentioned in the Doctrine and Covenants as being "filled with the spirit of Elias" (D&C 27:7) and the one called to "prepare the way" before the Savior (D&C 35:4). Several references to John in section 93 might refer to John the Baptist, John the Beloved, or both (see the entry for "John the Beloved" for details). Section 13 includes the immortal words of John the Baptist as he conferred the Aaronic Priesthood upon the heads of Joseph Smith and Oliver Cowdery on May 15, 1929: "Upon you my fellow servants, in the name of Messiah I confer the Priesthood of Aaron, which holds the keys of the ministering of angels, and of the gospel of repentance, and of baptism by immersion for the remission of sins; and this shall never be taken again from the earth, until the sons of Levi do offer again an offering unto the Lord in righteousness" (D&C 13:1).

JOHN THE BELOVED

John, son of Zebedee and brother of James, was one of the Lord's Twelve Apostles in the meridian of time (see Matt. 4:21–22; Luke 5:1–11). He belonged to the inner circle of three Apostles (Peter, James, and John) who were with the Savior on the Mount of Transfiguration (see Matt. 17: 1–13) and at Gethsemane (see Matt. 26:36–37; Mark 14:32–33; Luke 22:39). John was present at the crucifixion as the disciple "whom he [Jesus] loved" (John 19:26) and who would care for the bereaved Mary. John was permitted to remain on earth as a ministering servant of the Lord leading up to the Second Coming (see John 21:20–23; 3 Ne. 28:6; D&C 7). He participated with Peter and James in the latter-day restoration of the Melchizedek Priesthood, most likely in late May of 1829 (see D&C 27:12–13; 128:20), following the restoration of the Aaronic Priesthood under the hands of John the Baptist on May 15, 1829 (D&C 13).

John the Baptist

The text of the Doctrine and Covenants includes seventeen references to John that clearly refer to the Apostle John (D&C 7:1; 20:35; 27:12; 61:14; 76:15; 77:1, 2, 3, 5 [twice], 6, 14; 88:3; 128:6, 20; 130:3; 135:7). There is some uncertainty whether the seven references to John in section 93 (verses 6, 11, 12, 15, 16, 18, 26) apply to John the Apostle or John the Baptist (or both). Commentators Hyrum M. Smith and Janne M. Sjodahl indicate the "record" of John referred to in D&C 93:6 is that of John the Beloved, Apostle of the Lord (see *DCC*, 591). Historian Lyndon W. Cook takes an alternative position: "This revelation is of major doctrinal importance. The headnote of section 93 in the 1921 edition of the Doctrine and Covenants (and all subsequent reprints, 1921–1980) suggests that the text of the revelation contains a portion of the record of John the Apostle. Both John Taylor and Orson Pratt believed the record to be that of John the Baptist" (*RPJS*, 154–55). Author Richard O. Cowan shows how both positions can be harmonized: "In verses 7–17, the Lord refers to the testimony of John the Baptist as quoted in the gospel written by the apostle John; the Baptist had the privilege of beholding and bearing witness to Christ's glory" (*DCOMS*, 145).

According to this last position, both Johns are involved—John the Baptist, whose testimony is being cited, and John the Beloved, whose record is the source for this testimony. If this is correct, two noble and righteous voices uphold the divinity of the mission of Christ and the saving power of the gospel. The words of section 93, verses 7–10, are similar to those given by the John the Beloved in John 1:1–5; the words of section 93, verse 15, are similar to those given by John the Baptist in his report of the baptism of Jesus (see John 1:32; Matt. 3:16–17). Furthermore, the Savior's statement concerning the purpose for section 93 (verse 19) is similar to the words of John the Beloved in his gospel record (John 20:31). All of this is evidence for the consistency and integrity of the scriptural text.

Additional passages concerning John include his desire to remain on earth until the Second Coming: "And I will make thee [Peter] to minister for him [John] and for thy brother James; and unto you three I will give this power and the keys of this ministry until I come" (D&C 7:7); the future assembly of elect priesthood leaders who will partake of the sacrament with the Savior: "And also with Peter, and James, and John, whom I have sent unto you, by whom I have ordained you and confirmed you to be apostles, and especial witnesses of my name, and bear the keys of your ministry and of the same things which I revealed unto them" (D&C 27:12); and Joseph Smith's summation of the heavenly events comprising the restoration of the priesthood authority and keys: "The voice of Peter, James, and John in the wilderness between Harmony, Susquehanna county, and Colesville, Broome county, on the Susquehanna river, declaring themselves as possessing the keys of the kingdom, and of the dispensation of the fulness of times!" (D&C 128:20).

JOHN THE REVELATOR (SEE JOHN THE BELOVED)

JOHNSON, AARON

Aaron was born on June 22, 1806, at Haddam, Middlesex County, Connecticut. He was baptized on April 5, 1836, and moved the following

Aaron Johnson

year to Kirtland. Persecution forced him to move to Far West, Missouri, and then to Nauvoo, where his devoted service included being a member of the city council, filling officer duty in the Nauvoo Legion, being a municipal court judge, and participating as a member of the Nauvoo high council (see D&C 124:132). He also went to Carthage, Illinois, as a bondsman for the Prophet Joseph and Hyrum on the eve of the martyrdom. Aaron joined the westward migration as a captain of one of the companies, arriving in the Salt Lake Valley in 1850. Thereafter he was one of the principal settlers of Springville, Utah, where his devotion and community service were manifested in multiple ways. His civic accomplishments in the legislature were also notable. His last Church assignment was that of patriarch. He passed away on May 10, 1877.

JOHNSON, JOHN

John was born on April 11, 1778, at Chesterfield, Cheshire County, New Hampshire. Eventually he moved to Hiram, Ohio, and became a prosperous farmer. While visiting the Prophet Joseph Smith in Kirtland, John experienced the miraculous healing of his rheumatic wife, Elsa, under the hands of the Prophet. The couple was converted and subsequently baptized. In September 1831 they charitably opened their home in Hiram to the Prophet and his family. Joseph's productive time while living at the Johnson home was interrupted by a violent episode on March 24, 1832, in which a mob dragged him out and subjected him to a painful tarring and feathering. The Johnsons moved to Kirtland soon thereafter, where John (or Father Johnson, as he was called) was ordained an elder and subsequently—on June 4, 1833 (see *HC* 1:353)—a high priest:

> And again, verily I say unto you, it is wisdom and expedient in me, that my servant John Johnson whose offering I have accepted, and whose prayers I have heard, unto whom I give a promise of eternal life inasmuch as he keepeth my commandments from henceforth—
>
> For he is a descendant of Joseph and a partaker of the blessings of the promise made unto his fathers—
>
> Verily I say unto you, it is expedient in me that he should become a member of the order, that he may assist in bringing forth my word unto the children of men.
>
> Therefore ye shall ordain him unto this blessing, and he shall seek

diligently to take away incumbrances that are upon the house named among you, that he may dwell therein. Even so. Amen. (D&C 96:6–9)

John became a member of the Kirtland high council on February 17, 1834 (see D&C 102:3, 34). He is also mentioned in connection with his inheritance as a participant in the United Order (see D&C 104:24, 34). Among other things, he displayed the Michael Chandler mummies and papyri in his inn at Kirtland on July 3, 1835 (see *HC* 2:235–36) and contributed resources and service toward the building of the Kirtland Temple. Thereafter, financial and legal difficulties, together with his loss of commitment to gospel truths, led to his falling away from the Church in 1837. He died in Kirtland on July 30, 1843.

JOHNSON, LUKE S.

Luke was born on November 3, 1807, at Pomfret, Windsor County, Vermont, the son of John and Elsa Johnson. The conversion of his parents laid the groundwork for his own baptism into the restored Church on May 10, 1831, by the Prophet Joseph. He was called into missionary service by revelation in November 1831. It was on this occasion that the Lord declared the extraordinary promise given to Luke Johnson, Orson Hyde, Lyman Johnson, William McLellin, and "unto all the faithful elders of my church" (D&C 68:7) that their words, as inspired by the Holy Ghost, would in essence be scriptural: "And whatsoever they shall speak when moved upon by the Holy Ghost shall be scripture, shall be the will of the Lord, shall be the mind of the Lord, shall be the word of the Lord, shall be the voice of the Lord, and the power of God unto salvation" (D&C 68:4). In January 1832, Luke was called by revelation to serve a mission with William McLellin in the southern states (D&C 75:9–12).

He participated in Zion's Camp as a scout, and when he returned to Kirtland he was called to serve in the first high council of the Church (see D&C 102:3, 34). In February 1835 he became a member of the original Quorum of the Twelve (see the "Testimony of the Twelve Apostles to the Truth of the Book of Doctrine

Salt Lake Valley

78

Luke S. Johnson

and Covenants" in the Introduction to that volume of scripture). However, his faith weakened to the extent that he was excommunicated in Far West in 1838. Nevertheless, his support for the Prophet and the Smith family remained strong and he was rebaptized in March 1846. The following year he journeyed to the Salt Lake Valley with the original company of pioneers. In Utah he served in various Church leadership capacities, dying on December 9, 1861.

JOHNSON, LYMAN E.

Lyman, younger brother of Luke Johnson, was born on October 24, 1811, at Pomfret, Windsor County, Vermont. Following his baptism into the Church, Lyman was called by revelation in November 1831 to preach the gospel (see D&C 68:7). It was on this occasion that the Lord declared the extraordinary promise given to Lyman Johnson and others, as well as to "all the faithful elders of my church" (ibid.) that their words, as inspired by the Holy Ghost, would in fact be scripture: "And whatsoever they shall speak when moved upon by the Holy Ghost shall be scripture, shall be the will of the Lord, shall be the mind of the Lord, shall be the word of the Lord, shall be the voice of the Lord, and the power of God unto salvation" (D&C 68:4). He received a second mission call the following year to serve with Orson Pratt (see D&C 75:14). After his participation in Zion's Camp, Lyman was chosen on February 14, 1835, as the first apostle to serve in the Quorum of the Twelve in the dispensation of the fulness of times (see the "Testimony of the Twelve Apostles to the Truth of the Book of Doctrine and Covenants." He was disfellowshipped in 1837 over specious charges against the Prophet Joseph Smith, but he later repented and was reinstated. His return was

Lyman E. Johnson

short-lived. On April 13, 1838, Lyman was excommunicated for apostate actions, though he remained friendly toward the Saints and lamented his own downfall. He passed away in a sleighing accident in 1856.

JOSEPH

Joseph was the son of Jacob and Rachel and holder of the birthright in Israel (see Gen. 37–50). His dealings with his errant brothers who were sent by Jacob to gather provisions in Egypt during the time of acute famine attest to Joseph's Christlike nature (see Gen. 42–45). The fulfillment of the commission of the Abrahamic covenant to carry the gospel and the blessings of the priesthood to the four

Joseph

quarters of the earth (see Abr. 2:9–11) is accomplished largely through the lineage of Joseph. The Book of Mormon provides an abundance of additional scriptural material concerning Joseph and his commission (see 2 Ne. 3:4–22; 4:1–2; Alma 10:3; 46:23–27). Key passages in which Joseph is mentioned include a reference to the future event when Jesus Christ will participate in a glorious assemblage with all of His holy prophets down through the ages: "And also with Joseph and Jacob, and Isaac, and Abraham, your fathers, by whom the promises remain" (D&C 27:10). Joseph is also mentioned in connection with the "rod" that should come forth "out of the stem of Jesse" (Isa. 11:1): "Behold, thus saith the Lord: It [the rod] is a servant in the hands of Christ, who is partly a descendant of Jesse as well as of Ephraim, or of the house of Joseph, on whom there is laid much power" (D&C 113:4; compare also verse 6 in connection with the "root" of Jesse). The terms *rod* and *root* very likely refer to the Prophet Joseph Smith. Joseph, son of Jacob, is also mentioned in connection with the law of the Lord concerning the justification for war:

> Behold, this is the law I gave unto my servant Nephi, and thy fathers, Joseph, and Jacob, and Isaac, and Abraham, and all mine ancient prophets and apostles.
>
> And again, this is the law that I gave unto mine ancients, that they should not go out unto battle against any nation, kindred, tongue, or people, save I, the Lord, commanded them. (D&C 98:32–33)

JOSEPHITES

The Josephites (see D&C 3:17) were descendants of Joseph, the youngest brother of Nephi. They constituted one of the divisions of the

Nephite people. Jacob, brother of Nephi and Joseph wrote:

> Now the people which were not Lamanites were Nephites; nevertheless, they were called Nephites, Jacobites, Josephites, Zoramites, Lamanites, Lemuelites, and Ishmaelites. (Jacob 1:13)

JUDAH (SEE ALSO JEWS)

Judah, fourth son of Jacob and Leah (see Gen. 29:35; 37:26–27; 43:3, 8; 44:16; 49:8–12; Deut. 33:7), is mentioned three times in the Doctrine and Covenants: once in the dedicatory prayer for the Kirtland Temple—"And the yoke of bondage may begin to be broken off from the house of David; And the children of Judah may begin to return to the lands which thou didst give to Abraham, their father" (D&C 109:63–64); once in connection with the final gathering—"Let them, therefore, who are among the Gentiles flee unto Zion. And let them who be of Judah flee unto Jerusalem, unto the mountains of the Lord's house" (D&C 133:12–13); and once in relation to the eventual redemption of the house of Judah—"And they also of the tribe of Judah, after their pain, shall be sanctified in holiness before the Lord, to dwell in his presence day and night, forever and ever" (D&C 133:35).

KIMBALL, HEBER C.

Heber was born on June 14, 1801, at Sheldon, Franklin County, Vermont. In Kirtland he joined with the Prophet Joseph Smith as a faithful and loyal member of the restored Church. In February 1835 he was called as one of the original apostles in the Quorum of the Twelve and two years later journeyed to England to proclaim the gospel. Following a period of intense persecution in Missouri, Heber served a second mission in England with Brigham Young as his companion. The account of their departure is among the most famous of missionary stories of the Restoration.

On Saturday, September 14, 1839, amidst a severe malaria epidemic in the region, Brigham Young left his home in Montrose, Iowa, for his apostolic mission to Great Britain.

His health was very poor; he was unable to go thirty rods to the river without assistance. After he had crossed the ferry he got Brother Israel Barlow to carry him on his horse behind him to Heber C. Kimball's where he remained sick until the 18th. He left his wife sick with a babe only ten days old, and all his children sick, unable to wait upon each other. (*HC* 4:9)

Heber C. Kimball

On the 18th, the two Apostles, both still sick, left the Kimball household in Nauvoo, all ailing except four-year-old Heber Parley.

"It seemed to me," he [Brother Kimball] remarked afterwards in relating the circumstances, 'as though my very inmost parts would melt within me at the thought of leaving my family in such a condition, as it were, almost in the arms of death. I felt as though I could scarcely endure it." "Hold up!" said he to the teamster, who had just started, "Brother Brigham, this is pretty tough, but let us rise and give them a cheer!" Brigham, with much difficulty, rose to his feet, and joined Elder Kimball in swinging his hat and shouting, "Hurrah, hurrah, hurrah, for Israel!" The two sisters, hearing the cheer came to the door—Sister [Vilate] Kimball with much difficulty [Mary Ann Young having come to the Kimball household to help nurse her husband]—and waved a farewell; and the two apostles continued their journey, without purse, without scrip, for England. (*HC* 4:10)

After the Nauvoo period, Heber completed the trek west to the Salt Lake Valley and was called in December 1847 as First Counselor to Brigham Young in the First Presidency. During the remainder of his life he served with honor in Church and civic functions and was universally respected and admired. He passed away on June 22, 1868, having suffered a fall from a wagon. Although Heber is mentioned only one time in the Doctrine and Covenants—in a passage given on January 19, 1841, confirming his membership in the Quorum of the Twelve (see D&C 124:129), Joseph Smith once remarked, concerning the loyalty and devotion of Heber C. Kimball and Brigham Young: "Of the Twelve Apostles chosen in Kirtland, and ordained under the hands of Oliver Cowdery, David Whitmer and myself, there have been but two but what have lifted their heel against me—namely, Brigham Young and Heber C. Kimball" (*HC* 5:412; May 28, 1843). All of the others, to a greater or lesser degree, at one time or another, had differences with the Prophet or the Church—even Parley P. Pratt, who repented sorely for his temporary disaffection (see *HC* 2:488).

KIMBALL, SPENCER W. (SEE ALSO TANNER, NATHAN ELDON; ROMNEY, MARION G.)

Spencer W. Kimball

Spencer Kimball was born on March 28, 1895, in Salt Lake City, Utah. In his capacity as twelfth President of the Church, he issued Official Declaration—2, dated June 9, 1978, entitling all worthy males to hold the priesthood and enjoy the blessings of the temple. This Declaration was sustained by the Church at the semi-annual conference on September 30, 1978. His counselors in the First Presidency at the time were N. Eldon Tanner and Marion G. Romney. Leading up to this momentous event were many years of devoted service by President Kimball, including his appointment as a member of the Quorum of the Twelve Apostles on July 8, 1943, his untiring efforts to expand the outreach of the gospel among the Lamanites, his exemplary teaching that set the stage for memorable publications such as *The Miracle of Forgiveness* (1969) and *Faith Precedes the Miracle* (1972), and his encouragement of the Saints to lengthen their stride in all aspects of gospel living and service. He served as President of the Church from December 30, 1973, until his death on November 5, 1985.

KNIGHT, JOSEPH, SR.

Joseph was born on November 3, 1772, at Oakham, Worcester County, Massachusetts. He operated a farm and gristmill at Colesville, New York. In 1826 he learned from Joseph Smith about the Restoration of the gospel and allowed Joseph to use his horse and carriage to transport the plates when they were turned over to him by Moroni. In May 1829, as a result of a request by Joseph Knight, the Prophet Joseph inquired of the Lord and received what is now section 12 of the Doctrine and Covenants, consisting of the following counsel to Joseph Knight, which applies equally well to all Saints:

"Whosoever will thrust in his sickle . . ."

A great and marvelous work is about to come forth among the children of men.

Behold, I am God; give heed to my word, which is quick and powerful, sharper than a two-edged sword, to the dividing asunder of both joints and marrow; therefore, give heed unto my word.

Behold, the field is white already to harvest; therefore, whoso desireth to reap let him thrust in his sickle with his might, and reap while the day lasts, that he may treasure up for his soul everlasting salvation in the kingdom of God.

Yea, whosoever will thrust in his sickle and reap, the same is called of God.

Therefore, if you will ask of me you shall receive; if you will knock it shall be opened unto you.

Now, as you have asked, behold, I say unto you, keep my commandments, and seek to bring forth and establish the cause of Zion.

Behold, I speak unto you, and also to all those who have desires to bring forth and establish this work;

And no one can assist in this work except he shall be humble and full of love, having faith, hope, and charity, being temperate in all things, whatsoever shall be entrusted to his care.

Behold, I am the light and the life of the world, that speak these words, therefore give heed with your might, and then you are called. Amen. (D&C 12:1–9)

Father Knight, as he was known, gave encouragement and financial support to the young prophet and was baptized on June 28, 1830, by Oliver Cowdery. He and his family later moved to Ohio and then to Jackson Country, Missouri, finally relocating to Nauvoo in 1839. He was ever supportive of the Prophet Joseph and the Church. His final years were marked by ill health and feebleness—though he remained strong in the gospel. He died on February 2, 1847, at Mount Pisgah, Harrison County, Iowa.

Nauvoo

KNIGHT, NEWEL

Newel, born on September 13, 1800, at Windham County, Vermont, was a son of Joseph Knight. Newel became acquainted with Joseph Smith when the latter was boarding with the Knight family in Colesville, New York, in 1826. During the month of April 1830, Joseph miraculously rescued Newel from the effects of an evil influence—an event the Prophet characterized as "the first miracle that was done in the Church" (*HC* 1:83). Newel was baptized in May of 1830 and remained ever faithful to the Church. Persecution and hardship were his lot during two sojourns in Missouri and later in Nauvoo. His first wife, Sally, died because of the suffering she experienced in Missouri. While en route westward with the Saints fleeing from the mobs, Newel, beset with a lung disorder, died in Iowa Territory on January 11, 1847, leaving his second wife, Lydia, and their seven young children. Concerning Newel and his brother, Joseph Knight Jr., the Prophet stated that he had recorded their names "in the Book of the Law of the Lord with unspeakable delight, for they are my friends" (*HC* 5:125).

Newel is mentioned in the Doctrine and Covenants in connection with a mission call issued June 7, 1831 (see D&C 52:32); concerning how to proceed as branch president in Thompson, Ohio, in leading the faithful Saints to Missouri (see D&C 54:2–10); in connection with additional counsel concerning how to deal with the rebellious Saints in Thompson (see D&C 56:6, 7); and concerning Newel's involvement as a member of the high council in Nauvoo (see D&C 124:132).

KNIGHT, VINSON

Vinson was born on March 14, 1804, at Norwich, Hampshire County, Massachusetts. In

March 1834, Vinson and his wife heard of the restored gospel directly from Joseph Smith and Parley P. Pratt. The Knights were baptized that spring and moved to Kirtland, Ohio, where Vinson worked as a druggist. He was ordained an elder on January 2, 1836, and a high priest shortly thereafter as he took his place as a counselor to bishop Newel K. Whitney. Vinson attended the School of the Prophets and the dedication of the Kirtland Temple. His loyalty to the Prophet Joseph was unassailable. In Missouri he was appointed acting bishop in Adam-ondi-Ahman. Persecution robbed him of his holdings—which he willingly abandoned rather than deny the Prophet Joseph. Relocating to Illinois, he was made a local bishop on May 4, 1839. On January 19, 1841, he was named Presiding Bishop of the Church:

> And again, I say unto you, I give unto you Vinson Knight, Samuel H. Smith, and Shadrach Roundy, if he will receive it, to preside over the bishopric; a knowledge of said bishopric is given unto you in the book of Doctrine and Covenants. (D&C 124:141)

In the same revelation, Vinson was named a stockholder in the Nauvoo House (see D&C 124:74). He also served on the Nauvoo city council and as a regent of the University of Nauvoo. He passed away on July 31, 1842.

LABAN

Laban, the curator of the sacred brass plates in Jerusalem in the days of Lehi, is mentioned only once in the Doctrine and Covenants—in a revelation in June 1829 directed to Oliver Cowdery, David Whitmer, and Martin Harris prior to their viewing the plates containing the Book of Mormon record: "Behold, . . . you shall have a view of the plates, and also of the breast-plate, the sword of Laban, the Urim and Thummim, which were given to the brother of Jared upon the mount, when he talked with the Lord face to face, and the miraculous directors which were given to Lehi while in the wilderness, on the borders of the Red Sea" (D&C 17:1).

Laban, a descendant of Joseph of Egypt, was living in Jerusalem at the time of Lehi's exodus (1 Ne. 5:16). Laban and his forefathers had kept the records of their progenitors on the plates of brass, beginning with the creation of the world and continuing through Adam, Moses, and the other holy prophets down to the time of Jeremiah, the contemporary of Zedekiah, at the time the king of Judah (see 1 Ne. 5:10–16). It was therefore expedient that Lehi should have these records to take with him to the Promised Land to preserve the written record of the covenant truths of the gospel and a genealogy of his ancestors.

Laban at the feet of Nephi

87

LAMANITES (SEE ALSO JEWS)

Throughout the Book of Mormon, the descendants of Laman, son of Lehi, are called Lamanites. Into succeeding generations were integrated the descendants of associated family lines, including those of Lemuel and Ishmael. Jacob, brother of Nephi and Joseph, wrote of the various branches of the offspring of Lehi and his associates:

> Now the people which were not Lamanites were Nephites; nevertheless, they were called Nephites, Jacobites, Josephites, Zoramites, Lamanites, Lemuelites, and Ishmaelites.
>
> But I, Jacob, . . . shall call them Lamanites that seek to destroy the people of Nephi, and those who are friendly to Nephi I shall call Nephites, or the people of Nephi, according to the reigns of the kings. (Jacob 1:13–14; compare 4 Ne. 1:36–37; Morm. 1:8)

The Lamanites are referred to twelve times in the text of the Doctrine and Covenants consistently in the framework of the Lord's design to bless them by bringing them to the knowledge of the gospel plan. The Lord reminded Martin Harris, through the Prophet Joseph Smith, that "the Lamanites are a remnant [of the Jews]" (D&C 19:27).

In latter-day revelation, the Lamanites are given the promise that they shall have the blessings of God's covenant with Israel and unfold in their divine potential: "But before the great day of the Lord shall come, Jacob shall flourish in the wilderness, and the Lamanites shall blossom as the rose" (D&C 49:24).

Through the enlightenment of the gospel plan, the Lamanites would "rely upon the merits of Jesus Christ, and be glorified through faith in his name, and that through their repentance they might be saved" (D&C 3:20).

LAMECH

Lamech, the father of Noah (see Gen. 5:25–31; 1 Chr. 1:3; Luke 3:36), is mentioned in the Doctrine and Covenants in connection with the lineage of the priesthood: "Lamech was thirty-two years old when he was ordained under the hand of Seth" (D&C 107:51).

LAW, WILLIAM

William was born on September 8, 1809, at County Tyrone, Ireland. He became a convert to the restored Church and moved from Canada to Nauvoo, where he was called by revelation in 1841 to be the Second Counselor in the First Presidency (see D&C 124:91, 126). He served faithfully for two years but was removed from his position for speaking contemptuously of the Prophet. On April 18, 1844, he was excommunicated and established the anti-Mormon publication entitled the *Nauvoo Expositor*. The destruction of this press by city officials led to the arrest, imprisonment, and eventual martyrdom of the Prophet. William died on January 12, 1892.

The case of William Law is a remarkable study in the covenant relationship between the Lord and one of His promising servants. In section 124, given on January 19, 1841, William is first mentioned as a stockholder in the planned Nauvoo House (D&C 124:82). But then the full scope of the Lord's design for him is unfolded in subsequent verses, where William is mentioned in the context of his leadership potential:

Therefore, let my servant William put his trust in me, and cease to fear concerning his family, because of the sickness of the land. If ye love me, keep my commandments; and the sickness of the land shall redound to your glory.

Let my servant William go and proclaim my everlasting gospel with a loud voice, and with great joy, as he shall be moved upon by my Spirit, unto the inhabitants of Warsaw, . . . and await patiently and diligently for further instructions at my general conference, saith the Lord.

If he will do my will let him from henceforth hearken to the counsel of my servant Joseph, and with his interest support the cause of the poor, and publish the new translation of my holy word unto the inhabitants of the earth.

And if he will do this I will bless him with a multiplicity of blessings, that he shall not be forsaken, nor his seed be found begging bread.

And again, verily I say unto you, let my servant William be appointed, ordained, and anointed, as counselor unto my servant Joseph, in the room of my servant Hyrum, that my servant Hyrum may take the office of Priesthood and Patriarch, ...

Let my servant William Law also receive the keys by which he may ask and receive blessings; let him be humble before me, and be without guile, and he shall receive of my Spirit, even the Comforter, which shall manifest unto him the truth of all things, and shall give him, in the very hour, what he shall say.

And these signs shall follow him—he shall heal the sick, he shall cast out devils, and shall be delivered from those who would administer unto him deadly poison;

And he shall be led in paths where the poisonous serpent cannot lay hold upon his heel, and he shall mount up in the imagination of his thoughts as upon eagles' wings.

And what if I will that he should raise the dead, let him not withhold his voice.

Therefore, let my servant William cry aloud and spare not, with joy and rejoicing, and with hosannas to him that sitteth upon the throne forever and ever, saith the Lord your God. (D&C 124:87–91, 97–101)

Clearly, the Lord had a mission in store for William—and for Hyrum. Hyrum was one of the grand examples of boundless charity and enduring discipleship in the restored Church. By contrast, William Law was to perish spiritually through deceit and contempt for his covenants. Consider the "multiplicity of blessings" (v. 90) that the Lord promised him: health and nurture for himself and his family amidst the "sickness of the land" (v. 87), "the keys by which he may ask and receive blessings" (v. 97), "my Spirit, even the Comforter, which shall manifest unto him the truth of all things, and shall give him, in the very hour, what he shall say" (v. 97; compare D&C 100:5–8), gifts of the Spirit (healing, casting out evil spirits, protection, raising the dead), and the supreme opportunity to serve in the highest quorum in the Church in immediate association with the Lord's chosen Prophet. This grand covenant promise was conditioned upon William's fulfilling the Lord's agenda for him: "put his trust in me" (v. 87), "keep my commandments" (v. 87), proclaim the gospel by the Spirit, "hearken to the counsel of my servant Joseph" (v. 89), support the cause of the poor, publish the new translation of the Bible, serve as a counselor in the First Presidency, "be humble . . . and . . . without guile" (v. 97). Moreover, later verses identify William as one who was to help the Prophet Joseph with the proclamation to world leaders (v. 107), assist with the First Presidency's assignment to "lay the foundation of Zion" (v. 118), and facilitate the role of the First Presidency "to receive the oracles for the whole church" (v. 126). It was an agenda that would have granted William eternal blessings of glory and joy. Instead, he fell from his position within a short period of time and became a ruthless conspirator bent on destroying the Church and the Prophet.

Why would the Lord have lifted William to a station of such dignity in the Church with such promises of heavenly blessings when he would become so determined to destroy the Kingdom of God? The answer is that the Lord, knowing all, has infinite mercy and compassion and withholds His covenant promises from no one, leaving them in place and empowered for as long as possible, given the agency of man. He counseled the ancient Saints at Bountiful to cast no one from their midst "for ye know not but what they will return and repent, and come unto me with full purpose of heart, and I shall heal them; and ye shall be the means of bringing salvation unto them" (3 Ne. 18:32).

LEE, ANN (SEE ALSO COPLEY, LEMAN)

Ann is not mentioned in the text of the Doctrine and Covenants but is referenced in the current introduction to section 49. She was born on February 29, 1736, in Manchester, England. A person of deep spiritual conviction, she became associated with the Quakers (called the "Shaking Quakers") and eventually rose to a position of prominence in that association, identifying herself as the long-awaited Christ—appearing in the form of a woman. She immigrated to America and continued her religious campaign amidst much opposition and legal deterrence. She died on September 8, 1784 in Watervliet, New York; however, her influence spread to Ohio. The Prophet Joseph Smith received a revelation in March 1831 repudiating the doctrines of her followers, including their claims about the form of the Messiah at the Second Coming: "And again, verily I say unto you, that the Son of Man cometh not in the form of a woman, neither of a man traveling on the earth. Wherefore, be not deceived, but continue in steadfastness" (D&C 49:22–23). Sidney Rigdon, Parley P. Pratt, and Leman Copley delivered a copy of the revelation to the Shaker community near Cleveland, but the group rejected the word of the Lord.

LEHI

Lehi, the great patriarch of the Book of Mormon (see 1 Ne. and 2 Ne. 1–4:1–12), is mentioned only once in the Doctrine and Covenants in a revelation in June 1829 directed to the three witnesses, Oliver Cowdery, David Whitmer, and Martin Harris, prior to their viewing the plates containing the Book of Mormon record: "Behold, I say unto you, that you must rely upon my word, which if you do with full purpose of heart, you shall have a view of the plates, and also of the breastplate, the sword of Laban, the Urim and Thummim, which were given to the brother of Jared upon

Lehi

the mount, when he talked with the Lord face to face, and the miraculous directors which were given to Lehi while in the wilderness, on the borders of the Red Sea" (D&C 17:1).

Lehi, a descendant of Joseph through the lineage of Manasseh (Alma 10:3), is a model of many admirable characteristics: worthiness to commune with the Lord and receive through revelation a prophetic view of the divine plan of happiness for mankind, solemn witness of the divinity of the Messiah, powerful teacher of gospel principles, devoted and concerned father and patriarch in his family circle, and proponent and herald of the covenant of the Lord concerning the Promised Land. The reference to "miraculous directors" in D&C 17:1 has to do with the compass (or Liahona) provided by the Lord to assist Lehi and his faithful group in finding food and maintaining the proper course during their journey (see 1 Ne. 18:12, 21; 2 Ne. 5:12; Mosiah 1:16; Alma 37:38, 43–45).

LEMUELITES

The descendants of Lemuel, brother of Laman and second oldest son of Lehi, were known in the Book of Mormon as Lemuelites (Jacob 1:13; Alma 47:35; 4 Ne. 1:38; Morm. 1:8–9). The Lemuelites (see D&C 3:18) were absorbed into the generational flow stemming from Laman and thus became a part of the Lamanite peoples.

LEVI (SEE ALSO SONS OF LEVI)

Levi was the third son of Jacob by Leah (see Gen. 29:34; 35:23). The work of assisting the priests in the sanctuary of the Lord was assigned to the descendants of Levi as a tribe. Moses and Aaron were of the tribe of Levi. Levi is mentioned three times in the Doctrine and Covenants, in each case in the expression "sons of Levi" (see D&C 13:1; 124:39; 128:24). The following words of John the Baptist, uttered during the restoration of the Aaronic Priesthood in the latter days, are an example of this usage:

> Upon you my fellow servants, in the name of Messiah I confer the Priesthood of Aaron, which holds the keys of the ministering of angels, and of the gospel of repentance, and of baptism by immersion for the remission of sins; and this shall never be taken again from the earth, until the sons of Levi do offer again an offering unto the Lord in righteousness. (D&C 13:1)

LORD OF THE VINEYARD

The Lord of the vineyard in the parable on the redemption of Zion given in section 101 is the symbolic representation of the Almighty (see D&C 101:43–62). President Joseph Fielding Smith summarizes this parable:

In a revelation given December 16, 1833, the Lord in a parable spoke of the conditions in Missouri. A certain nobleman had a spot of land and he sent his servants in this choice land, and set watchmen round about and to build a tower for the protection of the land. While the workmen were yet building they questioned the need of the tower and said that the money required to build it could be put to better purpose. While they were at variance the enemy came by night and broke down the hedge and the servants were scattered. The Lord then commanded one of his servants to go and gather together the residue of his servants and go straightway to the land of his vineyard, for it was his; he had purchased it. They were to break down the walls of his enemies and possess the land. (CHMR 3:18)

The watchmen, workmen, and servants in the parable are symbolic representations of those called to build up the Kingdom of God, in their various functions and stewardships. The servant commanded to gather together the residue of the Lord's servants and complete the unfinished work represents the Prophet Joseph Smith (see D&C 103:21).

LYMAN, AMASA

Amasa was born on March 30, 1813, at Lyman, Grafton County, New Hampshire. He was baptized on April 27, 1832, and journeyed to Kirtland to join the Saints. He served a mission to the eastern states and then participated in Zion's Camp in 1834. After serving other short missions, he journeyed with his wife to Far West, Missouri, in 1837. Persecution forced them to flee to Illinois, where in Nauvoo he served as a counselor in the high priests quorum leadership (see D&C 124:136) before being called in August 1832 to fill the anticipated vacancy in the Quorum of the Twelve Apostles with the departure of Orson Pratt. When Orson repented, the Prophet Joseph instead appointed Amasa as a counselor to the First Presidency until such time as a future vacancy would occur (the Saints having upheld Sidney Rigdon in his counselorship). After the martyrdom, Amasa supported the Twelve and became a member of that body on August 12, 1844. He was appointed to organize a company for the exodus to the West (see D&C 136:14). Though a stalwart supporter of Brigham Young, Amasa eventually slipped from his position and lost his standing in the Church on January 12, 1870. He passed away on February 4, 1877, at Fillmore, Utah.

Amasa Lyman

M

MAHALALEEL

Mahalaleel, son of Cainan and great-great-grandson of Adam and Eve (Gen. 5:12–17; Moses 6:19–20), is mentioned twice in the Doctrine and Covenants: once in connection with the descent of the priesthood lineage—"Mahalaleel was four hundred and ninety-six years and seven days old when he was ordained by the hand of Adam, who also blessed him" (D&C 107:46); and again as one worthy to receive Adam's benedictory blessing: "Three years previous to the death of Adam, he called Seth, Enos, Cainan, Mahalaleel, Jared, Enoch, and Methuselah, who were all high priests, . . . into the valley of Adam-ondi-Ahman, and there bestowed upon them his last blessing" (D&C 107:53).

MALACHI

Malachi, the last of the Old Testament prophets, is referenced four times in the text of the Doctrine and Covenants (D&C 110:14; 128:17; 133:64; 138:46). Malachi delivered his prophetic message to the Jews around 430 BC—long after Lehi had left Jerusalem for the Promised Land.

So important were the words of Malachi, including truths about the law of tithing and the sealing commission of Elijah, that the resurrected Savior quoted them to the ancient American Saints during His visit (see 3 Ne. 24 and 25, including Mal. 3 and 4) and commanded that these words should be written down.

On the evening of September 21, 1823, Moroni, the last in a sequence of historians of the word of God, appeared to Joseph Smith to lay the foundation of the coming forth of the Book of Mormon in the context of the latter-day Restoration. Moroni cited the words of Malachi concerning the coming of the prophet Elijah: "And he shall plant in the hearts of the

Malachi

children the promises made to the fathers, and the hearts of the children shall turn to their fathers" (D&C 2:2; compare D&C 27:9). Six years after the publication of the Book of Mormon in this dispensation, the Savior appeared to Joseph Smith and Oliver Cowdery in the Kirtland Temple on April 3, 1836, accompanied by other heavenly beings, including Elijah, in fulfillment of the prophecy of Malachi:

> Elijah the prophet, who was taken to heaven without tasting death, stood before us, and said:
> Behold, the time has fully come, which was spoken of by the mouth of Malachi—testifying that he [Elijah] should be sent, before the great and dreadful day of the Lord come—
> To turn the hearts of the fathers to the children, and the children to the fathers, lest the whole earth be smitten with a curse—
> Therefore, the keys of this dispensation are committed into your hands; and by this ye may know that the great and dreadful day of the Lord is near, even at the doors. (D&C 110:13–16; compare D&C 128:17)

Thus, Malachi was the prophet of transition: transition from the Old Testament to the New Testament and from these sacred volumes to the Book of Mormon.

Malachi is also mentioned in section 133—the Lord's "appendix" to the Doctrine and Covenants given through Joseph Smith on November 3, 1831—in connection with the fate of those who are not prepared for the Second Coming: "And also that which was written by the prophet Malachi: For, behold, the day cometh that shall burn as an oven, and all the proud, yea, and all that do wickedly, shall be stubble; and the day that cometh shall burn them up, saith the Lord of hosts, that it shall leave them neither root nor branch" (D&C 133:64). Malachi is included among the elect whom President Joseph F. Smith beheld during his vision of the work of salvation going on in the spirit world (see D&C 138:46).

MARKS, WILLIAM

William was born on November 15, 1792, in Rutland, Rutland County, Virginia. He joined the Church in New York, was ordained a priest, and then moved his family to Kirtland, where he opened a bookstore. He was called to serve on the high council there on September 3, 1837, and soon thereafter became an agent working with Bishop Newel K. Whitney. On July 8, 1838, he was called by revelation to complete his business in Kirtland and move to Missouri (D&C 117:1) where he was to preside among the people at Far West: "Let my servant William Marks be faithful over a few things, and he shall be a ruler over many. Let him preside in the midst of my people in the city of Far West, and let him be blessed with the blessings of my people" (D&C 117:10). Mob violence in Missouri forced the Saints to leave before William could fulfill his calling there. He made his way to Commerce (later Nauvoo) and filled a number of Church and civic callings, including serving as president of the stake and helping the Church with land dealings, specifically being a stockholder in the planned Nauvoo House and ordaining Isaac Galland as a land agent (see D&C 124:79). When his testimony began to waver in 1844, he allied himself with the enemies of the Church after the Martyrdom. He then subsequently supported Sidney Rigdon's claim to succession of leadership. Later he retracted his support and returned to fellowship for a time. However, he again left the Church and became associated with other religious groups, including the Reorganized Church of Jesus Christ of Latter Day Saints. William died on May 22, 1872.

MARSH, THOMAS B.

Thomas was born on November 1, 1799, in Acton, Middlesex County, Massachusetts. Hungry for religious truth that accorded with the scriptures, he felt prompted to move to western New York, where he became acquainted with the mission of Joseph Smith. He was baptized by David Whitmer on September 3, 1830. A few days later he was ordained an elder and called by revelation to preach the gospel (section 31; his subsequent missionary assignments are recorded in D&C 52:22; 56:5; 75:31). Thomas is also mentioned in the Doctrine and Covenants regarding the assignment to assist in the publication of the revelations (see D&C 118:2). In 1835 he was called as a member of the Quorum of the Twelve and served as president of that quorum. In 1838 an altercation between his wife and the wife of an associate led to a dispute that burgeoned into a rift between Thomas and his priesthood brethren. He was excommunicated on March 17, 1839. For years he pursued a career as an itinerant teacher on biblical subjects. He moved to Utah in 1857 and sought fellowship once again in the Church, being rebaptized on July 16 of that year. He passed away in Ogden in poverty in January 1866.

Section 31 was given in September 1830 through the Prophet Joseph Smith following the baptism of Thomas and his ordination as an elder. In this revelation the Lord provides personal guidance to this new priesthood holder. The words have general application.

Thomas, my son, blessed are you because of your faith in my work.

Behold, you have had many afflictions because of your family; nevertheless, I will bless you and your family, yea, your little ones; and the day cometh that they will believe and know the truth and be one with you in my church.

Lift up your heart and rejoice, for the hour of your mission is come; and your tongue shall be loosed, and you shall declare glad tidings of great joy unto this generation.

You shall declare the things which have been revealed to my servant, Joseph Smith, Jun. You shall begin to preach from this time forth, yea, to reap in the field which is white already to be burned.

Therefore, thrust in your sickle with all your soul, and your sins are forgiven you, and you shall be laden with sheaves upon your back, for the laborer is worthy of his hire. Wherefore, your family shall live. . . .

Be patient in afflictions, revile not against those that revile. Govern your house in meekness, and be steadfast.

Behold, I say unto you that you shall be a physician unto the church, but not unto the world, for they will not receive you.

Go your way whithersoever I will, and it shall be given you by the Comforter what you shall do and whither you shall go.

Pray always, lest you enter into temptation and lose your reward.

Be faithful unto the end, and lo, I am with you. These words are not of man nor of men, but of me, even Jesus Christ, your Redeemer, by the will of the Father. Amen. (D&C 31:1–5, 9–13)

Section 112, given on July 23, 1837, when Thomas was serving as President of the Quorum of the Twelve Apostles, concerns the work of this quorum and Thomas's responsibility to provide exemplary leadership.

Verily thus saith the Lord unto you my servant Thomas: I have heard thy prayers; and thine alms have come up as a memorial before me, in behalf of those, thy brethren, who were chosen to bear testimony of my name and to send it abroad among all nations, kindreds, tongues, and people, and ordained through the instrumentality of my servants,

Verily I say unto you, there have been some few things in thine heart and with thee with which I, the Lord, was not well pleased.

Nevertheless, inasmuch as thou hast abased thyself thou shalt be exalted; therefore, all thy sins are forgiven thee.

Let thy heart be of good cheer before my face; and thou shalt bear record of my name, not only unto the Gentiles, but also unto the Jews; and thou shalt send forth my word unto the ends of the earth. . . .

Be thou humble; and the Lord thy God shall lead thee by the hand, and give thee answer to thy prayers.

I know thy heart, and have heard thy prayers concerning thy brethren.

Be not partial towards them in love above many others, but let thy love be for them as for thyself; and let thy love abound unto all men, and unto all who love my name. (D&C 112:1–4, 10–11)

In addition, the Lord warned Thomas and his associates that darkness and corruption prevail in the world and that the severe judgment of heaven would shortly commence (D&C 112:23–26). Thus, Thomas and his priesthood associates were warned to "cleanse your hearts and your garments, lest the blood of this generation be required at your hands" (D&C 112:33). The Twelve were reminded that their cause was to preach the gospel throughout the world according to the power of the priesthood vested in them (D&C 112:32–33). Although Thomas forgot this counsel for a period of time, he returned to the Church, humbled and meek, for the last decade of his life.

McLellin, William E.

William was born on January 18, 1806, in Smith County, Tennessee. He learned of the restored Church in the summer of 1831 and was baptized on August 20, 1831, by Hyrum Smith. He traveled to Ohio, where he stayed several weeks with the Prophet Joseph and received counsel from the Lord by revelation (section 66). At first receptive to the Lord's counsel, William soon thereafter criticized the language of the revelation and therefore came under the challenge of the Lord to anyone who felt so inclined to try to come up with revelations to equal the least of those given (see D&C 67:6–7). William soon learned that such was impossible. He went on to hold positions of responsibility in the Church and

William E. McLellin

became a member of the Quorum of the Twelve on February 15, 1835. The following year he apostatized, claiming that he had lost confidence in the leadership of the Church. His actions led to his excommunication in 1838. Subsequently, he joined the mobbers in persecuting the Saints and driving them from Missouri. After dabbling with various other religious organizations, he eventually abandoned his religious interests and passed away in obscurity on April 24, 1883. Of significance is that he remained true to his witness of the Book of Mormon.

In the revelations directed to William, much of the wording extended glorious promises based on loyalty and valor. On October 25, 1831, he inquired of the Prophet Joseph Smith, who received the following from the Lord:

> Behold, thus saith the Lord unto my servant William E. McLellin— Blessed are you, inasmuch as you have turned away from your iniquities, and have received my truths, saith the Lord your Redeemer, the Savior of the world, even of as many as believe on my name.
>
> Verily I say unto you, blessed are you for receiving mine everlasting covenant, even the fulness of my gospel, . . .
>
> Verily I say unto you, my servant William, that you are clean, but not all; repent, therefore, of those things which are not pleasing in my sight, saith the Lord, for the Lord will show them unto you. (D&C 66:1–3)

Thereupon the Lord instructed William to preach the gospel in the surrounding regions and in the eastern states:

> Be patient in affliction. Ask, and ye shall receive; knock, and it shall be opened unto you.
>
> Seek not to be cumbered. Forsake all unrighteousness. . . .
>
> Continue in these things even unto the end, and you shall have a crown of eternal life at the right hand of my Father, who is full of grace and truth. (D&C 66:9–10, 12)

In November 1831 he and three colleagues—Orson Hyde, Luke S. Johnson, and Lyman E. Johnson—were granted an extraordinary promise (also extended "unto all the faithful elders of my church," D&C 68:7) that their words, as inspired by the Holy Ghost, would in essence be scriptural: "And whatsoever they shall speak when moved upon by the Holy Ghost shall be scripture, shall be the will of the Lord, shall be the mind of the Lord, shall be the word of the Lord, shall be the voice of the Lord, and the power of God unto salvation" (D&C 68:4). William failed to rise to his potential and was censured by the Lord on January 25, 1832, and given an alternative assignment:

> Therefore, verily I say unto my servant William E. McLellin, I revoke the commission which I gave unto him to go unto the eastern countries;
> And I give unto him a new commission and a new commandment, in the which I, the Lord, chasten him for the murmurings of his heart;
> And he sinned; nevertheless, I forgive him and say unto him again, Go ye into the south countries.
> And let my servant Luke Johnson go with him, and proclaim the things which I have commanded them. (D&C 75:6–9)

Again, on March 3, 1833, the Lord revealed that He was "not well pleased with my servant William E. McLellin" (D&C 90:35). Nevertheless, William went forward with sufficient standing to become a member of the Quorum of the Twelve in 1835, but only briefly. His rancor against the Prophet and the Church cost him his membership in 1838 and brought him into alliance with those whose objective was destroying the work of the Lord. Thus he relinquished the divine promise to have "a crown of eternal life at the right hand of my Father, who is full of grace and truth" (D&C 66:12).

MELCHIZEDEK

Melchizedek was the great high priest and prophet—the king of Salem (Jerusalem)—who lived at the time of Abraham, around 2,000 years before Christ. The text of the Doctrine and Covenants uses the term Melchizedek numerous times, mostly in connection with the Melchizedek Priesthood (see, for example, D&C 68:15, 19; 76:57; 107:1, 6–10; 124:123). However, some references apply to the person of Melchizedek. For example, Abraham received the priesthood from Melchizedek (see D&C 84:14), and Melchizedek's name was appropriated for the higher priesthood to avoid using the name of Deity too frequently:

> There are, in the church, two priesthoods, namely, the Melchizedek and Aaronic, including the Levitical Priesthood.
> Why the first is called the Melchizedek Priesthood is because Melchizedek was such a great high priest.
> Before his day it was called *the Holy Priesthood, after the Order of the Son of God.*
> But out of respect or reverence to the name of the Supreme Being, to avoid the too frequent repetition of his name, they, the church, in ancient days, called that priesthood after Melchizedek, or the Melchizedek Priesthood. (D&C 107:1–4)

Other latter-day scripture sheds additional light on the person and character of Melchizedek. In his treatise on the priesthood before the leaders and citizens of the city of Ammonihah around 82 BC, Alma provides insights concerning the ancient king and priesthood leader:

> Now this Melchizedek was a king over the land of Salem; and his

people had waxed strong in iniquity and abomination; yea, they had all gone astray; they were full of all manner of wickedness;

But Melchizedek having exercised mighty faith, and received the office of the high priesthood according to the holy order of God, did preach repentance unto his people. And behold, they did repent; and Melchizedek did establish peace in the land in his days; therefore he was called the prince of peace, for he was the king of Salem; and he did reign under his father.

Now, there were many before him, and also there were many afterwards, but none were greater; therefore, of him they have more particularly made mention. (Alma 13:17–19; compare also JST Gen. 14:25–40)

METHUSELAH

Methuselah, son of Enoch, was the longest surviving of the ancient patriarchs (see Gen. 5:21–27; Luke 3:37; Moses 8:2–3). He is mentioned three times in the text of the Doctrine and Covenants: twice in connection with the descent of the priesthood lineage—"Methuselah was one hundred years old when he was ordained under the hand of Adam. Lamech was thirty-two years old when he was ordained under the hand of Seth. Noah was ten years old when he was ordained under the hand of Methuselah" (D&C 107:50–52)—and once again as a participant to receive Adam's benedictory blessing: "Three years previous to the death of Adam, he called Seth, Enos, Cainan, Mahalaleel, Jared, Enoch, and Methuselah, who were all high priests, . . . into the valley of Adam-ondi-Ahman, and there bestowed upon them his last blessing" (see D&C 107:53).

MICHAEL (SEE ADAM)

MILES, DANIEL

Daniel was born on July 22, 1772, at Sanbornton, Belknap County, New Hampshire. He joined the Church on April 22, 1832, and moved subsequently to Kirtland, Ohio. On April 6, 1837, he became one of the seven Presidents of the Seventy. He later moved to Far West, Missouri, but was forced to flee to Illinois because of the onslaught of the mobs. In Nauvoo, Daniel continued as a President of the Seventy (see D&C 124:138). He died on October 12, 1845, in Hancock County, Illinois.

MILLER, GEORGE

George was born on November 25, 1794, in Orange County, Virginia. Having heard the Prophet Joseph Smith preach, he became converted and was baptized on August 10, 1839. In

George Miller

a revelation dated January 19, 1841, the Lord declared:

> And again, verily I say unto you, my servant George Miller is without guile; he may be trusted because of the integrity of his heart; and for the love which he has to my testimony I, the Lord, love him.
>
> I therefore say unto you, I seal upon his head the office of a bishopric, like unto my servant Edward Partridge, that he may receive the consecrations of mine house, that he may administer blessings upon the heads of the poor of my people, saith the Lord. Let no man despise my servant George, for he shall honor me. (D&C 124:20–21)

In the same revelation, George, a carpenter by trade, was called to assist in the construction of the Nauvoo House (see D&C 124:22–23, 62, 70). In addition, he was an officer in the Nauvoo Legion and a regent of the University of Nauvoo. His association with the Prophet Joseph Smith was always very close. However, he later had differences with Brigham Young over administrative issues associated with the exodus and thus resigned from the Church in March 1847. Thereafter he sought affiliation with Lyman Wight and other apostates and later tried his fortune with the Strangites in Michigan. He died in 1856 while en route to California.

Morley, Isaac

Isaac, born on March 11, 1786, in Montague, Hampshire County, Massachusetts, became a prosperous farmer in the region of Ohio where Kirtland was established. He became infused with religious fervor through the preaching of Sidney Rigdon and organized a communal group known as "the family." Missionaries sent to the Lamanites also preached the restored gospel to this group and converted many, including Isaac and his wife. When Joseph Smith moved to Kirtland, he resided on the Morley property. Later, a frame house was built there for Joseph and Emma (see D&C 41:7). In June 1831 the fourth conference of the Church was held at the Morley farm. On that occasion, Isaac was ordained a high priest and called as a counselor to Bishop Edward Partridge. Additionally, he was asked to sell his farm and consecrate the proceeds to the Church, which he did, though at first reluctantly:

> Behold, I, the Lord, was angry with him who was my servant Ezra Booth, and also my servant Isaac Morley, for they kept not the law, neither the commandment;
>
> They sought evil in their hearts, and I, the Lord, withheld my Spirit. They condemned for evil that thing in which there was no evil; nevertheless I have forgiven my servant Isaac Morley. . . .
>
> And again, I say unto you, that my servant Isaac Morley may not be tempted above that which he is able to bear, and counsel wrongfully to your hurt, I gave commandment that his farm should be sold. (D&C 64:15–16, 20)

Isaac moved with his family to Independence, Missouri (in accordance with the commandment revealed in D&C 52:23). In Missouri mob violence caused him and his family great suffering and trauma, forcing them to flee to Clay County, Missouri, and then to Far West (where he was ordained a patriarch), and finally to Illinois. In Illinois he lived at Yelrome (Morley spelled in reverse), where he served as stake president until mobs destroyed his property and forced him to move to Nauvoo after the martyrdom. In 1847 he joined the pioneer exodus to the West, where he helped settle Manti. He died on June 24, 1865.

MORONI

Moroni, whose image graces the spires of modern-day temples of the Church throughout the world, was the angelic messenger who visited the young Joseph Smith for the first time on September 21, 1823, to inaugurate the era of the coming forth of the Book of Mormon. Moroni, son of Mormon, spent his last years performing service relating to the ancient records before depositing them on the crest of the Hill Cumorah. His valuable additions to the text include chapters 8 and 9 of his father's section (the Book of Mormon), his abridgement of the records of the Jaredite nation (the Book of Ether), and the Book of Moroni (which includes three treatises of his father Mormon, together with important observations by Moroni about the administration of the Church and farewell instructions about being perfected "in Christ"—Moroni 10:31–33). He also wrote the title page for the entire book, which makes clear that the work is designed for "the convincing of the Jew and Gentile that JESUS is the CHRIST, the ETERNAL GOD, manifesting himself unto all nations."

Moroni, the last in a millennium-long sequence of curators of the sacred chronicles of God in the New World, was entrusted with the keys of restoring this divine message of hope and exaltation in the latter days. He and, by

Moroni, with Joseph Smith

extension, his heavenly fellow-ministers of the Restoration, were viewed in vision by John the Revelator:

> And I saw another angel fly in the midst of heaven, having the everlasting gospel to preach unto them that dwell on the earth, and to every nation, and kindred, and tongue, and people,
>
> Saying with a loud voice, Fear God, and give glory to him; for the hour of his judgment is come: and worship him that made heaven, and earth, and the sea, and the fountains of waters. (Rev. 14:6–7)

Moroni lived from around AD 350 until around AD 421. He and his father, Mormon, experienced the cataclysmic battle of nations at Cumorah around AD 385 where nearly a quarter-million Nephite warriors were slain, including the ten thousand commanded by Moroni (see Morm. 6:12). Mormon himself was slain shortly thereafter by the Lamanite hordes. Thus Moroni was left alone for the better part of thirty-five years, wandering about the land defensively to protect his own life during a period of universal warfare among the Lamanite factions, taking care to invest his energy and devotion in preserving and augmenting the ancient records. During his lonely, vagabond existence, Moroni was nourished by the light of the gospel and sustained by the Spirit of God. His strength in the Lord derived from a confirmation of the mighty mission given unto him to speak eternal truth to future generations who would face the challenge of overcoming pride and embracing the plan of happiness. Moroni played an indispensable role in the design of the Lord regarding the "dispensation of the gospel for the last times; and for the fulness of times, in the which I will gather together in one all things, both which are in heaven, and which are on earth" (D&C 27:13).

Moroni is mentioned three times in the text of the Doctrine and Covenants: once in connection with the future event where Jesus Christ will participate in a glorious and sacred meeting with all of His holy prophets down through the ages, including "Moroni, whom I have sent unto you to reveal the Book of Mormon, containing the fulness of my everlasting gospel, to whom I have committed the keys of the record of the stick of Ephraim" (D&C 27:5); again in connection with the coming forth of the Book of Mormon—"Glad tidings from Cumorah! Moroni, an angel from heaven, declaring the fulfilment of the prophets—the book to be revealed" (D&C 128:20); and finally, in connection with the vision of the spirit realm revealed to President Joseph F. Smith, in which Elijah is mentioned—"of whom also Moroni spake to the Prophet Joseph Smith,

declaring that he should come before the ushering in of the great and dreadful day of the Lord" (D&C 138:46).

MOSES

Moses was the prophet of God who prefigured Christ's redeeming mission by liberating the Israelites from Egyptian bondage, serving as the agent for the revelation of the Ten Commandments, and providing leadership to guide the Israelites through the wilderness to the gateway of the Promised Land. It was Moses who appeared to Joseph Smith and Oliver Cowdery in the Kirtland Temple on April 3, 1836, to restore the keys of "the gathering of Israel from the four parts of the earth, and the leading of the ten tribes from the land of the north" (D&C 110:11). In all, Moses is mentioned twenty-seven times in the text of the Doctrine and Covenants. Some of the key passages depict Moses as an exemplar of one who receives and acts on the spirit of revelation (D&C 8:3);

Moses

as the prototype for the ministry of Joseph Smith—i.e., the only one appointed to receive commandments and revelations for God's people in a given dispensation (D&C 28:2); as a key figure in the lineage of the priesthood (D&C 84:6; 133:54–55; 136:37); as one given the mission to sanctify his people "that they might behold the face of God (D&C 84:23); as the forebear of those "sons of Moses" who shall serve with devotion in the temples of God and fulfill the commission of the Abrahamic covenant (D&C 84:31–34); as the prototype of the President of the High Priesthood, who is to "preside over the whole church, and to be like unto Moses" (D&C 107:91); as the one who restored the keys of the gathering of Israel in the latter days (D&C 110:11); as he who built the Tabernacle of the Lord as an ancient model of the temple (D&C 124:38); and as one of the "great and mighty ones" assembled in the "vast congregation of the righteous" perceived in vision by Joseph F. Smith (D&C 138:38–41). He is also noted in many passages concerning the law of Moses.

MURDOCK, JOHN

John, born on July 15, 1792, in Kortwright, Delaware County, New York, joined various religious organizations in sequence but was not satisfied that they were complying with the scriptures. In the winter of 1830 he became acquainted with the Book of Mormon and was convinced of its truth. On November 5, 1830, he was baptized by Parley P. Pratt. His wife, Julia, died on April 30, 1831, giving birth to twins, whom John, grief-stricken, gave to the Prophet Joseph and Emma to rear. In June 1831, John was called by revelation to journey with Hyrum Smith to Missouri (see D&C 52:8). Later, John Murdock was privileged to

John Murdock

receive a vision of the Savior and subsequently served a mission to the eastern states. All of section 99 is a revelation from the Lord given through Joseph Smith to John in August 1832 concerning this mission—and also the Lord's compassion for John's children:

> Behold, thus saith the Lord unto my servant John Murdock—thou art called to go into the eastern countries from house to house, from village to village, and from city to city, to proclaim mine everlasting gospel unto the inhabitants thereof, in the midst of persecution and wickedness.
>
> And who receiveth you receiveth me; and you shall have power to declare my word in the demonstration of my Holy Spirit.
>
> And who receiveth you as a little child, receiveth my kingdom; and blessed are they, for they shall obtain mercy.

And whoso rejecteth you shall be rejected of my Father and his house; and you shall cleanse your feet in the secret places by the way for a testimony against them. . . .

And now, verily I say unto you, that it is not expedient that you should go until your children are provided for, and sent up kindly unto the bishop of Zion. (D&C 99:1–4, 6)

John participated in Zion's Camp in 1834 and held positions of responsibility in Missouri. Because of mob violence in Missouri he moved to Nauvoo and later to the Salt Lake Valley, where he served as a high councilor and a bishop. He served as a missionary in Australia for a period of time, following which he was ordained a patriarch in Utah Valley. He died on December 23, 1871, a faithful servant of God.

NATHAN

Nathan, prophet of the Lord during the time of David (2 Sam. 7; 12; 1 Chron. 17:1–15), is mentioned once in the Doctrine and Covenants (see D&C 132:39). For more details, see the entry for "David."

NATHANAEL

Nathanael was an associate of Phillip during the ministry of the Savior in the Holy Land (see John 1:45–51; 21:2): "Jesus saw Nathanael coming to him, and saith of him, Behold an Israelite indeed, in whom is no guile!" (John 1:47). In section 41 of the Doctrine and Covenants, Edward Partridge is commended by the Lord "because his heart is pure before me, for he is like unto Nathanael of old, in whom there is no guile" (v. 11).

NEPHI

Among the most recognized and admired of the Lord's prophet-servants, Nephi exemplifies faith, obedience, steadfastness, visionary leadership, and valor in cultivating and upholding the

Nephi

testimony of Jesus Christ as the Redeemer and Savior. Nephi was one of the central figures in, and contributors to, the Book of Mormon. He labored all his days for the defense and welfare of his people. His faithful followers admired him and gloried in his example of integrity. And at the end of his long tenure as prophet and leader, Nephi counseled his people and all who followed after them to "feast upon the words of Christ" and "receive the Holy Ghost," thereby knowing of the Lord what to do to have eternal life and salvation (see 2 Ne. 32:3–5).

Nephi and his writings are mentioned ten times in the text of the Doctrine and Covenants. In one passage, the Lord refers to Nephi and other ancient prophets concerning His law of warfare (see D&C 98:32). In another passage Nephi is identified as an exemplar of courage in carrying out the commands of the Lord:

> Open your mouths and they shall be filled, and you shall become even as Nephi of old, who journeyed from Jerusalem in the wilderness.
>
> Yea, open your mouths and spare not, and you shall be laden with sheaves upon your backs, for lo, I am with you.
>
> Yea, open your mouths and they shall be filled, saying: Repent, repent, and prepare ye the way of the Lord, and make his paths straight; for the kingdom of heaven is at hand. (D&C 33:8–10)

NEPHITES

The descendants of Nephi, son of Lehi, were known throughout the Book of Mormon as Nephites. Into the Nephite generations were added the descendants of other individuals, including Jacob, Joseph, and Zoram.

> Now the people which were not Lamanites were Nephites; nevertheless, they were called Nephites, Jacobites, Josephites, Zoramites, Lamanites, Lemuelites, and Ishmaelites.

But I, Jacob, shall not hereafter distinguish them by these names, but I shall call them Lamanites that seek to destroy the people of Nephi, and those who are friendly to Nephi I shall call Nephites. (Jacob 1:13–14; compare 4 Ne. 1:36–37; Morm. 1:8)

The Nephites are referred to in the Doctrine and Covenants initially in connection with the coming forth of the Book of Mormon: "And after having received the record of the Nephites, yea, even my servant Joseph Smith, Jun., might have power to translate through the mercy of God, by the power of God, the Book of Mormon" (D&C 1:29). The Nephites are mentioned twice among the various Israelite peoples to whom the knowledge of a Savior shall come (see D&C 3:17, 18) and once in the Lord's warning to "beware of pride, lest ye become as the Nephites of old" (D&C 38:39).

NICOLAITANE BAND (SEE ALSO WHITNEY, NEWEL)

The term Nicolaitane band is used in the Doctrine and Covenants in the Lord's severe reprimand of Bishop Newel K. Whitney: "Let my servant Newel K. Whitney be ashamed of the Nicolaitane band and of all their secret abominations, and of all his littleness of soul before me, saith the Lord, and come up to the land of Adam-ondi-Ahman, and be a bishop unto my people, saith the Lord, not in name but in deed, saith the Lord" (D&C 117:11). Newel Whitney penitently redirected his ways and remained valiant in the faith. The reference to "Nicolaitane band" seems to relate to an unrighteous group referred to in the book of Revelation (Rev. 2:6, 15). Elder Bruce R. McConkie identifies them as

Noah

members of the Church who were trying to maintain their church standing while continuing to live after the manner of the world. They must have had some specific doctrinal teachings which they used to justify their course. In the counsel given to the Church in Pergamos, their doctrine is condemned as severely as that of Balaam who sought to lead Israel astray. (Rev. 2:14–16; 2 Pet. 2:10–22; Num. 22, 23, and 24.) Whatever their particular deeds and doctrines were, the designation has come to be used to identify those who want their names on the records of the Church, but do not want to devote themselves to the gospel cause with full purpose of heart [as in D&C 117:11, quoted]. (*DNTC* 3:446)

NOAH (SEE ALSO ELIAS)

Noah is the great patriarch of the Old Testament who stands next to Adam in authority (see *HC* 3:386). In the text of the Doctrine and Covenants, Noah is mentioned three times in connection with the descent of the priesthood (D&C 84:14–15; 107:52); once in connection with the assembly of elect prophets who will meet the Savior at His Second Coming (D&C 133:54); and three times as part of the vision granted to President Joseph F. Smith concerning the cause of salvation in the spirit world (D&C 138:9, 28, 41).

NOBLEMAN (SEE LORD OF THE VINEYARD)

ONE HUNDRED AND FORTY-FOUR THOUSAND

Section 77 of the Doctrine and Covenants provides inspired commentary on various passages written by John the Revelator, including the following reference: "And I heard the number of them which were sealed: and there were sealed an hundred and forty and four thousand of all the tribes of the children of Israel" (Rev. 7:4). Latter-day scripture asks the question:

Q. What are we to understand by sealing the one hundred and forty-four thousand, out of all the tribes of Israel—twelve thousand out of every tribe?

A. We are to understand that those who are sealed are high priests, ordained unto the holy order of God, to administer the everlasting gospel; for they are they who are ordained out of every nation, kindred, tongue, and people, by the angels to whom is given power over the nations of the earth, to bring as many as will come to the church of the Firstborn. (D&C 77:11)

Author Victor Ludlow comments that these are

righteous high priests, all of whom have honored the law of chastity, who will receive a special ordinance. (See Rev. 7:3–4; 14:3–4; D&C 77:11.) These 144,000 will be organized into groups or quorums of twelve thousand each according to the twelve tribes of Israel. (See Rev. 7:4–8.) . . . . Depending upon the earth's population when the Millennium is established, each of these 144,000 high priests could have responsibility for many thousands of people . . . to help the Messiah govern his kingdom on earth. (See D&C 133:18.) (*PPRG*, 612)

PACKARD, NOAH

Noah was born on May 7, 1796, at Plainfield, Hampshire County, Massachusetts. Having been introduced to the Book of Mormon, he was baptized by Parley P. Pratt in June 1832. Missionary work was his first assignment, and he enjoyed considerable success in his travels to various states. Upon moving to Kirtland, Noah generously contributed much revenue toward the building of the temple and covering the debts of the Church. He was ordained a high priest on January 15, 1836, and called to the Kirtland high council. After moving to Illinois, he was appointed a counselor to Don Carlos Smith in the presidency of the high priests quorum (see D&C 124:136), continuing for several years as a counselor after the death of Don Carlos. Subsequently, he served various missions for the Church. When persecution forced the Saints to abandon Nauvoo, Noah remained in Illinois and later went to Wisconsin to earn money for the exodus. He arrived in the Salt Lake Valley in 1850 and settled in Springville. Though service-minded and active in Church and civic affairs, Noah, a farmer and surveyor, disagreed with local authorities concerning the structural integrity of the Springville Tabernacle. Nonetheless, he remained devout and strong in the faith until his death on February 7, 1859.

PAGE, HIRAM

Hiram was born in 1800 in Vermont. In his travels as a medical practitioner he became acquainted with the Peter Whitmer family in Fayette, New York. He married Peter's oldest daughter Catherine on November 10, 1825. Through the Whitmers, Hiram learned of the mission of Joseph Smith and eventually became one of the eight witnesses of the Book of Mormon. He was baptized on April 11, 1830. Prior to the Church conference on September 26, 1830, Hiram came into possession of a small stone by means of which he claimed to receive revelations, for example, the location of the New Jerusalem. Section 28 constituted a firm rebuke of his claims, which he recanted at the September conference:

And again, thou [Oliver Cowdery] shalt take thy brother, Hiram Page, between him and thee alone, and tell him that those things which he hath written from that stone are not of me and that Satan deceiveth him;

For, behold, these things have not been appointed unto him, neither shall anything be appointed unto any of this church contrary to the church covenants.

For all things must be done in order, and by common consent in the church, by the prayer of faith. (D&C 28:11–13)

Hiram and his family later suffered abuse by the mobs in Missouri. Having lost his faith in the leadership of the Prophet Joseph, Hiram was eventually excommunicated, though he remained true to his testimony of the Book of Mormon. He died on his farm near Excelsior Springs, Ray County, Missouri, on August 12, 1852.

PAGE, JOHN E.

John was born on February 25, 1799, in Trenton Township, Oneida County, New York. He was baptized into the Church in 1833 and served two productive missions in Canada, guiding many converts to Missouri in 1838. Tragically, John's wife and two children were killed by mob violence that year. Still grieving, John was called by revelation to be a member of the Quorum of the Twelve Apostles on July 8, 1838: "Let my servant John Taylor, and also my servant John E. Page, and also my servant Wilford Woodruff, and also my servant Willard Richards, be appointed to fill the places of those who have fallen, and be officially notified of their appointment" (D&C 118:6). John

John E. Page

did not thereafter comply with a call to serve a mission in England, nor with a subsequent call in 1840 to accompany Orson Hyde on a mission to dedicate the Holy Land for the return of the Jews. He was still listed as a member of the Quorum of the Twelve in a revelation dated January 19, 1841 (see D&C 124:129). Over the next several years he professed repentance for his behavior and a desire to return to activity, but eventually he formed an allegiance with James J. Strang, who claimed to be the rightful successor to the martyred Prophet Joseph Smith. John lost his apostleship and was excommunicated on June 26, 1846. He took up affiliation with several other upstart groups thereafter and eventually helped the Hedrickites to secure the temple lot in Independence. John died on October 14, 1867.

PARTRIDGE, EDWARD

Edward was born on August 27, 1793, at Pittsfield, Berkshire County, Massachusetts. A

Edward Partridge

hatter by trade, he was at first reluctant to embrace the restored gospel. However, he was finally persuaded when he went with Sidney Rigdon to visit the Prophet Joseph Smith in 1830. The Prophet baptized him on December 11 of that year. On February 4, 1831, Edward was called by revelation to become the first bishop of the Church:

> And again, I have called my servant Edward Partridge; and I give a commandment, that he should be appointed by the voice of the church, and ordained a bishop unto the church, to leave his merchandise and to spend all his time in the labors of the church; . . .
>
> And this because his heart is pure before me, for he is like unto Nathanael of old, in whom there is no guile. (D&C 41:9, 11)

In May 1831, Bishop Partridge was instructed of the Lord on how to serve the stewardship and housing needs of the Saints moving to Kirtland (see D&C 51:1–4, 18). Sent to Missouri to assist the Saints (see D&C 52:24, 41; 57:7; 58:24, 62; 60:10; 82:11; 115:2), he was subjected to cruel abuse by the mobs. After returning to Kirtland, he spent his time serving the poor and preaching the gospel on various missions. On a subsequent sojourn in Missouri he was not only persecuted but imprisoned. On May 27, 1840, Edward passed away at the age of forty-six in Nauvoo. Though impoverished and frail in his final days, Edward Partridge was a person of eternal wealth, whom the Lord declared had been received "unto myself" (D&C 124:19). Even though Edward had been censured by the Lord because of his failings (see D&C 50:39; 58:14–16; 64:17), he was able to rise above his weaknesses. The Prophet Joseph characterized him as "a pattern of piety, and one of the Lord's great men" (*HC* 1:128).

PATTEN, DAVID W.

David, born November 14, 1799, near Indian River Falls, New York, was introduced to the restored gospel by his brother John. He was baptized and subsequently ordained an elder on June 19, 1832. He served several missions for the Church before the Prophet Joseph Smith sent him to aid the Saints in Missouri in 1834, where he blessed many with his gift of healing. He also journeyed to the southern states to preach the gospel before being called on February 15, 1835, as a member of the Quorum of the Twelve Apostles. Thereafter he served missions in the eastern states and the southern states (see, for example, D&C 114:1). At the battle of Crooked River, Missouri, in October

1838, David courageously led a charge against the mob in defense of the Saints. He received a severe gunshot wound and passed away on October 25, 1838. In a revelation dated January 19, 1841, the Lord declared: "David Patten . . . is with me at this time" (D&C 124:19). And also: "David Patten I have taken unto myself; behold, his priesthood no man taketh from him; but, verily I say unto you, another may be appointed unto the same calling" (D&C 124:130).

PAUL

The apostle Paul, one of the greatest of all missionaries, is mentioned six times in the text of the Doctrine and Covenants. Oliver Cowdery and David Whitmer were reminded by the Lord: "I speak unto you, even as unto Paul mine apostle, for you are called even with that same calling with which he was called" (D&C 18:9). In section 76, concerning the degrees of glory, those in the telestial kingdom are characterized as having denied the testimony of the Savior, though they might verbally claim allegiance to Christ, John, Moses, Elias, Isaiah, Enoch, Paul, or some other movement (see D&C 76:99). In the first epistle on baptism for

Paul

the dead (section 127), the Prophet Joseph Smith speaks of his adverse circumstances by relating to Paul:

> But nevertheless, deep water is what I am wont to swim in. It all has become a second nature to me; and I feel, like Paul, to glory in tribulation; for to this day has the God of my fathers delivered me out of them all, and will deliver me from henceforth; for behold, and lo, I shall triumph over all my enemies, for the Lord God hath spoken it. (D&C 127:2)

In section 128, a few weeks later, the Prophet Joseph cites Paul's teachings, this time in connection with the salvation of the deceased:

> And now, my dearly beloved brethren and sisters, let me assure you that these are principles in relation to the dead and the living that cannot be lightly passed over, as pertaining to our salvation. For their salvation is necessary and essential to our salvation, as Paul says concerning the fathers—that they without us cannot be made perfect—neither can we without our dead be made perfect.
>
> And now, in relation to the baptism for the dead, I will give you another quotation of Paul, 1 Corinthians 15:29: *Else what shall they do which are baptized for the dead, if the dead rise not at all? Why are they then baptized for the dead?* (D&C 128:15–16)

PERDITION (SEE SATAN; SONS OF PERDITION)

PETER

Peter was the leading Apostle among the Twelve Apostles called by the Lord during His mortal ministry (Matt. 4:18–22; Mark 1:16–18; Luke 5:1–11; and John 1:40–42). He, together with James and John, constituted the First Presidency of the Church. All three were with the Savior on the Mount of Transfiguration (see Matt. 17:1–13) and at Gethsemane (see Matt. 26:36–37; Mark 14:32–33; Luke 22:39). Peter's affirmation of the divine Sonship of Jesus (Matt. 16:16) preceded the Savior's celebrated declaration:

> Blessed art thou, Simon Bar-jona [his alternate name—also as the son of Jonah]: for flesh and blood hath not revealed it unto thee, but my Father which is in heaven.
>
> And I say also unto thee, That thou art Peter, and upon this rock [meaning the rock of the revealed word and will of the Lord] I will build my church; and the gates of hell shall not prevail against it.
>
> And I will give unto thee the keys of the kingdom of heaven: and whatsoever thou shalt bind on earth shall be bound in heaven: and whatsoever thou shalt loose on earth shall be loosed in heaven. (Matt. 16:17–19; compare the similar reference to Peter in D&C 128:10)

It was through the missionary work of Peter that the gospel was introduced among the Gentiles (Acts 10–11). Peter's pronouncement

Peter

to the people concerning the predicted "times of refreshing" and "times of restitution of all things" (Acts 3:19, 21) coming through the future ministry of the Lord foreshadowed the Restoration in the latter days. Peter and his writings are mentioned in the text of the Doctrine and Covenants eleven times. As part of Peter's great mission on behalf of the Kingdom of God, he participated with James and John in the latter-day restoration of the Melchizedek Priesthood, most likely in late May of 1829 (see D&C 27:12–13; 128:20).

Additional passages concerning Peter relate to John the Beloved's desire to remain on earth until the Second Coming: "And I will make thee [Peter] to minister for him [John] and for thy brother James; and unto you three I will give this power and the keys of this ministry until I come" (D&C 7:7; see also verses 4 and 5 where Peter is mentioned by name); the future assembly of elect priesthood leaders who will partake of the sacrament with the Savior: "And also with Peter, and James, and John, whom I have sent unto you, by whom I have ordained you and confirmed you to be apostles, and especial witnesses of my name, and bear the keys of your ministry and of the same things which I revealed unto them" (D&C 27:12); and Joseph Smith's summation of the heavenly events comprising the restoration of the priesthood authority and keys: "The voice of Peter, James, and John in the wilderness between Harmony, Susquehanna county, and Colesville, Broome county, on the Susquehanna river, declaring themselves as possessing the keys of the kingdom, and of the dispensation of the fulness of times!" (D&C 128:20).

When the Lord instructed Sidney Rigdon, Parley P. Pratt, and Leman Copley to go among the Shakers and proclaim the truths of the restored gospel, He told them to "go among this people, . . . like unto mine apostle of old, whose name was Peter" (D&C 49:11).

Peter is also mentioned in the current introductory heading of section 13, concerning the restoration of the Aaronic Priesthood. While pondering the writings of Peter, President Joseph F. Smith was granted his grand vision of the work of salvation taking place in the spirit world (see D&C 138:5–6, 9–10, 28).

PETERSON, ZIBA

Details concerning the birth of Ziba are not known. He was baptized as a young man on April 18, 1830, and was subsequently ordained an elder. In October of that same year he was called to serve a mission among the Lamanites along with Parley P. Pratt, Oliver Cowdery, and Peter Whitmer Jr. (see D&C 32:3). He was later chastened by the Lord for hiding his sins: "Let that which has been bestowed upon Ziba Peterson be taken from him; and let him stand as a member in the church, and labor with his own hands, with the brethren, until he is sufficiently chastened for all his sins; for he confesseth them not, and he thinketh to hide them" (D&C 58:60). Subsequently, he withdrew himself from fellowship in the Church and was excommunicated on June 25, 1833.

He moved to California with his family in 1848 where he became the sheriff in a mining community; he died in California.

PHELPS, WILLIAM W.

William was born on February 17, 1792, in Dover, Morris County, New Jersey. He purchased a copy of the Book of Mormon from Parley P. Pratt in April 1830 and was immediately persuaded of its divine authenticity. In June 1831 he moved to Kirtland and received a revelation through the Prophet Joseph Smith concerning his specific calling in the Church:

Behold, thus saith the Lord unto you, my servant William, . . . thou art called and chosen; and after thou hast been baptized by water, which if you do with an eye single to my glory, you shall have a remission of your sins and a reception of the Holy Spirit by the laying on of hands;

And then thou shalt be ordained by the hand of my servant Joseph

William W. Phelps

114

Smith, Jun., to be an elder unto this church, to preach repentance and remission of sins. . . .

And again, you shall be ordained to assist my servant Oliver Cowdery to do the work of printing, and of selecting and writing books for schools in this church, . . .

And again, . . . for this cause you shall take your journey with my servants Joseph Smith, Jun., and Sidney Rigdon, that you may be planted in the land of your inheritance to do this work. (D&C 55:1–2, 4–5)

William's baptism took place on June 10, 1831. Subsequently he was ordained an elder and journeyed with the Prophet to Missouri, where, by revelation on July 20, 1831, he was directed to set up shop as a printer (see D&C 57:11–13). On August 1, 1831, the Lord gave further instructions to William, which contain the oft-quoted statements of the Master concerning repentance:

And also let my servant William W. Phelps stand in the office to which I have appointed him, and receive his inheritance in the land;

And also he hath need to repent, for I, the Lord, am not well pleased with him, for he seeketh to excel, and he is not sufficiently meek before me.

Behold, he who has repented of his sins, the same is forgiven, and I, the Lord, remember them no more.

By this ye may know if a man repenteth of his sins—behold, he will confess them and forsake them. (D&C 58:40–43)

On the return trip back to Kirtland from Missouri on August 12, 1831, the Lord had additional instructions for William and his companion Sidney Gilbert:

Wherefore, it is expedient that my servant Sidney Gilbert and my servant William W. Phelps be in haste upon their errand and mission.

Nevertheless, I would not suffer that ye should part until you were chastened for all your sins, that you might be one, that you might not perish in wickedness;

But now, verily I say, it behooveth me that ye should part. Wherefore let my servants Sidney Gilbert and William W. Phelps take their former company, and let them take their journey in haste that they may fill their mission, and through faith they shall overcome;

And inasmuch as they are faithful they shall be preserved, and I, the Lord, will be with them. (D&C 61:7–10)

Then, on November 12, 1831, the Lord confirmed with strong language the commission to Joseph Smith, William W. Phelps, and their associates to complete the publication of the Book of Commandments, containing the revelations given to that point in time. They were also instructed that at the day of judgment an account of their stewardship would be requested (see D&C 70:1–5).

At a conference of the Church in Jackson County, Missouri, held on April 26, 1832, the Lord gave instructions to the assembled priesthood officers concerning their duties. Again, the name of William W. Phelps is mentioned in connection with several other brethren, all of whom were to be united in a covenant stewardship bond to attend to the duties of blessing the Saints (see D&C 82:11).

In July 1833 a mob attacked William's house and destroyed the press on which he was printing the Book of Commandments, the predecessor to the Doctrine and Covenants. He returned to Kirtland, where he assisted in the preparation of the 1835 edition of the Doctrine and Covenants and also the first Church hymnbook. He donated funds to support the building of the Kirtland Temple and composed the celebrated hymn sung at its dedication—"The Spirit of God Like a Fire Is Burning." Upon returning to Missouri he became involved in property arrangements in Far West, certain aspects of which caused concern among Church leaders. Although he turned his assets over to Bishop Edward Partridge for the building up of the Kingdom, he was chastened in a private revelation received by the Prophet (see *HC* 2:511) and excommunicated in March 1839. Though embittered, William repented and was forgiven. In Nauvoo he served on the city council and loyally stood by the Prophet in the hour of martyrdom. Thereafter he journeyed with the Saints to the Salt Lake Valley, where he spent his final years in civic and Church service, passing away on March 6, 1872. In addition to "The Spirit of God Like a Fire Is Burning," W. W. Phelps also wrote "Praise to the Man" and "Now Let Us Rejoice."

PRATT, ORSON

Orson was born on September 19, 1811, at Hartford, Washington County, New York. He was baptized on his nineteenth birthday by his brother Parley P. Pratt, with whom he was subsequently called to serve a mission in Missouri on November 4, 1830. This call came in a personal revelation through the Prophet Joseph:

> My son Orson, hearken and hear and behold what I, the Lord God, shall say unto you, even Jesus Christ your Redeemer;
>
> The light and the life of the world, a light which shineth in darkness and the darkness comprehendeth it not;
>
> Who so loved the world that he gave his own life, that as many as would believe might become the sons of God. Wherefore you are my son;
>
> And blessed are you because you have believed;
>
> And more blessed are you because you are called of me to preach my gospel—
>
> To lift up your voice as with the sound of a trump, both long and loud, and cry repentance unto a crooked

Orson Pratt

and perverse generation, preparing the way of the Lord for his second coming. . . .

Wherefore, lift up your voice and spare not, for the Lord God hath spoken; therefore prophesy, and it shall be given by the power of the Holy Ghost.

And if you are faithful, behold, I am with you until I come—

And verily, verily, I say unto you, I come quickly. I am your Lord and your Redeemer. Even so. Amen. (D&C 34:1–6, 10–12)

Orson was called to accompany his brother Parley to Missouri on June 7, 1831 (see D&C 52:26) and to go on a mission to the eastern states (see D&C 75:14). His career in the Church also included a call to participate in Zion's Camp in 1834 (see D&C 103:40) and to fill the office of apostle in the Quorum of the Twelve in 1835 (confirmed on January 19, 1841; D&C 124:129). He became proficient at teaching Hebrew. Because of a lapse into apostasy, he was excommunicated on August 20, 1842, but he repented and was rebaptized on January 20, 1843, and restored to his priesthood calling. As a participant in the western exodus (see D&C 136:13), he was one of the very first individuals to view the Salt Lake Valley. He crossed the Atlantic sixteen times as a missionary to the British Isles. He defended the Church and its doctrines with intensity, served in the Quorum of the Twelve in Utah, and filled the position of historian and general Church recorder beginning in 1874. He passed away on October 3, 1881, the last surviving member of the original Council of the Twelve, dating from 1835.

Parley P. Pratt

PRATT, PARLEY P.

Parley P. Pratt, one of the pillars of the Restoration, is mentioned in the text of the Doctrine and Covenants nine times. Parley was born on April 12, 1807, in Burlington, Otsego County, New York. The Book of Mormon brought the light of the gospel into his life, as this passage from his autobiography confirms:

I opened it [the Book of Mormon] with eagerness, and read its title page. I then read the testimony of several witnesses in relation to the manner of its being found and translated. After this I commenced its contents by course. I read all day; eating was a burden, I had no desire for food; sleep was a burden when the night came, for I preferred reading to sleep.

As I read, the spirit of the Lord was upon me, and I knew and comprehended that the book was true, as plainly and manifestly as a man comprehends and knows that he exists. My joy was now full, as it were, and I rejoiced sufficiently to more than pay me for all the sorrows, sacrifices and toils of my life. (*APPP*, 20)

Parley was baptized by Oliver Cowdery in September 1830 and ordained an elder soon after that. After converting his brother Orson, he was called in October 1830, along with Oliver Cowdery and several others, to serve a mission among the Lamanites in Ohio and Missouri (see D&C 32:1), traveling some 1,500 miles on foot. He was also sent in March 1831 with several others to preach the gospel to the Shakers in Ohio (see D&C 49:1, 3). Parley was an instrument in the hands of the Lord to strengthen the Church in various locations (see D&C 50:37). He was dispatched with many other priesthood leaders to Missouri (see D&C 52:26), where he directed the School of the Prophets with distinction:

> Behold, I say unto you, concerning the school in Zion, I, the Lord, am well pleased that there should be a school in Zion, and also with my servant Parley P. Pratt, for he abideth in me.
>
> And inasmuch as he continueth to abide in me he shall continue to preside over the school in the land of Zion until I shall give unto him other commandments.
>
> And I will bless him with a multiplicity of blessings, in expounding all scriptures and mysteries to the edification of the school, and of the church in Zion. (D&C 97:3–5; dated August 2, 1833)

Parley also participated in Zion's Camp in 1834 (see D&C 103:30, 37). On February 21, 1835, he was ordained an apostle and served on many missions for the Church (his apostolic appointment being confirmed on January 19, 1841, in D&C 124:129). Earlier, during the financial dislocations of the Kirtland years, he had lapsed into unfounded criticism of the Prophet Joseph, for which Parley went through a time of sore repentance. Of his temporary disaffection in the summer of 1837, Parley made the following comment in his autobiography: "I went to Brother Joseph in tears, and, with a broken heart and contrite spirit, confessed wherein I had erred in spirit, murmured, or done or said amiss. He frankly forgave me, prayed for me and blessed me. Thus, by experience, I learned more fully to discern and to contrast the two spirits, and to resist the one and cleave to the other. And, being tempted in all points, even as others, I learned how to bear with, and excuse, and succor those who are tempted" (*APPP*, 183–84; see also *HC* 2:488). No stranger to persecution and tribulation, he was imprisoned unjustly for a period of time in 1838–39. His service in the Kingdom of the Lord continued with additional missionary travels in England, the United States, and South America. He served the Saints with devotion in the Salt Lake Valley. In May 1857, while on yet another mission, this time in Arkansas, Parley was murdered. He, like Joseph and Hyrum, is considered a martyr.

PULSIPHER, ZERA

Zera was born on June 24, 1789, at Rockingham, Windham County, Vermont. A Baptist minister in Onondaga County, New York, Zera became interested in the restored gospel when news of the Book of Mormon reached him in

1831. Following his conversion, he proclaimed the gospel in the vicinity and baptized Wilford Woodruff, a future president of the Church, on December 31, 1833. In 1835, Zera moved to Ohio to be with the Saints. Subsequently, he filled missions in Canada and New York. On March 6, 1838, he was ordained as one of the seven Presidents of the Seventy (confirmed in D&C 124:138). As such, he assisted the poor Saints in their emigration to Missouri, he himself settling for a time in Adam-ondi-Ahman until the persecution became too severe. Following the Nauvoo and Iowa periods, he joined the westward trek in 1847. He continued as a General Authority until 1862, when he was released and called to serve as a patriarch in southern Utah. He passed away on January 1, 1872.

Zera Pulsipher

RAPHAEL

Raphael is mentioned once in the Doctrine and Covenants, in connection with the manifestations of various divine messengers during the foundation of the Restoration:

> And again, the voice of God in the chamber of old Father Whitmer, in Fayette, Seneca county, and at sundry times, and in divers places through all the travels and tribulations of this Church of Jesus Christ of Latter-day Saints! And the voice of Michael, the archangel; the voice of Gabriel, and of Raphael, and of divers angels, from Michael or Adam down to the present time, all declaring their dispensation, their rights, their keys, their honors, their majesty and glory, and the power of their priesthood; giving line upon line, precept upon precept; here a little, and there a little; giving us consolation by holding forth that which is to come, confirming our hope! (D&C 128:21)

The scriptures add nothing further concerning the identity and character of Raphael.

RICH, CHARLES C.

Charles was born on August 21, 1809, in Campbell County, Kentucky. Having been introduced to the restored gospel through the Book of

Charles C. Rich

Mormon, he was baptized in April 1832 in Illinois. After participating in Zion's Camp in 1834, he journeyed to Kirtland where he was ordained a high priest. In Far West, Missouri, he served on the high council until mob violence forced him to move to Nauvoo. There he served on the high council (see D&C 124:132), in the Nauvoo stake presidency, in the Nauvoo Legion, and as a regent of the University of Nauvoo. He was a leader during the exodus to the West and then served as a member of the Salt Lake Stake presidency until called as a member of the Council of the Twelve Apostles on February 12, 1849. As a General Authority he served in pioneering San Bernardino, California, presided over the European Mission, and pioneered in the Bear Lake region of Utah/Idaho. He died in Paris, Idaho, on November 17, 1883, following a series of strokes.

RICHARDS, WILLARD

Willard was born on June 24, 1804, at Hopkinton, Middlesex County, Massachusetts. He established a medical practice in Boston. When he acquired a copy of the Book of Mormon, he soon became convinced of its truth

Willard Richards

and journeyed to Kirtland in 1836 to continue his investigation of the Church. His cousin Brigham Young baptized him on December 31 of that year. Willard served a mission in the British Isles the following year and married one of his converts, Jennetta Richards, in 1838. While still in England, he learned of his call to the Quorum of the Twelve: "Let my servant John Taylor, and also my servant John E. Page, and also my servant Wilford Woodruff, and also my servant Willard Richards, be appointed to fill the places of those who have fallen, and be officially notified of their appointment" (D&C 118:6). He was ordained by visiting members of the Twelve on April 14, 1840. On January 19, 1841, his service as a member of the Quorum of the Twelve was confirmed by revelation (see D&C 124:129). After his return to America in April 1841, he was appointed private secretary to the Prophet Joseph in Nauvoo. On June 27, 1844, he was a witness to the Martyrdom in Carthage Jail: "John Taylor and Willard Richards, two of the Twelve, were the only persons in the room at the time; the former was wounded in a savage manner with four balls, but has since recovered; the latter, through the providence of God, escaped, without even a hole in his robe" (D&C 135:2). Thereafter he gave the same dedicated service to Brigham Young, whom he accompanied to the Salt Lake Valley in 1847. He served as Second Counselor to President Young from 1847 until his death on March 11, 1854.

RIGDON, SIDNEY

Sidney, born on February 19, 1793, near St. Clair Township, Allegheny County, Pennsylvania, became an accomplished orator, a Baptist minister, and later one of the founders of the Campbellite movement. Parley P. Pratt introduced him to the restored gospel and provided him with a copy of the Book of Mormon. Sidney was baptized on November 14, 1830. His service to the Church included participating in the dedication of Independence, Missouri, as the chosen land of Zion (see D&C 58:57), serving as a scribe for the Prophet Joseph for the inspired translation of the Bible, participating with Joseph Smith in a number of revelations (including section 76 on the degrees of glory), and generally being a spokesman and defender for the cause of Zion. He became a member of the First Presidency on March 18, 1833. He suffered greatly during the Missouri persecutions. Following a dispute with the Prophet Joseph, Sidney was severed from the Church on August 13, 1843, but was later reinstated. He moved to Pittsburgh, returning to Nauvoo following the Martyrdom in response to a vision he claimed had instructed him that he should become the guardian of the Church. Instead, the Church supported the Twelve under Brigham Young. Sidney was disfellowshipped in September of 1844. He returned to Pittsburgh and from thence to Friendship, New York, where he passed away in poverty on July 14, 1876.

Sidney is mentioned in the introductory heading/overview of thirteen sections of the Doctrine and Covenants (35, 36, 37, 40, 44, 49, 63, 71, 73, 76, 90, 100, 111). Of these revelations, eight were given jointly to the Prophet Joseph Smith and Sidney Rigdon (35, 37, 40, 44, 71, 73, 76, 100) and one was given through the Prophet to Sidney Rigdon, Parley P. Pratt, and Leman Copley (49, concerning the "Shakers"). Sidney is mentioned in the actual text of the Doctrine and Covenants some forty-four times, concerning instructions on his various travels, duties, and responsibilities.

Sidney Rigdon

These passages teach valuable lessons concerning the covenant operations in the Kingdom of God on earth—and the urgency of following through with devotion and dedication to the cause of Zion.

The Lord saw in Sidney great promise as a participant in the latter-day Restoration:

> I am Jesus Christ, the Son of God, who was crucified for the sins of the world, even as many as will believe on my name, that they may become the sons of God, even one in me as I am one in the Father, as the Father is one in me, that we may be one.
>
> Behold, verily, verily, I say unto my servant Sidney, I have looked upon thee and thy works. I have heard thy prayers, and prepared thee for a greater work.
>
> Thou art blessed, for thou shalt do great things. (D&C 35:2–4; dated December 1830)

The following year, in August 1831 at Kirtland, the Lord warned Sidney about his tendency toward pride—the cause of his eventual loss of fellowship in the Church: "I, the Lord, am not pleased with my servant Sidney Rigdon; he exalted himself in his heart, and received not counsel, but grieved the Spirit; Wherefore his writing [concerning a "description of the land of Zion"—D&C 58:50] is not acceptable unto the Lord, and he shall make another; and if the Lord receive it not, behold he standeth no longer in the office to which I have appointed him" (D&C 63:55–56).

In December 1831 a revelation was given to the Prophet Joseph and Sidney Rigdon in which a marvelous view concerning the calling of missionaries in the latter days was unfolded:

Behold, thus saith the Lord unto you my servants Joseph Smith, Jun., and Sidney Rigdon, that the time has verily come that it is necessary and expedient in me that you should open your mouths in proclaiming my gospel, the things of the kingdom, expounding the mysteries thereof out of the scriptures, according to that portion of Spirit and power which shall be given unto you, even as I will.

Verily I say unto you, proclaim unto the world in the regions round about, and in the church also, for the space of a season, even until it shall be made known unto you.

Verily this is a mission for a season, which I give unto you.

Wherefore, confound your enemies; call upon them to meet you both in public and in private; and inasmuch as ye are faithful their shame shall be made manifest.

Wherefore, let them bring forth their strong reasons against the Lord.

Verily, thus saith the Lord unto you—there is no weapon that is formed against you shall prosper;

And if any man lift his voice against you he shall be confounded in mine own due time. (D&C 71:1–3, 7–10)

Two months later the vision of the degrees of glory was given jointly to the Prophet Joseph and Sidney. This vision is the context for the well-known witness that these two recorded concerning the Savior:

We, Joseph Smith, Jun., and Sidney Rigdon, being in the Spirit on the sixteenth day of February, in the year of our Lord one thousand eight hundred and thirty-two—

By the power of the Spirit our eyes were opened and our understandings were enlightened, so as to see and understand the things of God—

Even those things which were from the beginning before the world was, which were ordained of the Father, through his Only Begotten Son, who was in the bosom of the Father, even from the beginning;

Of whom we bear record; and the record which we bear is the fulness of the gospel of Jesus Christ, who is the Son, whom we saw and with whom we conversed in the heavenly vision. . . .

And we beheld the glory of the Son, on the right hand of the Father, and received of his fulness;

And saw the holy angels, and them who are sanctified before his throne, worshiping God, and the Lamb, who worship him forever and ever.

And now, after the many testimonies which have been given of him, this is the testimony, last of all, which we give of him: That he lives!

For we saw him, even on the right hand of God; and we heard the voice bearing record that he is the Only Begotten of the Father—

That by him, and through him, and of him, the worlds are and were created, and the inhabitants thereof are begotten sons and daughters unto God. (D&C 76:11–14, 20–24); dated February 16, 1832)

In the ensuing years, Sidney participated in the United Order, instituted "to manage the affairs of the poor, and all things pertaining to the bishopric both in the land of Zion and in the land of Kirtland" (D&C 82:12): "I, the Lord, am bound when ye do what I say; but when ye do not what I say, ye have no promise. Therefore, verily I say unto you, that it is expedient for my servants Edward Partridge and Newel K. Whitney, A. Sidney Gilbert and Sidney Rigdon, and my servant Joseph Smith, and John Whitmer and Oliver Cowdery, and W. W. Phelps and Martin Harris to be bound together by a bond and covenant that cannot be broken by transgression, except judgment shall immediately follow, in your several stewardships" (D&C 82:10–11; see also D&C 104:20–23). Furthermore, Sidney and Frederick G. Williams, as counselors to the Prophet Joseph Smith, were admonished to treat the revelations of the Lord with utmost respect and honor (see D&C 90:5–6).

The Lord carefully observed the manner in which Sidney was conducting himself concerning covenant obligations: "Verily, I say unto my servant Sidney Rigdon, that in some things he hath not kept the commandments concerning his children; therefore, first set in order thy house. . . . Now, I say unto you, my friends, let my servant Sidney Rigdon go on his journey, and make haste, and also proclaim the acceptable year of the Lord, and the gospel of salvation, as I shall give him utterance; and by your prayer of faith with one consent I will uphold him" (D&C 93:44, 51). The promise of the Lord to give Sidney "utterance" as a missionary anticipates the wording of a revelation given on October 12, 1833, to the Prophet Joseph and Sidney Rigdon concerning missionary work (D&C 100) while they were serving a short-term proselyting mission to New York State and Canada (see HC 1:419–21). As with all missionaries, these brethren were anxious about their families, and thus the Lord gave them assurance: "Verily, thus saith the Lord unto you, my friends Sidney and Joseph, your families are well; they are in mine hands, and I will do with them as seemeth me good; for in me there is all power" (D&C 100:1).

As a member of the First Presidency, Sidney was involved in directing the affairs of the first high council organized in the Church (see D&C 102:3). He is mentioned, along with Hyrum Smith, as a counselor to the Prophet Joseph in the revelation proclaiming the name of the Church to be The Church of Jesus Christ of Latter-day Saints (see D&C 115:1–4; see also the earlier mention of Sidney as a counselor in D&C 112:17). Later, on January 19, 1841, Sidney was again identified as a counselor to the Prophet Joseph:

And again, verily I say unto you, if my servant Sidney will serve me and be counselor unto my servant Joseph, let him arise and come up and stand in the office of his calling, and humble himself before me.

And if he will offer unto me an acceptable offering, and acknowledgments, and remain with my people, behold, I, the Lord your God, will heal him that he shall be healed; and he shall lift up his voice again on the mountains, and be a spokesman before my face. (D&C 124:103–104)

A few years later Sidney attempted, outside the framework of succession established by the Lord, to take over the controls of leadership in the Church—and thus fell into a state of disgrace from which he never recovered.

RIGGS, BURR

Burr was born on April 17, 1811, at New Haven, New Haven County, Connecticut. Following his baptism into the Church, he was ordained a high priest on October 25, 1831, and subsequently received a missionary calling by revelation (see D&C 75:17)—a commission he apparently did not fulfill. He was excommunicated in February 1833 for failing to magnify his calling but subsequently repented and participated in Zion's Camp. Upon his return to Kirtland he established a medical practice. Persecution in Missouri in 1836 added more to the burdens he carried, and he later apostatized from the Church. On June 8, 1860, he passed away in Mt. Pleasant, Iowa.

ROLFE, SAMUEL

Samuel was born on August 26, 1794 (or 1796 by some accounts), in Concord, Merrimack County, New Hampshire. He joined the Church in 1835 and moved to Kirtland soon thereafter, where he performed carpentry service on the Kirtland Temple. For a period of time he lived in Missouri but was forced by persecution to relocate to Nauvoo, Illinois. In January 1841 he was called by revelation to preside over the priests' quorum (see D&C 124:142). He also devoted his carpentry service to the construction of the Nauvoo Temple. Samuel joined the westward exodus in 1846 and eventually moved to San Bernardino, California, where he was active in Church and civic duties. Later he returned to Utah where he died in July 1867.

ROMNEY, MARION G. (SEE ALSO KIMBALL, SPENCER W.; TANNER, NATHAN ELDON)

Marion Romney was born on September 19, 1897, in Colonia Juarez, Mexico. His family brought him back to the United States when he was fourteen years old. He served a mission

Marion G. Romney

in Australia, achieved considerable mastery as a scriptorian, and eventually went into law practice in Salt Lake City. He served as a bishop and stake president before being called in April 1941 as an Assistant to the Quorum of the Twelve Apostles, with the assignment to assist with the management of the welfare program of the Church. In October 1951 he was called to be a member of the Quorum of the Twelve. He became Second Counselor to President Harold B. Lee on July 7, 1972, and Second Counselor to President Spencer W. Kimball on December 30, 1973.

On June 8, 1978, the Church announced Official Declaration—2, the revealed word of the Lord that all worthy males could receive the priesthood and the blessings of the temple. In that context, N. Eldon Tanner and Marion G. Romney are listed with President Spencer W. Kimball as constituting the First Presidency in the confirming letter sent throughout the Church. On December 2, 1982, Marion Romney was called as First Counselor to President Spencer W. Kimball and then in 1985 sustained as President of the Quorum of the Twelve Apostles. He passed away on May 20, 1988.

ROOT OF JESSE (SEE EPHRAIM; JESSE; JOSEPH)

ROUNDY, SHADRACH

Shadrach was born on January 1, 1789, at Rockingham, Windham County, Vermont. In the winter of 1830, he journeyed to Fayette, New York, to meet with Joseph Smith and subsequently accepted the restored gospel. Shadrach moved to Ohio, then to Missouri, and eventually to Illinois. In Nauvoo he served as a member of the Nauvoo Legion and as a bodyguard to the Prophet Joseph Smith. On January 19, 1841, Shadrach was called as a counselor to Vinson Knight in the bishopric (see D&C 124:141). He assisted in the exodus from Nauvoo to Iowa, where he served as bishop of the Winter Quarters Fifth Ward, and on the trek westward in 1847. In the Salt Lake Valley he gave devoted service in Church and civic duties and was eventually ordained a patriarch. He passed away on July 4, 1872.

RYDER, SIMONDS

Simonds (also spelled Symonds) was born on November 20, 1792, at Hartford, Windsor County, Vermont. He moved to Ohio and settled in Hiram, where he became a prosperous farmer and a man of some repute. In 1831 he met the Prophet Joseph Smith and joined the Church in early June of that year. On June 6 he was ordained an elder and then called by revelation to replace Heman Basset in the ministry (see D&C 52:37). His call was signed by Joseph Smith and Sydney Rigdon, but the document had his name misspelled as "Rider," causing him to have misgivings about the inspiration behind the Church. This, and his misunderstanding of the law of consecration, caused him to rise up in league with apostate Ezra Booth in an effort to eradicate Mormonism. On March 24, 1832, a mob in Hiram, led by Simonds Ryder and Ezra Booth, tarred and feathered the Prophet Joseph and Sidney Rigdon. Simonds passed away on August 1, 1870.

SARAH

Sarah, wife of Abraham (see Gen. 11:29 through chapter 17; Gen. 21:2; 23:2; Isa. 51:2; Rom. 4:19; Heb. 11:11; 1 Pet. 3:6) is mentioned twice in the text of the Doctrine and Covenants:

Sarah

But if ye enter not into my law ye cannot receive the promise of my Father, which he made unto Abraham.

God commanded Abraham, and Sarah gave Hagar to Abraham to wife. And why did she do it? Because this was the law; and from Hagar sprang many people. This, therefore, was fulfilling, among other things, the promises. (D&C 132:33–34)

Therefore, it shall be lawful in me, if she [the wife of one who "holds the keys of this power" (v. 64)] receive not this law, for him to receive all things whatsoever I, the Lord his God, will give unto him, because she did not believe and administer unto him according to my word; and she then becomes the transgressor; and he is exempt from the law of Sarah, who administered unto Abraham according to the law when I commanded Abraham to take Hagar to wife. (D&C 132:65)

Satan

Satan, the enemy of righteousness, is referenced frequently in the text of the Doctrine and Covenants under various names. In one central passage from section 76 he is mentioned with several different designations:

> And this we saw also, and bear record, that an angel of God who was in authority in the presence of God, who rebelled against the Only Begotten Son whom the Father loved and who was in the bosom of the Father, was thrust down from the presence of God and the Son,
>
> And was called Perdition, for the heavens wept over him—he was Lucifer, a son of the morning.
>
> And we beheld, and lo, he is fallen! is fallen, even a son of the morning!
>
> And while we were yet in the Spirit, the Lord commanded us that we should write the vision; for we beheld Satan, that old serpent, even the devil, who rebelled against God, and sought to take the kingdom of our God and his Christ. (D&C 76:25–28)

The appellations for the adversary in this passage include fallen angel, Perdition, Lucifer, son of the morning, Satan, old serpent, and devil. The word *perdition* in English usage comes from the Latin verb *perdere*, meaning "to lose." Assuredly Satan is the archetype of the loser, for as an angel in authority in the premortal realm who rebelled against the Almighty God, he lost forever the divinely appointed opportunity to receive an inheritance of glory and exaltation. The word *Lucifer* means literally "the shining one" or "the light-bringer" (Bible Dictionary, 726). This name, which derives from the Latin word for light (compare the related word *lucid*), is the equivalent of the appellation "son of the morning." The word *Satan* in its Greek, Latin, and Hebrew sources means "adversary"—the perfect characterization of the fallen angel's defining role in opposing the Father's plan of redemption and rejecting the choice of Jehovah as Redeemer from the foundations of the world. The word *devil* in its Latin and Greek etymological derivation means "slanderer"—a further characterization of the fallen angel's strategy in opposing the eternal source of truth. The case of Lucifer (Perdition, Satan, devil, etc.) is the most fundamental example of irony in the scriptures. How could a being of light (son of the morning) transform himself into the arch-representative of darkness? Section 76 reveals the contrast between this benighted personality and the grandeur of the eternal source of light and truth, even the Father and the Son.

The heavens wept over Lucifer, for he was an angel "in authority in the presence of God" (D&C 76:25). He held high office. It was this tragic transformation, this total abdication of godly potential in one of the leading sons of God in the spirit realm that caused the heavens to weep. In the visions of eternity granted unto the prophet Enoch, he also beheld Satan "and he had a great chain in his hand, and it veiled the whole face of the earth with darkness; and he looked up and laughed, and his angels rejoiced" (Moses 7:26; compare also D&C 29:36; Moses 1:19; 4:1–3). The condition of those who followed Satan caused God to weep (Moses 7:28), much to the discomfort of Enoch—until he was told why: "Behold, their sins shall be upon the heads of their fathers;

Satan shall be their father, and misery shall be their doom; and the whole heavens shall weep over them, even all the workmanship of mine hands; wherefore should not the heavens weep, seeing these shall suffer?" (Moses 7:37). It is the inevitable suffering of the wicked brought about by their own choice that causes the heavens to weep—seeing that the divine plan of the atoning sacrifice would otherwise save God's children through the grace and truth of the Almighty and the obedience and righteousness of the faithful. But Lucifer and his followers would not have it so—hence the triumphant campaign of heaven to thwart his designs. The word *Satan* occurs thirty-five times in the Doctrine and Covenants; *devil* twenty-five times; *Perdition* three times; *serpent* and *son of the morning* twice each; and *Lucifer* once.

SCOTT, JACOB

The details of Jacob's birth and death are not known. On the occasion of the fourth conference of the Church, held on the Morley farm in Kirtland in June of 1831, Jacob was ordained a high priest and was called thereafter by revelation to serve a mission (see D&C 52:28). However, he refused to respond and immediately apostatized from the Church and began persecuting the Saints.

SERVANT(S)

Symbolic figures in the parable concerning the vineyard of the Lord. See the entry for "Lord of the Vineyard." Alternately, the term *servant* or *servants* appears pervasively throughout the Doctrine and Covenants in connection with those who serve or minister.

SETH

Seth, son of Adam and Eve (Luke 3:38; Moses 6:1–3, 10–11), is mentioned five times in the text of the Doctrine and Covenants. The following passage indicates the priesthood lineage through Seth, and also gives a profile of his character:

> This order [of the priesthood] was instituted in the days of Adam, and came down by lineage in the following manner:
> From Adam to Seth, who was ordained by Adam at the age of sixty-nine years, and was blessed by him three years previous to his (Adam's) death, and received the promise of God by his father, that his posterity should be the chosen of the Lord, and that they should be preserved unto the end of the earth;
> Because he (Seth) was a perfect man, and his likeness was the express likeness of his father, insomuch that he seemed to be like unto his father in all things, and could be distinguished from him only by his age. (D&C 107:41–43)

Additionally, Seth is mentioned as one of the elect individuals to receive Adam's benedictory blessing: "Three years previous to the death of Adam, he called Seth, Enos, Cainan, Mahalaleel, Jared, Enoch, and Methuselah, . . . into the valley of Adam-ondi-Ahman, and there bestowed upon them his last blessing" (see D&C 107:53). Seth is also mentioned as one of the noble personages viewed by President Joseph F. Smith in his vision of the spirit realm: "Abel, the first martyr, was there, and his brother Seth, one of the mighty ones, who was in the express image of his father, Adam" (D&C 138:40).

Seven Angels

Section 77 of the Doctrine and Covenants provides inspired commentary on various passages written by John the Revelator, including the following reference: "And I saw the seven angels which stood before God; and to them were given seven trumpets" (Rev. 8:2). Latter-day scripture asks:

Q. What are we to understand by the sounding of the trumpets, mentioned in the 8th chapter of Revelation?

A. We are to understand that as God made the world in six days, and on the seventh day he finished his work, and sanctified it, and also formed man out of the dust of the earth, even so, in the beginning of the seventh thousand years will the Lord God sanctify the earth, and complete the salvation of man, and judge all things, and shall redeem all things, except that which he hath not put into his power, when he shall have sealed all things, unto the end of all things; and the sounding of the trumpets of the seven angels are the preparing and finishing of his work, in the beginning of the seventh thousand years—the preparing of the way before the time of his coming. (D&C 77:12)

President Joseph Fielding Smith explains the chronology of this reference:

In this instruction the Lord sets days against thousand years, as days, in speaking of the creation and the continuance of the earth during its mortal existence. At the close of the sixth thousand years and at the opening of the seventh, since the fall, the earth and all that remain upon its face will be changed from the telestial condition of wickedness to the terrestrial condition of peace and order. This is the day when the earth "will be renewed and receive its paradisiacal glory," as declared in the Tenth Article of Faith.

We are now in the great day of restoration of all things, and the renewal of the earth is the bringing of it back to a comparable condition to that which existed before the fall. (CHMR, 1:293)

Shem

Shem, son of Noah (see Gen. 5:32; 6:10; 7:13; 8:16; 9:26; Moses 8:12), is mentioned in the Doctrine and Covenants in connection with President Joseph F. Smith's vision of the work of salvation in the spirit world, among whom were "Noah, who gave warning of the flood; Shem, the great high priest; Abraham, the father of the faithful; Isaac, Jacob, and Moses, the great law-giver of Israel" (D&C 138:41).

Sherman, Lyman

Lyman was born on May 22, 1804, at Monkton, Addison County, Vermont. Through his interest in the Book of Mormon, he became a member of the Church and was ordained a high priest. He was also ordained a seventy on

February 28, 1835, and served for a time as a President of the Seventies. Later that year he sought clarification from the Prophet concerning his duty. The resulting revelation on his behalf (section 108) provided counsel for his future service:

> Verily thus saith the Lord unto you, my servant Lyman: Your sins are forgiven you, because you have obeyed my voice in coming up hither this morning to receive counsel of him whom I have appointed.
>
> Therefore, let your soul be at rest concerning your spiritual standing, and resist no more my voice.
>
> And arise up and be more careful henceforth in observing your vows, which you have made and do make, and you shall be blessed with exceeding great blessings.
>
> Wait patiently until the solemn assembly shall be called of my servants, then you shall be remembered with the first of mine elders, and receive right by ordination with the rest of mine elders whom I have chosen.
>
> Behold, this is the promise of the Father unto you if you continue faithful.
>
> And it shall be fulfilled upon you in that day that you shall have right to preach my gospel wheresoever I shall send you, from henceforth from that time.
>
> Therefore, strengthen your brethren in all your conversation, in all your prayers, in all your exhortations, and in all your doings.
>
> And behold, and lo, I am with you to bless you and deliver you forever. Amen. (D&C 108:1–8; dated December 26, 1835, at Kirtland)

Lyman participated in the dedication of the Kirtland temple in 1836 and was called to be a member of the Kirtland high council. He defended the Church and its leaders with courage. Lyman moved to Missouri in 1838 and became a member of the Far West high council. From Liberty Jail, the Prophet sent a letter dated January 16, 1839, calling Lyman to the apostleship to replace Orson Hyde, but Lyman passed away a few days later, on January 27.

SHERWOOD, HENRY G.

Henry, born on April 20, 1785, at Kingsbury, Washington County, New York, was baptized in August 1832 and ordained an elder that same month. He moved to Kirtland soon thereafter and subsequently engaged in missionary work for the Church. In September 1837 he was appointed to the Kirtland high council. Following periods of persecution in Ohio and Missouri, Henry moved to Illinois where his life was saved from malaria miraculously through a blessing by the Prophet Joseph Smith. Thereafter Henry served with devotion in numerous callings, including as a member of the Nauvoo high council (see D&C 124:132) and the first marshal of Nauvoo. He was also a stockholder in the Nauvoo House project (see D&C 124:81). Following the martyrdom of the Prophet, Henry joined the vanguard camp in 1847 and journeyed west, where he made the initial drawing of the survey plan for Salt Lake City. A dispute with Church leaders in 1855 led to Henry's departure from the Church. He passed away in California on November 24, in 1862 (or, according to some records, in 1867).

SMITH, ALVIN

Alvin was born February 11, 1798 (or 1799), at Tunbridge, Orange County, Vermont, son of Joseph Smith Sr. and Lucy Mack Smith. He had a strong work ethic and was a great help to his family in their years of financial struggle, including arranging to build a home for them across the street from their log cabin in the Palmyra area. He likewise encouraged his younger brother Joseph at the commencement of the latter's work of the Restoration. Alvin became seriously ill in November 1823. The attending physician administered a medication that resulted in unanticipated and lethal side effects, and Alvin died on November 19, 1823. On January 21, 1836, the Prophet Joseph beheld his brother once again, this time as a resident of the celestial kingdom:

> I saw Father Adam and Abraham; and my father and my mother; my brother Alvin, that has long since slept;
>
> And marveled how it was that he had obtained an inheritance in that kingdom, seeing that he had departed this life before the Lord had set his hand to gather Israel the second time, and had not been baptized for the remission of sins.
>
> Thus came the voice of the Lord unto me, saying: All who have died without a knowledge of this gospel, who would have received it if they had been permitted to tarry, shall be heirs of the celestial kingdom of God;
>
> Also all that shall die henceforth without a knowledge of it, who would have received it with all their hearts, shall be heirs of that kingdom;

> For I, the Lord, will judge all men according to their works, according to the desire of their hearts. (D&C 137:5–9)

Of Alvin, the Prophet said:

> He was the oldest and the noblest of my father's family. He was one of the noblest of the sons of men. . . . In him there was no guile. He lived without spot from the time he was a child. From the time of his birth he never knew mirth. He was candid and sober and never would play; and minded his father and mother in toiling all day. He was one of the soberest of men, and when he died the angel of the Lord visited him in his last moments. (HC 5:126)

SMITH, DON CARLOS

Don Carlos Smith, younger brother of Joseph, was born March 25, 1816, at Norwich, Windsor County, Vermont. He was baptized on June 9, 1830, by David Whitmer, and soon thereafter journeyed with his family to Kirtland, Ohio. He was ordained a high priest at age nineteen and became president of the high priests quorum in Kirtland. In 1838 the family moved to Missouri. Don Carlos and his cousin George A. Smith traveled to Tennessee and Kentucky to obtain revenue for buying property. While they were away, Don Carlos's wife and two children suffered unspeakable hardships because of mob violence. When they were reunited again in Illinois, Don Carlos contributed devoted service on behalf of the poor and sick. During his Nauvoo years, he served as editor of the *Times and Seasons* from 1839 to 1840 and also was president of the high priests quorum (see D&C 124:133). Later he was elected to the city council, filled an assignment in the Nauvoo Legion, and served as regent of the University of Nauvoo. He was overtaken by a sudden illness on August 7, 1841, and passed away at the age of twenty-five.

SMITH, EDEN

Eden was born in 1806 in Indiana. After joining the Church, he was called by revelation in January 1832 as a missionary (see D&C 75:36). A second missionary call was received in March of that year (see D&C 80:1–2). In light of Eden's somewhat contentious nature, he was disfellowshipped on July 2, 1833, but he repented and came back into fellowship in the Church. He joined the Saints in Missouri and later moved to Nauvoo, where he served in the Nauvoo Legion. He died in Iowa on December 7, 1851.

SMITH, EMMA (SEE ALSO SMITH, JOSEPH, JR.; SMITH, JOSEPH, III)

Emma was born on July 10, 1804, in Harmony, Susquehanna County, Pennsylvania, daughter of Isaac Hale and Elizabeth Lewis Hale. Her father having withheld consent for her to marry Joseph, the two eloped and were married in January 1827. She assisted her husband as a scribe in the translation of the Book of Mormon. She was baptized on June 28, 1830, by Oliver Cowdery. Emma was instrumental in preparing a selection of hymns for the Church, a commission given to her through the Prophet Joseph in the remarkable revelation (D&C 25) outlining her role in the Restoration:

Emma Smith

A revelation I give unto you [Emma Smith] concerning my will; and if thou art faithful and walk in the paths of virtue before me, I will preserve thy life, and thou shalt receive an inheritance in Zion.

Behold, thy sins are forgiven thee, and thou art an elect lady, whom I have called.

Murmur not because of the things which thou hast not seen, for they are withheld from thee and from the world, which is wisdom in me in a time to come.

And the office of thy calling shall be for a comfort unto my servant, Joseph Smith, Jun., thy husband, in his afflictions, with consoling words, in the spirit of meekness.

And thou shalt go with him at the time of his going, and be unto him for a scribe, while there is no one to be a scribe for him, that I may send my servant, Oliver Cowdery, whithersoever I will.

And thou shalt be ordained [i.e., set apart] under his hand to expound scriptures, and to exhort the church, according as it shall be given thee by my Spirit.

For he shall lay his hands upon thee, and thou shalt receive the Holy Ghost, and thy time shall be given to writing, and to learning much. . . .

And thou needest not fear, for thy husband shall support thee in the church; for unto them is his calling, that all things might be revealed unto them, whatsoever I will, according to their fair.

And verily I say unto thee that thou shalt lay aside the things of this world and seek for the things of a better.

And it shall be given thee, also, to make a selection of sacred hymns, as it shall be given thee, which is pleasing unto me, to be had in my church.

For my soul delighteth in the song of the heart; yea, the song of the righteous is a prayer unto me, and it shall be answered with a blessing upon their heads.

Wherefore, lift up thy heart and rejoice, and cleave unto the covenants which thou hast made.

Continue in the spirit of meekness, and beware of pride. Let thy soul delight in thy husband, and the glory which shall come upon him.

Keep my commandments continually, and a crown of righteousness thou shalt receive. And except thou do this, where I am you cannot come. (D&C 25:2–8, 11–15; dated July 1830)

Emma is also mentioned in section 132 concerning the Lord's law of marriage. When the Relief Society was organized by the Prophet Joseph Smith on March 17, 1842, she was named president of the organization. Joseph and Emma had nine children, of whom only four grew to maturity. Her life was filled with abundant tribulation and adversity, but she remained supportive and loyal to her husband. Following the Martyrdom, she declined to go West with the Saints. Her second marriage was to Major Lewis Bidamon. She passed away on April 30, 1879, at Nauvoo, Illinois, at the age of seventy-four and was buried next to the plot where the Prophet Joseph was buried.

SMITH, GEORGE A.

George was born on June 26, 1817, at Potsdam, St. Lawrence County, New York. After reading the Book of Mormon, he was baptized on September 10, 1832, and moved with his family to Kirtland the following year. At age sixteen he became a member of Zion's Camp and acted as a personal guard for his cousin, the Prophet Joseph Smith. Thereafter he served two missions for the Church and subsequently moved to Missouri, where persecution and mob abuse were the common lot of the Saints. By January 19, 1841, he was a member of the Quorum of the Twelve (see D&C 124:129), having filled one of the vacancies created by the departure of apostates. He served a successful mission in England as one of the Twelve and then returned to Nauvoo to take up married life. He helped build the Nauvoo Temple before joining Brigham Young and the Saints on the westward trek in 1847. As part of that exodus, George was placed in charge of organizing a company (see D&C 136:14). In Utah he helped with the settlement of the Saints in the

George A. Smith

southern part of the area—the community of St. George was named in his honor. His activities also included service as Church historian and recorder. From 1868 until his death on September 1, 1875, he served as First Counselor in the First Presidency of the Church, succeeding Heber C. Kimball.

SMITH, HYRUM

Hyrum, older brother of Joseph, was born on February 9, 1800, at Tunbridge, Orange County, Vermont. He was baptized by Joseph in June 1829, and on April 6, 1830, became one of the six original members of the Church. Following Joseph's counsel, he moved to Kirtland, Ohio, where he became an elder and later a high priest. Beginning in 1831, he served an extended mission in the area extending between Ohio and Missouri. In the period 1836–37 he was given higher priesthood duties, including serving on the high council and as Second Counselor in the First Presidency (see

D&C 112:17). From November 1838 until April 1839 he was imprisoned, along with Joseph and others, in the squalor of Liberty Jail. He later settled in Nauvoo and was called as Patriarch to the Church by revelation on January 19, 1841 (see D&C 124:91) and sustained to that office on January 24, 1841. Joseph revered his brother. The two gave their lives in sustaining the cause of Zion as martyrs on June 27, 1844, at Carthage, Hancock County, Illinois. In the words of John Taylor: "They lived for glory; they died for glory; and glory is their eternal reward. From age to age shall their names go down to posterity as gems for the sanctified" (D&C 135:6).

Hyrum is named twenty-four times in the text of the Doctrine and Covenants and is also mentioned in the introductory headings of sections 11, 23, 94, 111, 124, 135. Section 11, which was received through the Prophet Joseph in May 1829 on behalf of Hyrum, contains counsel for all readers of the Doctrine and Covenants:

> Behold, I say unto you, keep my commandments, and seek to bring forth and establish the cause of Zion.
>
> Seek not for riches but for wisdom; and, behold, the mysteries of God shall be unfolded unto you, and then shall you be made rich. Behold, he that hath eternal life is rich.
>
> Verily, verily, I say unto you, even as you desire of me so it shall be done unto you; and, if you desire, you shall be the means of doing much good in this generation.
>
> Say nothing but repentance unto this generation. Keep my commandments, and assist to bring forth my work, according to my commandments, and you shall be blessed. . . .

Hyrum Smith, with Joseph

I say unto thee, put your trust in that Spirit which leadeth to do good—yea, to do justly, to walk humbly, to judge righteously; and this is my Spirit.

Verily, . . . I will impart unto you of my Spirit, which shall enlighten your mind, which shall fill your soul with joy;

And then shall ye know . . . whatsoever you desire of me, which are pertaining unto things of righteousness, in faith believing in me that you shall receive.

Behold, . . . you need not suppose that you are called to preach until you are called.

Wait a little longer, until you shall have my word, my rock, my church, and my gospel, that you may know of a surety my doctrine. . . .

Keep my commandments; hold your peace; appeal unto my Spirit;

Yea, cleave unto me with all your heart, that you may assist in bringing to light . . . the translation of my work;

Behold, this is your work, to keep my commandments, yea, with all your might, mind and strength.

Seek not to declare my word, but first seek to obtain my word, and then shall your tongue be loosed; then, if you desire, you shall have my Spirit and my word, yea, the power of God unto the convincing of men.

But now hold your peace; study my word which hath gone forth among the children of men, and also study my word which shall come forth among the children of men, . . . yea, until you have obtained all which I shall grant unto the children of men in this generation, and then shall all things be added thereto.

Behold thou art Hyrum, my son; seek the kingdom of God, and all things shall be added according to that which is just.

Build upon my rock, which is my gospel;

Deny not the spirit of revelation, nor the spirit of prophecy, for wo unto him that denieth these things;

Therefore, treasure up in your heart until the time which is in my wisdom that you shall go forth.

Behold, I speak unto all who have good desires, and have thrust in their sickle to reap.

Behold, I am Jesus Christ, the Son of God. I am the life and the light of the world.

I am the same who came unto mine own and mine own received me not;

But verily, verily, I say unto you, that as many as receive me, to them will I give power to become the sons of God, even to them that believe on my name. Amen. (D&C 11:6–9, 12–16, 18–30)

On January 19, 1841, William Law was named by revelation (see D&C 124:91–96; compare also v. 124) as a counselor to Joseph Smith in the First Presidency, replacing Hyrum, who was called on that occasion as Patriarch to the Church and also appointed to share the office of presidency with his brother Joseph:

And again, verily I say unto you, let my servant William be appointed, ordained, and anointed, as counselor unto my servant Joseph, in the room of my servant Hyrum, that my servant Hyrum may take the office of Priesthood and Patriarch, which was appointed unto him by his father, by blessing and also by right;

That from henceforth he shall hold the keys of the patriarchal blessings upon the heads of all my people . . .

And from this time forth I appoint unto him that he may be a prophet, and a seer, and a revelator unto my church, as well as my servant Joseph. (D&C 124:91–92, 94)

On October 3, 1918, President Joseph F. Smith, son of the martyred Hyrum, received the revelation concerning the glorious ongoing work of salvation in the spirit realm. How inspiring it must have been to President Smith to see in vision, among the noble and elect of the Restoration, "the Prophet Joseph Smith, and [his] father, Hyrum Smith, . . . and other choice spirits who were reserved to come forth in the fulness of times to take part in laying the foundations of the great Latter-day work" (D&C 138:53).

SMITH, JOHN

John, brother of Joseph Smith Sr., was born on July 16, 1781, at Derryfield, Rockingham County, New Hampshire. After receiving a copy of the Book of Mormon from his brother, he joined the restored Church on January 9, 1832. He moved to Kirtland in May 1833 where he was called to the Kirtland high

John Smith

council on February 17, 1834 (see D&C 102:3, 34). He suffered persecution by mobs in Kirtland and later at Adam-ondi-Ahman, Missouri, while serving as president of the local stake. He served faithfully in many additional capacities in the Church, including that of fifth Patriarch to the Church following his move to the West with the Saints. He died on May 23, 1854.

SMITH, JOSEPH, JR.

Joseph was born on December 23, 1805, at Sharon, Windsor County, Vermont. He was the son of Joseph Smith Sr. and Lucy Mack Smith. A perceptive and inquisitive lad with a desire for spiritual enlightenment, Joseph refused to become part of the competing religious factions of his day and invested his efforts instead in the holy scriptures. The turning point was his obedience to the counsel of the Apostle James: "If any of you lack wisdom, let him ask of God" (James 1:5). Joseph did ask—and the response of heaven was the extraordinary sequence of visions, revelations, and visitations constituting the Restoration of the gospel of Jesus Christ in the dispensation of the fulness of times (see Joseph Smith—History). The Book of Mormon, foretold by Isaiah (Isa. 29:14), restored the fulness of the gospel (see D&C 20:9; 42:12) in the form of another witness for Jesus Christ. The pages of the Doctrine and Covenants brought forth the essence of covenant wisdom and priesthood power, allowing the Church and Kingdom of God to arise "out of obscurity and out of darkness, the only true and living church upon the face of the whole earth, with which I, the Lord, am well pleased" (D&C 1:30). It was the work of Joseph Smith that made possible the formal organization of the Church on April 6, 1830. It was his service that ensured the advancement

Joseph Smith Jr.

of the Church as the gateway to salvation and exaltation and the means to prepare the world for the Second Coming of the Savior.

This glorious process was inaugurated in the year 1820 when the First Vision was experienced by the fourteen-year-old Joseph, who first uttered prayer in a shady grove in New York State and subsequently changed the history of the world. From the foundations of the world, this moment had been planned and anticipated as an essential step in Heavenly Father's design: "That in the dispensation of the fulness of times he might gather together in one all things in Christ, both which are in heaven, and which are on earth; *even* in him" (Eph. 1:10). The First Vision ended generations of spiritual darkness fostered by the great apostasy.

The sequence of events inaugurated by the First Vision resulted in the complete restoration of the gospel of redemption and the reestablishment of the living Church and Kingdom of God through the Prophet Joseph Smith. The birth of the restored Church was a process of supreme joy, tempered however by intense sacrifice and the need to overcome daunting challenges. Following that inaugural moment, the process of restoring the gospel unfolded systematically over the ensuing years under divine guidance until the Prophet's mission was complete and he had sealed his work and his testimony through martyrdom on June 27, 1844. In the pages of the Doctrine and Covenants the steps of the Restoration are recounted as administered by the Prophet Joseph Smith under the direct guidance of the Lord Jesus Christ.

Joseph Smith was the chosen mouthpiece of the Lord in the dispensation of the fulness of times through which the oracles of heaven were again unfolded to a world hungry and thirsty for the mysteries (i.e., principles, doctrines, ordinances) of salvation and exaltation. His influence and presence are pervasive throughout the Doctrine and Covenants. His name is invoked in the text 138 times, as well as in the current introductory headings to all of the sections except sections 109 (which refers to the "Prophet's written statement"), 134 (a declaration of belief concerning governments and laws drafted by Oliver Cowdery), and 138 (the vision of President Joseph F. Smith concerning the spirit realm). The word most often used in the Doctrine and Covenants in conjunction with the name of the Prophet Joseph Smith is *revelation*. Most of the sectional headings that include his name begin with the phrase, "Revelation given through Joseph Smith the Prophet." Exceptions are the headings to the following:

- Section 102: "Minutes of the organization of the first high council of the Church, at Kirtland, Ohio, February 17, 1834"—to which verses 30–32 "were added by the Prophet Joseph Smith in 1835 when he prepared this section for publication."

- Section 109: "Prayer offered at the dedication of the temple at Kirtland"; it goes on to mention that the words were given by revelation.

- Section 110: "Visions manifested to Joseph Smith the Prophet"; section 137: "A vision given to Joseph Smith the Prophet."

- Section 113: "Answers to certain questions on the writings of Isaiah, given by Joseph Smith the Prophet."

- Sections 121–23: "Prayer and prophecies written by Joseph Smith the Prophet," "The word of the Lord to Joseph Smith the Prophet," and "Duties of the saints in relation to their persecutors, as set forth by Joseph Smith the Prophet," respectively.

- Sections 127 and 128: "An epistle from Joseph Smith the Prophet."

- Sections 129–31: "Instruction(s) given by Joseph Smith the Prophet."

- Section 134: "A declaration of belief regarding governments and laws in general, adopted by unanimous vote at a general conference of the Church at Kirtland, Ohio, August 17, 1835."

Whether the words given through the Prophet Joseph Smith are designated as revelations, visions, instructions, epistles, answers, prophecies, or other terms, the essence of his pronouncements accords fully with the sacred

Joseph Smith Jr.

office he held, characterized as "a presiding elder over all [the Lord's] church, to be a translator, a revelator, a seer, and prophet" (D&C 124:125). In all of this, Joseph Smith was not the author of the Doctrine and Covenants but the conveyor of the truths of the Almighty. The Lord is thus the Author of the Doctrine and Covenants, with Joseph Smith the curator of the revealed word of heaven and the spokesperson for Jesus Christ in the dispensation of the fulness of times. After the Prophet Joseph had sealed his witness with his life on June 27, 1844, the mantle of authority shifted by divine design to Brigham Young, who penned the words to section 136 under inspiration. John Taylor, as well, who wrote the statement concerning the Martyrdom now included as section 135, would serve as president of the Church following the tenure of Brigham Young. And President Joseph F. Smith, whose vision of the work of salvation in the spirit realm is included as section 138 in the Doctrine and Covenants, provides a further illustration of the continuity and perpetuity of the office of prophet, seer, and revelator, with the commission to bring forth the words of the Savior "even as they are in mine own bosom, to the salvation of mine own elect" (D&C 35:20).

In the pages of the Doctrine and Covenants one finds the sequence of steps relating to the commission given to the Prophet Joseph and the manner in which his life unfolded as an example of repentance and triumph, contrition and ascendancy.

From the Lord's preface to the Doctrine and Covenants—revealed on November 1,

140

1831, and now placed as section 1—it is clear that the divine action to call Joseph Smith to the ministry occurred in the context of preparing the inhabitants of the world through the gospel of eternal truth and thus protecting them from chaos and disaster associated with the judgments of God leading up the Second Coming:

> Wherefore, I the Lord, knowing the calamity which should come upon the inhabitants of the earth, called upon my servant Joseph Smith, Jun., and spake unto him from heaven, and gave him commandments;
>
> And also gave commandments to others, that they should proclaim these things unto the world; and all this that it might be fulfilled, which was written by the prophets—
>
> The weak things of the world shall come forth and break down the mighty and strong ones, that man should not counsel his fellow man, neither trust in the arm of flesh—
>
> But that every man might speak in the name of God the Lord, even the Savior of the world. (D&C 1:17–20)

From the beginning of his prophetic calling, Joseph Smith was constrained to learn obedience. When he allowed the first 116 pages of the translation of the Book of Mormon to disappear into the hands of a careless and disobedient Martin Harris, the Lord was firm, yet compassionate in His response:

> Behold, thou art Joseph, and thou wast chosen to do the work of the Lord, but because of transgression, if thou art not aware thou wilt fall.

> But remember, God is merciful; therefore, repent of that which thou hast done which is contrary to the commandment which I gave you . . . ;
>
> Except thou do this, thou shalt be delivered up and become as other men, and have no more gift. (D&C 3:9–11; compare also D&C 10)

The divine commission stood, and the Lord later declared that "this generation shall have my word through you" (D&C 5:10). Hence Joseph was commanded to rise to the stature of his foreordained premortal calling as the Prophet of the Restoration (see *TPJS*, 365). Oliver Cowdery was reminded by the Lord of Joseph's sacred calling and promise: "And now, marvel not that I have called him unto mine own purpose, which purpose is known in me; wherefore, if he shall be diligent in keeping my commandments he shall be blessed unto eternal life; and his name is Joseph" (D&C 18:8). Having accomplished many preparatory assignments, Joseph presided over the formal organization of the Church on April 6, 1830, according to the will and commandments of God, "which commandments were given to Joseph Smith, Jun., who was called of God, and ordained an apostle of Jesus Christ, to be the first elder of this church" (D&C 20:2).

In September 1830, Oliver Cowdery, not without his tendencies toward pride and ambition, was directed by the Lord not to "write by way of commandment, but by wisdom" (D&C 28:5), because "no one shall be appointed to receive commandments and revelations in this church excepting my servant Joseph Smith, Jun., for he receiveth them even as Moses. And thou shalt be obedient unto the things which I shall give unto him, even as Aaron, to declare faithfully the commandments and the revelations, with power and authority unto the church" (D&C 28:2–3). Thus Oliver was reminded not to "command him who is at thy head, and at the head of the church; For I have given him the keys of the mysteries, and the revelations which are sealed, until I shall appoint unto them another in his stead" (D&C 28:6–7). With this wording, the Lord made clear at this early stage of the Restoration that Joseph still held a probationary commission, and another could be appointed in his place if necessary. This was confirmed in December 1830 to Sidney Rigdon: "And I have sent forth the fulness of my gospel by the hand of my servant Joseph; and in weakness have I blessed him; And I have given unto him the keys of the mystery of those things which have been sealed, . . . if he abide in me, and if not, another will I plant in his stead" (D&C 35:17–18). In February 1831, the Lord confirmed the exclusive commission of Joseph Smith as revelator (though Joseph is not mentioned by name until later in this section):

> For behold, verily, verily, I say unto you, that ye have received a commandment for a law unto my church, through him whom I have appointed unto you to receive commandments and revelations from my hand.
>
> And this ye shall know assuredly—that there is none other appointed unto you to receive commandments and revelations until he be taken, if he abide in me.
>
> For verily I say unto you, that he that is ordained of me shall come in at the gate and be ordained as I have told you before, to teach those revelations which you have received and

shall receive through him whom I have appointed. (D&C 43:2–3, 7)

Later that same year, the Lord's word conveyed the sense that Joseph's commission was assured throughout the remainder of his days on earth, based on his obedience: "And the keys of the mysteries of the kingdom shall not be taken from my servant Joseph Smith, Jun., through the means I have appointed, while he liveth, inasmuch as he obeyeth mine ordinances" (D&C 64:5).

Nevertheless, Joseph was not perfect. When on one occasion his associates complained against him, without cause, the Lord confirmed that he had "sinned; but verily I say unto you, I, the Lord, forgive sins unto those who confess their sins before me and ask forgiveness, who have not sinned unto death. . . . I, the Lord, will forgive whom I will forgive, but of you it is required to forgive all men" (D&C 64:7, 10). When some complained of the language in Joseph's rendition of the revelations, the Lord declared: "Your eyes have been upon my servant Joseph Smith, Jun., and his language you have known, and his imperfections you have known; and you have sought in your hearts knowledge that you might express beyond his language; this you also know" (D&C 67:5). When no one was capable of measuring up to the Lord's challenge to write a revelation surpassing in quality and substance even the least of the revelations received through the Prophet Joseph, the naysayers were humbled into submission. On March 8, 1833, the Lord reformulated his covenant commission and promise to the Prophet Joseph in a significant way:

> Thus saith the Lord, verily, verily I say unto you my son, thy sins are

forgiven thee, according to thy petition, for thy prayers and the prayers of thy brethren have come up into my ears.

Therefore, thou art blessed from henceforth that bear the keys of the kingdom given unto you; which kingdom is coming forth for the last time.

Verily I say unto you, the keys of this kingdom shall never be taken from you, while thou art in the world, neither in the world to come;

Nevertheless, through you shall the oracles be given to another, yea, even unto the church. (D&C 90:1–4)

Thus Joseph's ministry was not confined to his mortal years but was extended into the world to come. Still, there was occasion in the future where he would stand rebuked: "You have not kept the commandments, and must needs stand rebuked before the Lord; Your family must needs repent and forsake some things, and give more earnest heed unto your sayings, or be removed out of their place" (D&C 93:47–48). Nevertheless, the commission of the Prophet Joseph went forward, so that, as the Lord said, he could "preside in the midst of my people, and organize my kingdom upon the consecrated land, and establish the children of Zion upon the laws and commandments which have been and which shall be given unto you" (D&C 103:35). In his inspired dedicatory prayer for the Kirtland Temple, the Prophet supplicated the Lord on behalf of himself and his family:

O Lord, remember thy servant, Joseph Smith, Jun., and all his afflictions and persecutions—how he has covenanted with Jehovah, and vowed

Joseph Smith Jr.

to thee, O Mighty God of Jacob—and the commandments which thou hast given unto him, and that he hath sincerely striven to do thy will. Have mercy, O Lord, upon his wife and children, that they may be exalted in thy presence, and preserved by thy fostering hand. (D&C 109:68–69; dated March 27, 1836)

The scope of the Prophet Joseph Smith's ministry is truly remarkable. It was by authority of the Prophet Joseph Smith that stakes were to be appointed, because "the keys of [the Lord's] kingdom and ministry" were given to him (D&C 115:18–19; compare D&C 125:2). It was through the Prophet Joseph that the principles and operation of the priesthood were manifested (see D&C 20, 84, 107, 121, 122). It was through Joseph Smith that the Abrahamic covenant was to be extended as a blessing to mankind (D&C 124:57–58). Because of Joseph Smith, the office of "a prophet, and a seer, and a revelator unto [the Lord's] church" (D&C 124:94; compare D&C 124:125) could be extended to others when directed by the Lord—as it was to Hyrum Smith (see D&C 124:94–96). It was in Joseph Smith that the sealing blessings for celestial marriage were vested and through him that they were administered (see D&C 132:7), thus assuring the perpetuity and expansion of the family through the eternities.

Indeed, the commission given by the Lord to Joseph Smith was to "restore all things" (D&C 132:40): "For I am the Lord thy God, and ye shall obey my voice; and I give unto my servant Joseph that he shall be made ruler over many things; for he hath been faithful over a few things, and from henceforth I will strengthen him" (D&C 132:53). When Joseph made the decision to consign himself into the hands of officials at Carthage, he said: "I am going like a lamb to the slaughter; but I am calm as a summer's morning; I have a conscience void of offense towards God, and towards all men. I SHALL DIE INNOCENT, AND IT SHALL YET BE SAID OF ME—HE WAS MURDERED IN COLD BLOOD" (D&C 135:4). And so it was. The Prophet Joseph Smith honored his divine commission as the agent of the Restoration of the gospel of Jesus Christ. John Taylor, an eyewitness to the Martyrdom, described it with solemnity and historical accuracy:

Joseph Smith, the Prophet and Seer of the Lord, has done more, save Jesus only, for the salvation of men in this world, than any other man that ever lived in it. In the short space of twenty years, he has brought forth the Book of Mormon, which he translated by the gift and power of God, and has been the means of publishing it on two continents; has sent the fulness of the everlasting gospel, which it contained, to the four quarters of the earth; has brought forth the revelations and commandments which compose this book of Doctrine and Covenants, and many other wise documents and instructions for the benefit of the children of men; gathered many thousands of the Latter-day Saints, founded a great city, and left a fame and name that cannot be slain. He lived great, and he died great in the eyes of God and his people; and like most of the Lord's anointed in ancient times, has sealed his mission and his works with his own blood; and so has his brother Hyrum. In life they were not divided, and in death they were not separated! (D&C 135:3)

When President Joseph F. Smith had his remarkable vision of the ongoing work of salvation in the spirit realm, he saw, through spiritual eyes, "the Prophet Joseph Smith, and my father, Hyrum Smith, Brigham Young, John Taylor, Wilford Woodruff, and other choice spirits who were reserved to come forth in the fulness of times to take part in laying the foundations of the great Latter-day work, . . . I observed that they were also among the noble and great ones who were chosen in the beginning to be rulers in the Church of God" (D&C 138:53–55). As one privileged to observe the Father and the Son in Their celestial glory, the Prophet Joseph Smith (along with his companion on that occasion, Sidney Rigdon) could utter this splendid testimony of them:

> And now, after the many testimonies which have been given of him, this is the testimony, last of all, which we give of him: That he lives!
>
> For we saw him, even on the right hand of God; and we heard the voice bearing record that he is the Only Begotten of the Father—
>
> That by him, and through him, and of him, the worlds are and were created, and the inhabitants thereof are begotten sons and daughters unto God. (D&C 76:22–24)

SMITH, JOSEPH, III

Joseph, the eldest son of the Prophet Joseph Smith, is alluded to in Doctrine and Covenants section 122, verse 6:

> If thou art accused with all manner of false accusations; if thine enemies fall upon thee; if they tear thee from the society of thy father and mother and brethren and sisters; and if with a drawn sword thine enemies tear thee from the bosom of thy wife, and of thine offspring, and thine elder son, although but six years of age, shall cling to thy garments, and shall say, My father, my father, why can't you stay with us? O, my father, what are the men going to do with you? and if then he shall be thrust from thee by

Joseph Smith III

the sword, and thou be dragged to prison . . .

> . . . All these things shall give thee experience and shall be for thy good. (D&C 122:6–7)

Lyman Wight gives background about this event in the Prophet's life:

> About the hour the prisoners were to have been shot on the public square in Far West, they were exhibited in a wagon in the town, all of them having families there, but myself; . . . The aged father and mother of Joseph Smith were not permitted to see his face, but to reach their hands through the curtains of the wagon, . . . When passing his own house, he was taken out of the wagon and permitted to go into the house, but not without a strong guard, and not permitted to speak with his family but in the presence of his guard and his eldest son,

Joseph, about six or eight years old, hanging to the tail of his coat, crying father, is the mob going to kill you? The guard said to him, 'you d—d little brat, go back, you will see your father no more.'" (Cited in *RPJS*, 240; compare the account by the Prophet Joseph Smith in *HC* 3:193.)

SMITH, JOSEPH, SR.

Joseph Smith Sr. was born on July 12, 1771, in Essex County, Massachusetts. He pursued farming and teaching as a profession, moving with his family from location to location in Vermont and New Hampshire, only to find that prosperity was elusive. In 1816 the family moved to Palmyra, New York. Father Smith had faith in the reports of his son Joseph concerning the events of the Restoration that commenced there and was ever supportive of the young prophet. Joseph Sr. was one of the eight witnesses of the Book of Mormon. He was baptized on April 6, 1830, the day the Church was organized. On December 18, 1833, he was ordained the first Patriarch of the Church in the new dispensation. He is also mentioned as a member of the first high council in the Church, organized in Kirtland on February 17, 1834 (see D&C 102:3, 34). He later served an extended mission in the eastern states. Suffering from ill health in his final years in Nauvoo, he died on September 14, 1840, and inherited a place in the eternal realm as one "who sitteth with Abraham at his right hand, and blessed and holy is he, for he is mine" (D&C 124:19). The Prophet Joseph Smith beheld his father and mother in his vision of the celestial realm (see D&C 137:5). Perhaps the most memorable record left in honor of Joseph Smith Sr. is the fourth section of the Doctrine and Covenants, given through the Prophet Joseph Smith to his father in February 1829:

> Now behold, a marvelous work is about to come forth among the children of men.
>
> Therefore, O ye that embark in the service of God, see that ye serve him with all your heart, might, mind and strength, that ye may stand blameless before God at the last day.
>
> Therefore, if ye have desires to serve God ye are called to the work;
>
> For behold the field is white already to harvest; and lo, he that thrusteth in his sickle with his might, the same layeth up in store that he perisheth not, but bringeth salvation to his soul;
>
> And faith, hope, charity and love, with an eye single to the glory of God, qualify him for the work.

Joseph Smith Sr.

Remember faith, virtue, knowledge, temperance, patience, brotherly kindness, godliness, charity, humility, diligence.

Ask, and ye shall receive; knock, and it shall be opened unto you. Amen. (D&C 4:1–7; compare 2 Pet. 1:4–8)

SMITH, JOSEPH F.

Joseph was born on November 13, 1838, at Far West, Caldwell County, Missouri, the son of Hyrum Smith and Mary Fielding Smith. His father was martyred along with the Prophet Joseph, on June 27, 1844. His mother brought young Joseph to the Salt Lake Valley during the westward exodus of the Saints. He served a mission to the Hawaiian Islands when only a teenager. Following several other missionary excursions, he was ordained at age twenty-seven as an apostle in the Quorum of the Twelve and served as a counselor to President

Joseph F. Smith

Brigham Young and later as a counselor to John Taylor, Wilford Woodruff, and Lorenzo Snow. Joseph F. Smith was active in civil affairs for many years and served as the President of the Church from 1901 until his death in 1918. On October 3, 1918, he was privileged to behold the extraordinary vision of the Savior's mission to the spirit world and the work of salvation inaugurated there (see D&C 138). Joseph F. Smith passed away on November 19, 1918. His discourses on the doctrine of Christ and the principles of salvation and exaltation are among the most eloquent and inspiring of the teachings of the modern prophets.

SMITH, LUCY MACK

Lucy was born on July 8, 1776, in New Hampshire. She married Joseph Smith Sr. on January 24, 1796. Thereafter they embarked on the historical and spiritual journey that placed them in the center of the Restoration of the gospel. Both Lucy and her husband were unshakably supportive of their prophet son. On Wednesday, October 8, 1845, Lucy Mack Smith, revered and aging mother of the Prophet Joseph, rose and spoke before some 5,000 Saints assembled for the last conference of the Church in Nauvoo—and the first in the nearly completed temple—held October 6–8 under the direction of Brigham Young (*HC* 7:456–77). She exhorted all to protect their children from idleness by giving them work to do and books to read. She counseled all "to be full of love, goodness and kindness, and never to do in secret, what they would not do in the presence of millions" (*HC* 7:470–71). In his vision of the celestial realm on January 21, 1836, in the Kirtland Temple, the Prophet Joseph Smith was permitted to view both of his parents (not mentioned by name, though still

Lucy Mack Smith

alive), together with his deceased brother Alvin (see D&C 137:5). Lucy passed away on May 5, 1855.

SMITH, SAMUEL H.

Samuel was born on March 13, 1808, at Tunbridge, Orange County, Vermont, son of Joseph Smith Sr. and Lucy Mack. He was convinced of the divine mission of his older brother Joseph and was baptized by Oliver Cowdery on May 25, 1829, the third person to be baptized in the new dispensation. He was one of the eight witnesses of the Book of Mormon and one of the six original members of the Church upon its organization. The Lord had the following counsel for Samuel in April 1830: "Behold, I speak a few words unto you, Samuel; for thou also art under no condemnation, and thy calling is to exhortation, and to strengthen the church; and thou art not as yet called to preach before the world" (D&C 23:4).

Considered the first missionary of the Church, he performed labors that resulted in the conversion of Heber C. Kimball and Brigham Young. Brigham Young was baptized on Saturday, April 14, 1832, after two years of intensive study and prayer centered on the Book of Mormon, a copy of which his brother Phineas had given him. Phineas had purchased the copy from Samuel in April 1830 during his early missionary labors. Samuel also provided a copy to Reverend John P. Greene, husband of Phineas's sister, Rhoda. Both were subsequently converted. Brigham Young had given his copy of the Book of Mormon to his sister, Fanny Young Murray, the mother-in-law of Heber C. Kimball, who, along with his family, also became converted because of it. These families were thus brought into the Church through the Book of Mormon and the devoted missionary labors of twenty-two-year-old Samuel Harrison Smith. Young Samuel had returned home somewhat discouraged from this early mission to upstate New York—unaware at the time that his labors would eventually yield such extraordinary fruit (see *CHFT*, 74–75).

Samuel was tireless in contributing to the building up of the Kingdom in callings that ranged from being a member of the high council in Kirtland (see D&C 102:3, 34) to serving as a counselor in Nauvoo to Vinson Knight, Presiding Bishop of the Church (see D&C 124:141), and later to serving as bishop of the Nauvoo Ward. He was foiled by mobs in his attempt to come to the rescue of Joseph and Hyrum in Carthage, but he later accompanied the bodies back to Nauvoo. He died on July 30, 1844, a little over a month after his brothers.

SMITH, SYLVESTER

Sylvester was born in 1805. He was ordained a high priest on October 25, 1831, by Oliver Cowdery and was called by revelation in January 1832 to serve as a missionary (see D&C 75:34). As a participant in Zion's Camp he was distinguished by his quarrelsome nature, evoking the reproach of the Prophet Joseph Smith. Upon his return to Kirtland, Sylvester vilified the Prophet with false accusations but repented when a court verdict exonerated Joseph Smith. Sylvester later served on the Kirtland high council (see D&C 102:3, 34) and was for a time a president of the Seventy. By 1838 he had withdrawn his affiliation with the Church.

SMITH, WILLIAM

William was born on March 13, 1811, at Royalton, Windsor County, Vermont. He was baptized by David Whitmer on June 9, 1830. Following his service as a missionary, he was ordained an elder and then, in February 1835, he became a member of the original Quorum of Twelve Apostles (see *HC* 2:187; D&C 124:129; "Testimony of the Twelve Apostles to the Truth of the Book of Doctrine and Covenants"). As a person given to outbursts of anger, even against his brother the Prophet Joseph, William demonstrated that his faith in the gospel was unstable. He did not heed warnings to correct his ways and even declined to serve a mission with the Twelve in England. Though the Prophet Joseph attempted with patience and love to redirect William's behavior, the latter's animosity toward his brother was persistent, even up to the time of the martyrdom in 1844. Thereafter, William supported the Twelve and was, by lineage, ordained Patriarch to the Church on May 24, 1845—a calling that he felt entitled him to lead the Church. Because of his attitude, his calling as an apostle was revoked on October 6, 1845 (see *HC* 7:458). He was excommunicated on October 12 of that year for using Church funds for his own private purposes. Embittered, William attempted, unsuccessfully, to form his own church. Later he joined the Reorganized Church of Jesus Christ of Latter Day Saints. On November 13, 1893, he died at Osterdock, Iowa.

William Smith

SNIDER, JOHN

John was born on February 11, 1800, in Pleasant Valley, New Brunswick. Having heard the preaching of John Taylor and Parley P. Pratt, he joined the Church in June 1836. The following year he served his first mission to the British Isles and by 1838 was residing in Far West, Missouri. Persecution forced him to relocate to Illinois. By 1841 he was active on the personal staff of the Prophet Joseph Smith

John Snider (at the left), with his wife, Silvia, and family

and in the Nauvoo Legion. A mason by training, he was called by revelation on January 19, 1841, to assist with the construction of the Nauvoo House (see D&C 124:22–24, 62, 70). John was also sent again to England, this time to help raise funds for the construction of the Nauvoo House and the Nauvoo Temple. He later served as one of the bodyguards accompanying the body of the martyred Prophet to Nauvoo. He and his family ultimately settled in the Salt Lake Valley where John earned a living by constructing homes. He died on December 18, 1875.

SNOW, ERASTUS

Erastus was born on November 9, 1818, at St. Johnsbury, Caledonia County, Vermont. He was baptized in 1833 and ordained a teacher.

In 1835 he moved to Kirtland and was ordained a member of the Second Quorum of Seventy. An avid missionary, he served several times as a messenger of the restored gospel. After a period of persecution in Missouri, Erastus moved with his family in April 1839 to Quincy, Illinois, and then later to Nauvoo. With faithfulness, he continued his missionary travels. Following the exodus from Nauvoo, Erastus participated in the vanguard company traveling to the Salt Lake Valley (see D&C 136:12) and was one of the first to view the destination site. After months of helping other Saints travel to the West, Erastus was able to bring his own family to the Salt Lake Valley on September 20, 1846. He was ordained an apostle on February 12, 1849, and served tirelessly in missionary work, leadership, and community service. He passed away on May 27, 1888.

150

Erastus Snow

SNOW, LORENZO

Lorenzo Snow, fifth President of the Church, was born on April 3, 1814, in Mantua, Portage County, Ohio. His interest in the Church was stimulated through the Book of Mormon and his contacts with the Prophet Joseph Smith at nearby Hiram, Ohio, in 1831. He was baptized on June 19, 1836. Setting aside his academic studies at Oberlin College, Lorenzo devoted his time and energy to missionary work, including time in England. After the Nauvoo period, he brought his family westward in 1848 as part of the pioneer exodus. On February 12, 1849, he was ordained an apostle in the Quorum of the Twelve. His life was one of exemplary service in ecclesiastical and civic leadership from that point on. On September 13, 1898, he was sustained as the fifth President of the Church. He is remembered particularly for his inspired program to renew the Saints' commitment to

the law of tithing. Lorenzo Snow is not named in the sections of the Doctrine and Covenants but is mentioned in connection with Official Declaration—1 as the General Authority who, on October 6, 1890, presented the motion for acceptance of the Manifesto issued by Wilford Woodruff authorizing the cessation of the practice of plural marriage in the Church in compliance with the laws of the land.

SOLOMON

Solomon, the son of David and Bathsheba (see 2 Sam. 5:14; 12:24; 1 Chr. 3:5; 14:4; Matt. 1:6), is mentioned twice in the text of the Doctrine and Covenants, both times in connection with the practice of plural marriage (see D&C 132:1–2, 38). The governing principle involved is stated by the Lord: "David also received many wives and concubines, and also

Lorenzo Snow

Solomon

Solomon and Moses my servants, as also many others of my servants, from the beginning of creation until this time; and in nothing did they sin save in those things which they received not of me" (D&C 132:38).

SON AHMAN

The Savior refers to Himself as Son Ahman in the following two passages: "Wherefore, do the things which I have commanded you, saith your Redeemer, even the Son Ahman, who prepareth all things before he taketh you" (D&C 78:20). "And let the higher part of the inner court [of the house of the Lord] be dedicated unto me for the school of mine apostles, saith Son Ahman; or, in other words, Alphus; or, in other words, Omegus; even Jesus Christ your Lord. Amen" (D&C 95:17). Concerning the name "Ahman," Elder Bruce R. McConkie observes that "since *Ahman* is the name of God the Father in the pure language spoken by

Adam, *Son Ahman* is the name of his Only Begotten Son" (*MD*, 740).

SONS OF AARON

The precise expression "sons of Aaron" is used twice in the text of the Doctrine and Covenants. The first instance concerns those who are to serve as bishops:

> Wherefore they shall be high priests who are worthy, and they shall be appointed by the First Presidency of the Melchizedek Priesthood, except they be literal descendants of Aaron.
>
> And if they be literal descendants of Aaron they have a legal right to the bishopric, if they are the firstborn among the sons of Aaron. (D&C 68:15–16)

The second instance concerns the worthiness of priesthood holders in serving in the house of the Lord and honoring the oath and covenant of the priesthood:

> Therefore, as I said concerning the sons of Moses—for the sons of Moses and also the sons of Aaron shall offer an acceptable offering and sacrifice in the house of the Lord, . . .
>
> And the sons of Moses and of Aaron shall be filled with the glory of the Lord, . . .
>
> For whoso is faithful unto the obtaining these two priesthoods of which I have spoken, and the magnifying their calling, are sanctified by the Spirit unto the renewing of their bodies.
>
> They become the sons of Moses and of Aaron and the seed of Abra-

ham, and the church and kingdom, and the elect of God. (D&C 84:31–34)

SONS OF GOD

The expression "sons of God" is used five times in the text of the Doctrine and Covenants to characterize those who, through their faith and obedience, inherit the blessings and glory of the celestial kingdom: "I came unto mine own, and mine own received me not; but unto as many as received me gave I power to do many miracles, and to become the sons of God; and even unto them that believed on my name gave I power to obtain eternal life" (D&C 45:8; compare also D&C 11:30; 34:3; 76:58; 128:23).

SONS OF JACOB

"Sons of Jacob" occurs only once in the text of the Doctrine and Covenants as part of the dedicatory prayer for the Kirtland Temple delivered on March 27, 1836: "That from among all these, thy servants, the sons of Jacob, may gather out the righteous to build a holy city to thy name, as thou hast commanded them" (D&C 109:58). The sons of Jacob include all those who have embraced the covenants of the Lord and who go forth for the purpose of gathering to Zion the scattered remnants of Israel and those of the Gentiles who are adopted into the fold of Christ through obedience and faith.

SONS OF LEVI

The expression "sons of Levi" is used three times in the text of the Doctrine and Covenants. In the first instance, it occurs in the words spoken by John the Baptist in restoring the Aaronic Priesthood in the latter days:

"Upon you my fellow servants, in the name of Messiah I confer the Priesthood of Aaron, which holds the keys of the ministering of angels, and of the gospel of repentance, and of baptism by immersion for the remission of sins; and this shall never be taken again from the earth, until the sons of Levi do offer again an offering unto the Lord in righteousness" (D&C 13).

The second instance of the ordination of Joseph Smith and Oliver Cowdery to the Aaronic Priesthood along the banks of the Susquehanna River near Harmony, Pennsylvania, on May 15, 1829, under the hands of John the Baptist (see JS—H 1:68–73).

The expression "sons of Levi" occurs in connection with "the sacrifices by the sons of Levi" associated with temple work (see D&C 124:39), and the third time in connection with the purification process required of those who provide leadership for temple work:

Behold, the great day of the Lord is at hand; and who can abide the day of his coming, and who can stand when he appeareth? For he is like a refiner's fire, and like fuller's soap; and he shall sit as a refiner and purifier of silver, and he shall purify the sons of Levi, and purge them as gold and silver, that they may offer unto the Lord an offering in righteousness. Let us, therefore, as a church and a people, and as Latter-day Saints, offer unto the Lord an offering in righteousness; and let us present in his holy temple, when it is finished, a book containing the records of our dead, which shall be worthy of all acceptation. (D&C 128:24; compare 3 Ne. 24:3, where the Savior quotes Mal. 3:3)

What is the doctrinal context for references such as "the sons of Levi"? The Doctrine and Covenants is the principal scriptural medium in the latter-days for codifying, understanding, and applying the principles embodied in the priesthood. As declared in section 13, the initial step in the restoration of priesthood powers and keys was the visit of John the Baptist on May 15, 1829. The bishop, as president of the priests' quorum, holds the keys of baptism within the ward. The Aaronic Priesthood will never be taken from the earth until the sons of Levi, successors of those who administered basic priesthood ordinances in ancient Israel, become purified and offer a righteous sacrifice unto the Lord.

What is to be understood about the offering in righteousness of the sons of Levi? Scholar Richard Cowan explains:

The answer to this question may be understood on at least two levels. On the literal level, Joseph Smith explained that the Savior's atonement did not completely end blood offerings. "These sacrifices as well as every ordinance, belonging to the priesthood, will, when the Temple of the Lord shall be built, and the sons of Levi be purified, be fully restored and attended to" (*TPJS*, 173). . . .

On a more figurative level, the Lord promised that faithful bearers of the Melchizedek and Aaronic Priesthood who magnify their callings "become the sons of Moses and of Aaron" respectively (D&C 84:33–34). Because Moses and Aaron were members of the tribe of Levi, faithful latter-day priesthood bearers become the "sons of Levi," and their "offering" is the

faithful service they render (see, for example, D&C 128:24). (*AQDC*, 19)

SONS OF MEN

The expression "sons of men" is used in the text of the Doctrine and Covenants to refer to mortals in general (as in D&C 93:4) or to those receiving specific directions from the Lord who, through no fault of their own, are unable to comply with these directions:

Verily, verily, I say unto you, that when I give a commandment to any of the sons of men to do a work unto my name, and those sons of men go with all their might and with all they have to perform that work, and cease not their diligence, and their enemies come upon them and hinder them from performing that work, behold, it behooveth me to require that work no more at the hands of those sons of men, but to accept of their offerings. (D&C 124:49)

SONS OF MOSES

The expression "sons of Moses" is used in the text of the Doctrine and Covenants, in the first instance, with the lineage of the priesthood: "And the sons of Moses, according to the Holy Priesthood which he [Moses] received under the hand of his father-in-law, Jethro" (D&C 84:6). In addition, the expression is used concerning the worthiness of priesthood holders in serving in the house of the Lord and honoring the oath and covenant of the priesthood (see D&C 84:31–34). As a blessing for their obedience, they shall be filled with the glory of the Lord.

154

Sons of Perdition

This term is used only twice in the scriptures, both times in the Doctrine and Covenants (D&C 76:32, 43). The sons of perdition are characterized by the Lord as those who "know my power, and have been made partakers thereof, and suffered themselves through the power of the devil to be overcome, and to deny the truth and defy my power—They are they who are the sons of perdition, of whom I say that it had been better for them never to have been born" (D&C 76:31–32). The sons of perdition not only "deny" the truth after having known it, but also "defy" the power of God, i.e., come out in open rebellion after the pattern of Lucifer. "For they are vessels of wrath, doomed to suffer the wrath of God, with the devil and his angels in eternity; Concerning whom I have said there is no forgiveness in this world nor in the world to come—" (D&C 76:33–34). Section 76 makes clear that the Lord "saves all the works of his [the Father's] hands, except those sons of perdition who deny the Son after the Father has revealed him" (D&C 76:44; compare D&C 132:27).

Spirits of Just Men Made Perfect

In a revelation given through the Prophet Joseph Smith at Nauvoo, February 9, 1843, the Lord declared:

> There are two kinds of beings in heaven, namely: Angels, who are resurrected personages, having bodies of flesh and bones—
>
> For instance, Jesus said: Handle me and see, for a spirit hath not flesh and bones, as ye see me have.
>
> Secondly: the spirits of just men made perfect, they who are not resurrected, but inherit the same glory. (D&C 129:1–3; compare *HC* 5:267)

The Prophet distinguishes between embodied (resurrected) beings and disembodied beings (spirits prior to their resurrected state). The reference to "the spirits of just men made perfect" (v. 3) concerns the state of those beings who will eventually inherit the highest degree of the celestial kingdom as resurrected beings: "These are they who have come to an innumerable company of angels, to the general assembly and church of Enoch, and of the Firstborn. . . . These are they who are just men made perfect through Jesus the mediator of the new covenant, who wrought out this perfect atonement through the shedding of his own blood. These are they whose bodies are celestial" (D&C 76:67, 69–70; compare the similar language in Heb. 12:22–23). Prior to this exalted and resurrected condition, the unembodied spirits of "just men made perfect" can be commissioned of the Lord as emissaries to perform missions unto God's children, just as the Savior did between His crucifixion and His resurrection. At a general conference of the Church held in Nauvoo on Sunday, October 3, 1841, the Prophet

> explained the difference between an angel and a ministering spirit; the one a resurrected or translated body, with its spirit ministering to embodied spirits—the other a disembodied spirit, visiting and ministering to disembodied spirits. Jesus Christ became a ministering spirit (while His body was lying in the sepulchre) to the spirits in prison [see 1 Pet. 3:18–20], to fulfill an important part of His

mission, without which He could not have perfected His work, or entered into His rest. After His resurrection He appeared as an angel to His disciples [see D&C 129:2, above, in reference to Luke 24:39].

Translated bodies cannot enter into rest until they have undergone a change equivalent to death. Translated bodies are designed for future missions. (HC 4:425)

President George Q. Cannon commented on section 129 as follows:

In the broadest sense, any being who acts as a messenger for our Heavenly Father, is an angel, be he a God, a resurrected man, or the spirit of a just man; and the term is so used in all these senses in the ancient scriptures. In the stricter and more limited sense, an angel is, as the Prophet Joseph Smith states, a resurrected personage, having a body of flesh and bones; but it must be remembered that *none* of the angels who appeared to men before the death of the Savior could be of that class, for none of them was resurrected. (*Juvenile Instructor*, Vol. 26; January 15, 1891; cited in *DCC*, 811–12)

STANTON, DANIEL

Daniel was born on May 28, 1795, in Manlius, Onondaga County, New York. On November 3, 1830, he was baptized a member of the Church in Kirtland by Parley P. Pratt. Oliver Cowdery ordained him a high priest. In January 1832 he was called as a missionary by revelation (see D&C 75:33). Following the

mission, he moved to Jackson County, Missouri, and then, because of religious persecution, to Clay County. After serving another mission for the Church, he returned to Missouri and became a member of the Adam-ondi-Ahman high council. He was tireless in assisting suffering Saints in the area but was forced by the mobs to flee to Illinois. He continued his faithful priesthood service as stake president in Quincy, Illinois, and later as a member of the high council in Lima, Illinois. Daniel joined with the Saints in the exodus to the Salt Lake Valley and became one of the earliest settlers in Springville. He passed away in Panaca, Nevada, on October 26, 1872.

STEM OF JESSE (SEE JESSE)

SWEET, NORTHROP

Northrop was born in 1802 in New York. He was baptized by Parley P. Pratt in October 1830 and was ordained an elder the following June. At first he honored the revelation calling him and an associate on a mission:

Behold, I say unto you, my servants Ezra and Northrop, open ye your ears and hearken to the voice of the Lord your God, . . .

For verily, verily, I say unto you that ye are called to lift up your voices as with the sound of a trump, to declare my gospel unto a crooked and perverse generation. . . .

Open your mouths and they shall be filled, and you shall become even as Nephi of old, who journeyed from Jerusalem in the wilderness.

Yea, open your mouths and spare not, and you shall be laden with sheaves upon your backs, for lo, I am with you.

Yea, open your mouths and they shall be filled, saying: Repent, repent, and prepare ye the way of the Lord, and make his paths straight; for the kingdom of heaven is at hand. (D&C 33:1–2, 8–10)

However, Northrop soon fell away from the restored Church and formed a church of his own in Kirtland. When his church failed to prosper, he moved to Ohio and then later to Michigan.

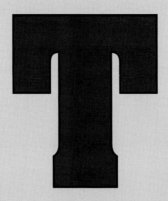

TANNER, NATHAN ELDON (SEE ALSO KIMBALL, SPENCER W.; ROMNEY, MARION G.)

N. Eldon Tanner was born on May 9, 1898, in Salt Lake City, Utah. He grew up in a small farming community in Alberta, Canada, and eventually became the principal of the high school in Cardston. He made his mark in government service and achieved prominence in the petroleum industry. He served as the president of the Calgary Stake before being called by President David O. McKay in 1960 as an Assistant to the Council of the Twelve Apostles. He became a member of that council in 1962 and on October 3, 1963, was called as the Second Counselor in the First Presidency of the Church. In his leadership service, N. Eldon Tanner was a counselor to four presidents: David O. McKay, Joseph Fielding Smith, Harold B. Lee, and Spencer W. Kimball. President Kimball requested that N. Eldon Tanner, First Counselor in the First Presidency, read the text of the Official Declaration—2, dated June 8, 1978, before the semi-annual conference of

the Church on September 30, 1978. The Declaration revealed the word of the Lord that all worthy males could receive the priesthood and the blessings of the temple. In that context, N. Eldon Tanner and Marion G. Romney are listed with President Spencer W. Kimball as

Nathan Eldon Tanner

constituting the First Presidency in the confirming letter sent throughout the Church. N. Eldon Tanner passed away on November 27, 1982.

Taylor, John

John was born on November 1, 1808, at Milnthorpe, Westmoreland County, England. He immigrated to Toronto, Canada, where he learned of the restored Church through the preaching of Parley P. Pratt. John was baptized by Apostle Pratt on May 9, 1836, and subsequently ordained an elder and then a high priest. He was called by revelation on July 8, 1838, to be a member of the Quorum of the Twelve (D&C 118:6; confirmed in D&C 124:129). He served a mission in Great Britain and then filled important civic offices in Nauvoo upon his return. He witnessed firsthand the martyrdom of the Prophet Joseph at Carthage on June 27, 1844, and was severely wounded himself. He penned section 135 concerning the Martyrdom and the significance of the mission of the Prophet Joseph Smith and Joseph's brother Hyrum. John is mentioned in verse 2: "John Taylor and Willard Richards, two of the Twelve, were the only persons in the room at the time; the former was wounded in a savage manner with four balls, but has since recovered; the latter, through the providence of God, escaped, without even a hole in his robe." After the exodus from Nauvoo, John served additional missions for the Church. In the West, he was active in the establishment and development of new settlements and occupied various civic positions of leadership. With the death of Brigham Young, John Taylor became the third President of the Church, serving during perilous and difficult times with devotion and leadership until his own death on July 25, 1887.

John Taylor

John Taylor is also named in President Joseph F. Smith's vision of the work of salvation in the spirit realm as one of the noble and elect leaders participating in the work of salvation in the spirit realm (see D&C 138:53).

Thayre, Ezra

Ezra was born on October 14, 1791, at Randolph, Windsor County, Vermont. He became a builder of bridges, dams, and mills in the Palmyra area of New York where he was converted through the teaching of Hyrum Smith. Baptized by Parley P. Pratt in October 1830, he soon was called on a mission by the Lord, along with Northrop Sweet (D&C 33). Many joined the Church through Ezra's service. He was ordained a high priest in June 1831 but failed to heed the Lord's directive to go on another mission (see D&C 52:22). Thereafter he was called to repentance by the Lord, who revoked

Ezra's commission (see D&C 56:5) and added these words:

> And again, verily I say unto you, that my servant Ezra Thayre must repent of his pride, and of his selfishness, and obey the former commandment which I have given him concerning the place upon which he lives.
>
> And if he will do this, . . . he shall be appointed still to go to the land of Missouri;
>
> Otherwise he shall receive the money which he has paid, and shall leave the place, and shall be cut off out of my church, . . .
>
> And though the heaven and the earth pass away, these words shall not pass away, but shall be fulfilled. (D&C 56:8–11)

A subsequent mission call (see D&C 75:31) found Ezra obedient. He participated in Zion's Camp in 1834, later served on the high council in Adam-ondi-Ahman, Missouri, and subsequently moved to Rochester, New York, and then to Michigan. After the martyrdom of the Prophet, he joined the ranks of the Reorganized Church of Jesus Christ of Latter Day Saints.

THOMPSON, ROBERT B.

Robert was born on October 1, 1811, at Great Driffield, Yorkshire, England. He was a Methodist preacher before immigrating to Canada in 1834. Through the missionary work of Parley P. Pratt, Robert joined the Church in May 1836 and then journeyed to Kirtland the following year before returning to Canada on a mission. After a period of time in Missouri, where he fought for the cause of the Saints in the Battle of Crooked River, he moved to Illinois and served as a scribe for the Prophet Joseph Smith. Robert also served as general clerk for the Church, colonel in the Nauvoo Legion, city treasurer, and regent of the University of Nauvoo. In a revelation dated January 19, 1841, Robert was appointed to assist in the preparation of a proclamation to the leaders of the nations:

> And again, verily I say unto you, let my servant Robert B. Thompson help you to write this proclamation, for I am well pleased with him, and that he should be with you;
>
> Let him, therefore, hearken to your counsel, and I will bless him with a multiplicity of blessings; let him be faithful and true in all things from henceforth, and he shall be great in mine eyes;
>
> But let him remember that his stewardship will I require at his hands. (D&C 124:12–14)

In addition, he assisted Don Carlos Smith as associate editor of the *Times and Seasons*. He was suddenly overcome with a serious illness (the same that had taken the life of Don Carlos Smith) and passed away on August 27, 1841, at the age of twenty-nine.

THREE WITNESSES

The three witnesses of the Book of Mormon were Oliver Cowdery, David Whitmer, and Martin Harris. (See "The Testimony of Three Witnesses" included in the Introduction to the Book of Mormon.)

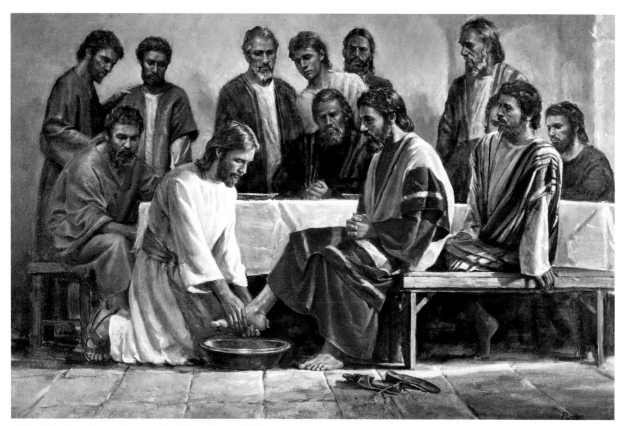

The Twelve Apostles in the Meridian of Time

TWELVE APOSTLES IN THE MERIDIAN OF TIME

In the revelation known as section 29, the Lord refers to His original Twelve Apostles in connection with the Second Coming:

> And again, verily, verily, I say unto you, and it hath gone forth in a firm decree, by the will of the Father, that mine apostles, the Twelve which were with me in my ministry at Jerusalem, shall stand at my right hand at the day of my coming in a pillar of fire, being clothed with robes of righteousness, with crowns upon their heads, in glory even as I am, to judge the whole house of Israel, even as many as have loved me and kept my commandments, and none else. (D&C 29:12)

In this context, the term "holy apostles" occurs once in the text of the Doctrine and Covenants (see D&C 133:55; compare Eph. 3:5; Rev. 18:20).

TWELVE APOSTLES OF THE RESTORATION

The original members of the latter-day Quorum of the Twelve Apostles (called in February 1835) included Lyman E. Johnson, Brigham Young, Heber C. Kimball, Orson Hyde, David W. Patten, Luke S. Johnson, William E. McLellin, John F. Boynton, Orson Pratt, William Smith, Thomas B. Marsh, and Parley P. Pratt (see *HC* 2:187; see also the "Testimony of the Twelve Apostles to the Truth of the Doctrine and Covenants"). By January 1841, the Quorum had been adjusted:

I give unto you my servant Brigham Young to be a president over the Twelve traveling council;

Which Twelve hold the keys to open up the authority of my kingdom upon the four corners of the earth, and after that to send my word to every creature.

They are Heber C. Kimball, Parley P. Pratt, Orson Pratt, Orson Hyde, William Smith, John Taylor, John E. Page, Wilford Woodruff, Willard Richards, George A. Smith;

David Patten I have taken unto myself; behold, his priesthood no man taketh from him; but, verily I say unto you, another may be appointed unto the same calling. (D&C 124:127–30)

Thus, Lyman E. Johnson, Luke S. Johnson, William E. McLellin, John F. Boynton, and Thomas B. Marsh had been replaced by John Taylor, John E. Page, Wilford Woodruff, Willard Richards, and George A. Smith. David Patten died as a martyr on October 25, 1838, at the battle of Crooked River while defending the Saints in Missouri from attacks by the mobs.

The Doctrine and Covenants frequently refers to the office and duties of the Twelve (see, for example, D&C 18:27, 31, 37; 102:30; 112:12, 14, 16, 21, 30; 136:3). The Twelve are called to be "special witnesses of the name of Christ in all the world—thus differing from other officers in the church in the duties of their calling" (D&C 107:23).

TWO WITNESSES

Section 77 of the Doctrine and Covenants provides inspired commentary on various passages written by John the Revelator, including the following reference: "And I will give power unto my two witnesses, and they shall prophesy a thousand two hundred and threescore days, clothed in sackcloth" (Rev. 11:3). Latter-day scripture asks:

Q. What is to be understood by the two witnesses, in the eleventh chapter of Revelation?

A. They are two prophets that are to be raised up to the Jewish nation in the last days, at the time of the restoration, and to prophesy to the Jews after they are gathered and have built the city of Jerusalem in the land of their fathers. (D&C 77:15)

Elder Bruce R. McConkie comments:

'In the mouth of two or three witnesses shall every word be established.' (2 Cor. 13:1.) Such is God's eternal law. And these two shall be followers of that humble man, Joseph Smith, . . . No doubt they will be members of the Council of the Twelve or of the First Presidency of the Church. Their prophetic ministry to rebellious Jewry shall be the same in length as was our Lord's personal ministry among their rebellious forebears. (*DNTC* 3:510; compare the reference in the Book of Mormon to the two sons in the streets of Jerusalem in the last days: 2 Ne. 8:18–20; Isa. 51:17–20; see also Ezek. 38:17–23)

Unjust Judge

The unjust judge in the parable given by the Lord in section 101 is a figurative representation of the civil leadership to which the Saints of the Restoration appealed as they sought for redress in the face of daunting suffering and persecution:

Now, unto what shall I liken the children of Zion? I will liken them unto the parable of the woman and the unjust judge, for men ought always to pray and not to faint, which saith—

There was in a city a judge which feared not God, neither regarded man.

And there was a widow in that city, and she came unto him, saying: Avenge me of mine adversary.

And he would not for a while, but afterward he said within himself: Though I fear not God, nor regard man, yet because this widow troubleth me I will avenge her, lest by her continual coming she weary me.

Thus will I liken the children of Zion. (D&C 101:81–85)

If the unjust judge would give relief to the widow, how much more would the Almighty, in His perfection and majesty, hear the pleas of His righteous Saints and grant them relief in their time of misery as they appealed to their civil leaders for help? If the Saints were righteous and wholly dependent upon the Lord—and continued their petitions for redress in good faith—then relief would come—or the perpetrators would be punished in the due time of the Lord.

Uriah

Uriah, warrior in the army of David and husband of Bathsheba (2 Sam. 11), is mentioned once in the Doctrine and Covenants (see D&C 132:39). For more detail, see the entry for "David."

WAKEFIELD, JOSEPH

Joseph was born around 1792 in New York State. He was baptized around 1831 and moved to Kirtland, Ohio. He accompanied Parley P. Pratt on a mission to the Western Reserve (see D&C 50:37). He was ordained a high priest on June 3, 1831, and subsequently served another mission, this time in the eastern states (see D&C 52:35), where, in 1832, he was privileged to baptize George A. Smith (the future apostle). Not long thereafter, Joseph Wakefield fell into apostasy and was excommunicated. He turned his bitterness into persecution against the Prophet and the Church.

WATCHMEN

Symbolic figures in the parable concerning the vineyard of the Lord. (See the entry for "Lord of the Vineyard.")

WELTON, MICAH B.

Micah was born on August 13, 1792, at Watertown, Litchfield County, Connecticut. He was baptized into the Church on June 23, 1831, and was ordained a priest, then an elder. In January 1832 he was called by revelation as a missionary (see D&C 75:36) and served in that capacity. He attended the Kirtland Temple dedication in March 1836 and later that year became a resident in Clay County, Missouri. Persecution forced him to move to Illinois, where he was ordained a seventy in 1839 in Quincy and later became a member of the Third Quorum of the Seventy in Nauvoo. He also served another mission for the Church in 1844 and helped in the construction of the temple. He died on August 9, 1861, at Knox County, Illinois.

WHITLOCK, HARVEY

Harvey was born in 1809 in Massachusetts. At the fourth conference of the Church held in June 1831, he was ordained a high priest by Joseph Smith and immediately experienced the influence of Satan, whom the Prophet cast out of him. Thereafter he was called by revelation to serve a mission with David Whitmer: "Let my servants David Whitmer and Harvey Whitlock also take their journey, and preach by the way unto this same land [Missouri]" (D&C

52:25). In 1833 he was expelled from Missouri by the mobs and subsequently fell into apostasy, returning to fellowship for a short time before abdicating his membership again in 1838 at the time of the ongoing Missouri difficulties. By 1850 he was again living among the Saints in Utah County where he practiced medicine. Again he denied the faith and was again rebaptized. By 1864 he had moved to California, where he joined the Reorganized Church of Jesus Christ of Latter Day Saints and served a mission for that group.

WHITMER, DAVID

David was born on January 7, 1805, near Harrisburg, Dauphin County, Pennsylvania, the son of Peter Whitmer Sr. He learned in 1828 of the mission of Joseph Smith and became one of the three witnesses of the Book of Mormon. He was also one of the original six members of the Church at its organization on April 6, 1830, and was ordained an elder that day. He and his family suffered great persecution along with the other Saints in Missouri. He became president of the Clay County high council on July 3, 1834, and a few days later was appointed president of the Church in Missouri. His service for the Church was considerable, but he fell prey in 1836 to pride and apostasy. On April 13, 1838, he was excommunicated and took up residence in Richmond, Missouri. For the next half-century he pursued a business and community service career in Richmond, where he established a reputation of honesty and respect. Though he remained aloof from the Church, he consistently confirmed his witness of the Book of Mormon, even to his dying day on January 25, 1888, at Richmond, Ray County, Missouri.

David is mentioned by name five times in the text of the Doctrine and Covenants.

David Whitmer

Counsel given to him provides significant lessons for all who read this volume of scripture.

For example, in section 14, a revelation given specifically to David in June 1829, there is confirmation of the personal nature of the covenant relationship offered by the Lord to His servants:

> And it shall come to pass, that if you [David] shall ask the Father in my name, in faith believing, you shall receive the Holy Ghost, which giveth utterance, that you may stand as a witness of the things of which you shall both hear and see, and also that you may declare repentance unto this generation.
>
> Behold, I am Jesus Christ, the Son of the living God, who created the heavens and the earth, a light which cannot be hid in darkness; . . .
>
> And behold, thou art David, and thou art called to assist; which thing if

ye do, and are faithful, ye shall be blessed both spiritually and temporally, and great shall be your reward. Amen. (D&C 14:8–9, 11)

The spirit of the intimate, personal relationship conveyed by the expression "I am Jesus Christ"/"thou art David" is continued in section 18, also dated June 1829, where the Lord reminds both Oliver Cowdery and David Whitmer personally of the essential role of repentance in the plan of salvation. Oliver and David are to go forth to call people to repentance that joy might abound for the convert as well as the missionary (see D&C 18:9–16).

In the service of their calling to proclaim the gospel, Oliver and David, as witnesses to the Book of Mormon, were to be commissioned (with Martin Harris later) to select the Twelve Apostles of the Lord in the latter days—a process which took place in February 1835:

And now, behold, I give unto you, Oliver Cowdery, and also unto David Whitmer, that you shall search out the Twelve, who shall have the desires of which I have spoken;

And by their desires and their works you shall know them.

And when you have found them you shall show these things unto them.

And you shall fall down and worship the Father in my name.

And you must preach unto the world, saying: You must repent and be baptized, in the name of Jesus Christ. (D&C 18:37–41)

However, the spiritual development of David Whitmer was not without its reversals, as the Lord's counsel to him in September 1830 demonstrates:

Behold, I say unto you, David, that you have feared man and have not relied on me for strength as you ought.

But your mind has been on the things of the earth more than on the things of me, your Maker, and the ministry whereunto you have been called; and you have not given heed unto my Spirit, and to those who were set over you, but have been persuaded by those whom I have not commanded. (D&C 30:1–2)

Taken in its broadest scope, the ministry assigned to David Whitmer was of grand proportions: to be one of the three witnesses of the Book of Mormon, to be one of the six Saints on hand at the formal organization of the Church, to be part of the organizing campaign in Missouri (see D&C 52:25), and to participate in the selection of the original members of the Quorum of the Twelve. But he forgot the covenant obligations inherent in the wording of the Lord's commission to him: "I am Jesus Christ"/"thou art David" (D&C 14:9, 11). He forgot the admonition of the Lord to give "heed unto my Spirit, and to those who were set over you" (D&C 30:2). And thus he was "left to inquire for [himself]" (D&C 30:3)—for fifty years, outside the Church—though he preserved at least his witness to the truth of the Book of Mormon.

WHITMER, JOHN

John was born on August 27, 1802, at Fayette Township, Seneca County, New York, son of Peter Whitmer Sr. He learned in 1828 of the mission of Joseph Smith and assisted the young prophet as scribe in the translation of the Book of Mormon. He was baptized by Oliver Cowdery. He was one of the eight witnesses of the Book of Mormon and contributed loyal service to the building of the Kingdom at Colesville, New York. Tirelessly he engaged in proselyting work for the restored Church (see D&C 30:9) and also assisted the Prophet with scribal duties, including writing a segment of the history of the Church (see D&C 47:1; 69:2–3, 7–8) and assisting in the commission to care for and publish the revelations of the Lord as part of the covenant obligation of the Church leadership (see D&C 70:1–3; 82:11). On July 3, 1834, he became a member of the presidency of the Church in Missouri. Later, in Kirtland, he became editor of the *Messenger and Advocate* publication. Upon his return to Missouri, he helped the Saints by becoming involved in financial transactions for purchasing tracts of lands. Because of allegations concerning irregularities in these transactions, an investigation was carried out, and John, who refused to cooperate with Church leaders, was excommunicated on March 10, 1838. Though acrimonious about this action, he privately yearned for forgiveness. He remained in Far West, aloof from the Church, and acquired at bargain prices many properties the Saints were forced to abandon. Though he remained bitter against the Prophet and the Church, John never recanted his firm testimony of the Book of Mormon. He died on July 11, 1878, at Far West, Caldwell County, Missouri.

The earliest incident of personal revelation given to John occurred in June 1829 when the Lord identified for him, through the Prophet Joseph Smith, what his most important duty in the Kingdom would be:

John Whitmer

Hearken, my servant John, and listen to the words of Jesus Christ, your Lord and your Redeemer. . . .

And I will tell you that which no man knoweth save me and thee alone—

For many times you have desired of me to know that which would be of the most worth unto you.

Behold, blessed are you for this thing, and for speaking my words which I have given you according to my commandments.

And now, behold, I say unto you, that the thing which will be of the most worth unto you will be to declare repentance unto this people, that you may bring souls unto me, that you may rest with them in the kingdom of my Father. Amen. (D&C 15:1, 3–6)

The following month, the Lord revealed to both Oliver Cowdery and John Whitmer how they should be using their time: "Behold, I say unto you that you shall let your time be devoted to the studying of the scriptures, and to preaching, and to confirming the church at Colesville, and to performing your labors on the land, such as is required" (D&C 26:1). Soon thereafter, John was called to engage in missionary work (see D&C 30:9). John's writing commission was revealed on March 8, 1831:

> Behold, it is expedient in me that my servant John should write and keep a regular history, and assist you, my servant Joseph, in transcribing all things which shall be given you, until he is called to further duties. . . .
> Wherefore, it shall be given him, inasmuch as he is faithful, by the Comforter, to write these things. (D&C 47:1, 4)

In fact, John Whitmer was included in the select circle of leaders to whom was given the monumental assignment to be stewards over the revelations of the Lord and see that they were published (first as the Book of Commandments and then later as the Doctrine and Covenants):

> Behold, . . . and hear the word of the Lord which I give unto my servant Joseph Smith, Jun., and also unto my servant Martin Harris, and also unto my servant Oliver Cowdery, and also unto my servant John Whitmer, and also unto my servant Sidney Rigdon, and also unto my servant William W. Phelps, by the way of commandment unto them.

> I, the Lord, have appointed them, and ordained them to be stewards over the revelations and commandments which I have given unto them, and which I shall hereafter give unto them. (D&C 70:1–3; dated November 12, 1831)

John participated with his associates in a stewardship covenant according to the principles of the law of consecration (United Order) for the purpose of carrying out these sacred duties (see D&C 82:11). However, he did not remain faithful to this covenant bond and thus lost his membership in the Church—though, to his credit, he upheld his witness to the Book of Mormon to his last day.

WHITMER, PETER, JR.

Peter was born on September 27, 1809, at Fayette Township, Seneca County, New York, the son of Peter Whitmer Sr. Peter became acquainted with the Prophet Joseph Smith in the summer of 1829 when Joseph resided for a time in the family residence. The Lord's counsel to Peter (named in D&C 16:1) was the same as to his brother John: "And now, behold, I say unto you, that the thing which will be of the most worth unto you will be to declare repentance unto this people, that you may bring souls unto me, that you may rest with them in the kingdom of my Father" (D&C 16:6). Peter served as a scribe on occasion in the work of translation and became one of the eight witnesses of the Book of Mormon. He was baptized in June 1830 by Oliver Cowdery and was then ordained an elder. In the period 1830–31, he accompanied Parley P. Pratt, Oliver Cowdery, and Ziba Peterson on a mission among the Lamanites (see D&C 32:2–3; compare also the earlier missionary exhortation given to John in D&C 30:5). In Independence, Missouri, he established a trade as a tailor. On October 25, 1831, he was ordained a high priest. Beset by aggressive mob action and persecution in Independence, Peter relocated to Clay County, where he provided charitable service to many, despite his ill health. He died on September 22, 1836, at Liberty, Clay County, Missouri.

WHITMER, PETER, SR.

Peter was born on April 14, 1773, in Pennsylvania. Three of his eight children—David, Peter Jr., and John—are also mentioned in the Doctrine and Covenants. By 1809, Peter had settled with his family in Fayette, New York. It was in his log home that the Prophet Joseph Smith completed the translation of the Book of Mormon in 1829. Near the home, the three witnesses of the Book of Mormon—Oliver Cowdery, David Whitmer, and Martin Harris—experienced their divine confirmation of the truth of that volume of scripture. And it was in that same home that the Church was formally organized on April 6, 1830. Peter and his wife were baptized by Oliver Cowdery on April 18, 1830. The Whitmer family moved to Kirtland in 1831 and to Missouri soon thereafter, where persecution was severe. Peter slipped into apostasy along with his sons Jacob, John, and David and moved with the dissenters to Richmond, Missouri. He passed away on August 12, 1854. The text of the Doctrine and Covenants refers to the senior Whitmer in connection with the events of the restoration: "And again, the voice of God in the chamber of old Father Whitmer, in Fayette, Seneca county, and at sundry times, and in divers places through all the travels and tribulations of this Church of Jesus Christ of Latter-day Saints!" (D&C 128:21; Peter Whitmer Sr. is also mentioned in the introductory headings to sections 14, 21, 34).

WHITNEY, NEWEL K.

Newel was born on February 5, 1795, in Marlborough, Windham County, Vermont. He settled in Ohio as a merchandiser and worked with Sidney Gilbert in the capacity of clerk and bookkeeper. Newel and his wife, Elizabeth, had spiritual promptings about receiving the word of the Lord. Soon thereafter, the missionaries taught them the gospel and they were baptized in November 1830. In a vision the Prophet Joseph Smith saw Newel and his wife pleading with the Lord that the Prophet would come to Kirtland. In response, the Prophet showed up at the Gilbert and Whitney store around February 1, 1831, and greeted the astonished young man warmly with the words, "Newel K. Whitney! Thou art the man." Newel then shook the extended hand of the Prophet and said, "You have the

Newel K. Whitney

advantage of me. . . . I could not call you by name as you have me." "I am Joseph the Prophet," said the stranger smiling. "You've prayed me here, now what do you want of me?" (*HC* 1:146). The Whitneys considered the Prophet's arrival in Kirtland the fulfillment of their earnest supplication to the Lord. On December 4, 1831, Newel was called by revelation to serve as a bishop. Ever beloved of the Prophet, Newel was later called as Presiding Bishop of the Church following the Martyrdom. He and his family joined the westward trek in 1848. He passed away of severe chest pains on September 23, 1850, at his home in Salt Lake City.

Newel is mentioned by name thirteen times in the text of the Doctrine and Covenants. Among those passages is the following, which provides details of his calling as a bishop on December 4, 1831:

> Hearken, and listen to the voice of the Lord, . . .
>
> For verily thus saith the Lord, it is expedient in me for a bishop to be appointed unto you, or of you, unto the church in this part of the Lord's vineyard. . . .
>
> And the duty of the bishop shall be made known by the commandments which have been given, and the voice of the conference.
>
> And now, verily I say unto you, my servant Newel K. Whitney is the man who shall be appointed and ordained unto this power. This is the will of the Lord your God, your Redeemer. Even so. Amen. (D&C 72:1–2, 7–8; see also D&C 78:9; 82:11; 84:112; 96:2; 104:39–41; 117:1, 11)

In another passage the Lord emphasizes that "my servant Newel K. Whitney also, a bishop of my church, hath need to be chastened, and set in order his family, and see that they are more diligent and concerned at home, and pray always, or they shall be removed out of their place" (D&C 93:50). Two months later, the Lord again commands Newel and one of his associates to be urgently engaged in the Lord's business and not delay their journey to Missouri out of concern for temporal matters:

> Verily thus saith the Lord unto my servant William Marks, and also unto my servant Newel K. Whitney, let them settle up their business speedily and journey from the land of Kirtland, before I, the Lord, send again the snows upon the earth.
>
> Let them awake, and arise, and come forth, and not tarry, for I, the Lord, command it.
>
> Therefore, if they tarry it shall not be well with them.
>
> Let them repent of all their sins, and of all their covetous desires, before me, saith the Lord; for what is property unto me? saith the Lord.
>
> Let the properties of Kirtland be turned out for debts, saith the Lord. Let them go, saith the Lord, and whatsoever remaineth, let it remain in your hands, saith the Lord. . . .
>
> Therefore, come up hither unto the land of my people, even Zion. (D&C 117:1–5, 9; dated July 8, 1838)

Then, without equivocation, the Lord makes plain to Newel what is required: "Let my servant Newel K. Whitney be ashamed of the

Nicolaitane band and of all their secret abominations, and of all his littleness of soul before me, saith the Lord, and come up to the land of Adam-ondi-Ahman, and be a bishop unto my people, saith the Lord, not in name but in deed, saith the Lord" (D&C 117:11).

Fortunately, Newel Whitney repented and rose to the stature of his high potential as a leader in the Kingdom of God:

Blessed of the Lord is Brother Whitney, even the Bishop of the Church of Latter-day Saints, for the Bishopric shall never be taken away from him while he liveth . . . and he shall deal with a liberal hand to the poor and the needy, the sick and afflicted, the widow and the fatherless. And marvelously and miraculously shall the Lord his God provide for him, even that he shall be blessed with a fullness of the good things of this earth, and his seed after him from generation to generation. And it shall come to pass, that according to the measure that he meteth out with a liberal hand to the poor, so shall it be measured to him again by the hand of his God, even an hundred fold. Angels shall guard his house, and shall guard the lives of his posterity, and they shall become very great and very numerous on the earth. (HC 2:288)

Later, in August 1842, the Prophet Joseph told Newel:

Thou art a faithful friend in whom the afflicted sons of men can confide with the most perfect safety. Let the blessings of the Eternal also be crowned upon his head. How warm that heart! how anxious that soul! for the welfare of one who has been cast out, and hated of almost all men. Brother Whitney, thou knowest not how strong those ties are that bind my soul and heart to thee. (HC 5:108)

WIGHT, LYMAN

Lyman was born on May 9, 1796, at Fairfield Township, Herkimer County, New York. He moved to Ohio and became affiliated with the communal group on the Isaac Morley farm in Kirtland. Like Isaac and many others in that group, Lyman embraced the restored gospel. He was baptized on November 14, 1830, by Oliver Cowdery. At the fourth conference of the Church in June 1831, Lyman was the first man ordained a high priest by Joseph Smith. Subsequently, he was called on a mission to Missouri by revelation (see D&C 52:7). At that time he

Lyman Wight

was warned of the Lord to be on guard "for Satan desireth to sift him as chaff. And behold, he that is faithful shall be made ruler over many things" (D&C 52:12–13). His preaching was powerful and effective. He then became a resident in Jackson County, Missouri, where he witnessed the violent treatment of the Saints. He and Parley P. Pratt traveled to inform the Prophet of the crisis, leading to the formation of Zion's Camp and the trek to bring relief. Lyman marched as Joseph's deputy, walking much of the way without stockings on his feet. (Concerning his commission to be involved with this campaign, see D&C 103:30, 38, and the heading to that section.)

In the ensuing years he encountered difficulties with Church authorities because of his outspoken manner and questionable doctrinal positions. Nevertheless, he was called as a counselor in the Adam-ondi-Ahman stake on June 28, 1838. Shortly thereafter he was seized by the mob militia who offered him his life if he would swear against the Prophet Joseph Smith. Lyman defiantly refused to do so. His life was spared, though he was imprisoned with the Prophet at Richmond and then in Liberty Jail. In a revelation on January 19, 1841, he was commissioned to assist in the building of the Nauvoo House (see D&C 124:22, 62, 70) and was on that occasion given an extraordinary promise of the Lord:

It is my will that my servant Lyman Wight should continue in preaching for Zion, in the spirit of meekness, confessing me before the world; and I will bear him up as on eagles' wings; and he shall beget glory and honor to himself and unto my name.

That when he shall finish his work I may receive him unto myself,

even as I did my servant David Patten, who is with me at this time, and also my servant Edward Partridge, and also my aged servant Joseph Smith, Sen., who sitteth with Abraham at his right hand, and blessed and holy is he, for he is mine. (D&C 124:18–19)

Lyman was ordained to the apostleship on April 8, 1841. Nevertheless, he failed to support Brigham Young as successor to Joseph Smith after the Martyrdom and called for the Saints to join him in Texas, where he felt he was commissioned of God to start a new colony. His fellowship was withdrawn on December 3, 1848, by Church leaders in Salt Lake City. He passed away suddenly in Texas on March 31, 1858.

WILLIAMS, FREDERICK G.

Frederick was born on October 28, 1787, at Suffield, Hartford County, Connecticut. A self-trained medical practitioner, he found his way to Kirtland where he and his wife were converted by the missionaries. He was baptized in October 1830 and then ordained an elder. In March 1832 he was called by revelation to be a counselor to Joseph Smith:

Verily, verily, I say unto you my servant Frederick G. Williams: Listen to the voice of him who speaketh, to the word of the Lord your God, and hearken to the calling wherewith you are called, even to be a high priest in my church, and a counselor unto my servant Joseph Smith, Jun.; . . .

Wherefore, be faithful; stand in the office which I have appointed unto you; succor the weak, lift up the hands which hang down, and strengthen the feeble knees.

And if thou art faithful unto the end thou shalt have a crown of immortality, and eternal life in the mansions which I have prepared in the house of my Father. (D&C 81:1, 5–6; the current heading to that section notes: "The historical records show that when this revelation was received in March 1832, it called Jesse Gause to the office of counselor to Joseph Smith in the Presidency. However, when he failed to continue in a manner consistent with this appointment, the call was subsequently transferred to Frederick G. Williams.")

The Prophet placed a great deal of trust in Frederick. In May 1834 Frederick deeded his farm to the Prophet and then subsequently participated in Zion's Camp as paymaster. He continued his devoted service in Kirtland, but by 1837 he had lost his counselorship and his

Frederick G. Williams

membership, though he was rebaptized the following year prior to joining the Saints in Missouri (see *HC* 3:55). In Missouri the process of stumbling and being received again into fellowship took place once more for Frederick, but he maintained his association with the Prophet and passed away in poor health in Quincy, Illinois, in October 1842, faithful to the cause of the Kingdom.

In confirmation of the revealed commission to serve as a counselor to Joseph Smith (quoted above), the Doctrine and Covenants includes the following passage addressed to Frederick and Sidney Rigdon: "And again, verily I say unto thy brethren, Sidney Rigdon and Frederick G. Williams, their sins are forgiven them also, and they are accounted as equal with thee [Joseph Smith] in holding the keys of this last kingdom" (D&C 90:6; according to the current heading of this section the two counselors were ordained on March 18, 1833). On May 6, 1833, the Lord revealed a warning to Frederick that offers valuable counsel to all readers of the Doctrine and Covenants:

> But I have commanded you to bring up your children in light and truth.
>
> But verily I say unto you, my servant Frederick G. Williams, . . .
>
> You have not taught your children light and truth, according to the commandments; and that wicked one hath power, as yet, over you, and this is the cause of your affliction. (D&C 93:40–42)

WILLIAMS, SAMUEL

Samuel was born on March 22, 1789, at Russell, Hampden County, Massachusetts. He was living in Kirtland, Ohio, when he joined the

Church. For a time he resided in Missouri until persecution forced him to move to Nauvoo. On January 19, 1841, he was called by revelation as a counselor to John Hicks in the presidency of the elders' quorum (see D&C 124:137). Samuel took the place of John Hicks after the latter's apostasy and also served as a temporary member of the Nauvoo high council. When persecution forced the Saints to abandon their beloved Nauvoo, Samuel moved to the Iowa Territory. He was ordained a high priest on December 24, 1846, in Winter Quarters, later traveling to the Salt Lake Valley where he was a stonecutter. He died on November 10, 1855, in Ogden.

WILSON, CALVES

Birth and death dates for Calves Wilson are unknown. As a baptized member, he was ordained a priest on October 25, 1831, by Oliver Cowdery. In January 1832 he was called by revelation to serve a mission for the Church (see D&C 75:15). It is not known whether he accepted and fulfilled that calling; however, in the spring of 1832 he accompanied Lyman Wight on a productive mission to Cincinnati, Ohio.

WILSON, DUNBAR

Lewis Dunbar Wilson was born on June 2, 1805, in Chittenden County, Vermont. He was baptized on May 23, 1836, in Ohio and subsequently served a short mission. He lived for a time in Far West, Missouri, but was forced to leave because of persecution. In Nauvoo he was called to the high council (see D&C 124:132). In July 1843 he participated in the rescue of the Prophet Joseph Smith, who was being sought on illegal charges by the Missourians, and

served thereafter as one of his bodyguards. He was part of the westward migration, arriving in the Salt Lake Valley in 1853. He settled in Ogden and served again as a member of the high council. Dunbar died on March 11, 1856.

THE WOMAN AND THE UNJUST JUDGE

The woman in the parable given by the Lord in section 101 is a figurative representation of the Saints of the Restoration as they sought for redress in the face of daunting suffering and persecution.

WOODRUFF, WILFORD

Wilford was born on March 1, 1807, at Farmington, Hartford County, Connecticut. A meditative and religiously inclined individual, Wilford learned of the Church in 1833 and was baptized on December 31 of that same year. He journeyed to Kirtland to meet the Prophet Joseph in April 1834 and directly joined Zion's Camp. After serving a mission to the southern states, he returned to Kirtland, and thence journeyed to the eastern states to continue his missionary labors. While active in this service he learned of his calling to the Quorum of the Twelve Apostles (D&C 118:6) and was ordained to that position on April 26, 1839, at the Far West temple site. This position was confirmed in the revelation given on January 19, 1841 (see D&C 124:129). He next served a mission in England where he brought more than 1,800 souls into the Church. Thereafter he served another mission to the eastern states, during which time the Martyrdom took place. Following a second productive mission to Great Britain, Wilford returned to America, spending his time in devoted service to the

Church throughout the years of the exodus (for which he was appointed to organize a company of Saints—D&C 136:13) and the trials and tribulation endured by the Saints as they created a new environment in the Rocky Mountains.

Following the death of John Taylor, Wilford Woodruff became the fourth President of the Church. The "Manifesto" (Official Declaration—1) issued by Wilford Woodruff with the date of September 24, 1890, and sustained unanimously by the Church at the general conference on October 6, 1890, proclaims the cessation of the practice of plural marriage in the Church in compliance with the laws of the land. Wilford Woodruff passed away on September 2, 1898. He was among the elect leaders viewed by President Joseph F. Smith in his vision of the work being carried on in the spirit realm (D&C 138:53).

Throughout his days of service in the Kingdom of God he was known as "Wilford the Faithful." This title is authenticated by the record of his accomplishments:

From the year 1834 to the close of 1895 he traveled 172,369 miles, held 7,555 meetings, attended 75 semi-annual conferences and 344 quarterly conferences; preached 3,526 discourses; established 77 preaching places in the missionary field; organized 51 branches of the Church; received 18,977 letters; wrote 11,519 letters; assisted in the confirmation into the Church of 8,952 persons, and in addition to his work in the St. George temple, labored 603 days in the Endowment House in Salt Lake City. He traveled through England, Scotland, Wales, six islands of the sea, and twenty-three States and five Territories of the United States. (*LDSBE* 1:26)

Wilford Woodruff

YOUNG, BRIGHAM (SEE ALSO KIMBALL, HEBER C.)

Brigham was born on June 1, 1801, at Whittingham, Windham County, Vermont. After his conversion, he embarked on a career of service in the Kingdom of God that was to continue unabated until his dying day. He was ordained a member of the Quorum of the Twelve Apostles on February 14, 1835, and served as president of that Quorum (see D&C 124:127–28). On July 9, 1841, the Prophet Joseph Smith received a revelation commending him for his labors:

> Dear and well-beloved brother, Brigham Young, verily thus saith the Lord unto you: My servant Brigham, it is no more required at your hand to leave your family as in times past, for your offering is acceptable to me.
>
> I have seen your labor and toil in journeyings for my name.
>
> I therefore command you to send my word abroad, and take especial care of your family from this time,

henceforth and forever. Amen. (D&C 126:1–3)

Following the Martyrdom of the Prophet Joseph Smith, Brigham Young applied the keys of

Brigham Young

the priesthood vested in the Quorum of the Twelve and moved the Kingdom forward. Section 136, given through Brigham Young on January 14, 1847, provided the inspired framework for the exodus to the Rocky Mountains. Brigham Young was sustained as Prophet and President of the Church in December 1847. He passed away on August 29, 1877, in Salt Lake City. He was among the elect leaders viewed by President Joseph F. Smith in his vision of the work of salvation being carried on in the spirit realm.

YOUNG, JOSEPH

Joseph, older brother of Brigham Young, was born on April 7, 1797, at Hopkinton, Middlesex County, Massachusetts. As a young man with a spiritual disposition, Joseph went on a quest to find the truth—and found it, in the form of the Book of Mormon. He was baptized on April 6, 1832, and ordained an elder soon thereafter. By 1834 he was living in Kirtland, where he responded to the call to join Zion's Camp. In 1835 the Prophet Joseph Smith advised him that he was to serve as one of the Presidents of the Seventy—something that indeed took place (see D&C 124:138–39). For the remainder of his life, he occupied that position. During the Missouri years, he and his family endured the adversity heaped upon the Saints by the mobs. He later settled in Nauvoo where he supported his family as a painter and glazier. By 1846 he and his family had fled their home once more because of persecution. In 1850 they made the trek to the Salt Lake Valley, where Joseph rendered great service in the Kingdom of God, including serving a mission in the British Isles. He passed away on July 16, 1881, having never left the straight and narrow pathway of truth.

Joseph Young

Zion

As an appellation referring to a group of people, the word *Zion* is used frequently in the Doctrine and Covenants and is defined in the following passage: "Therefore, verily, thus saith the Lord, let Zion rejoice, for this is Zion—THE PURE IN HEART; therefore, let Zion rejoice, while all the wicked shall mourn" (D&C 97:21). The ultimate design of the Lord is plainly manifest through the voice of the His latter-day prophet: "For I will raise up unto myself a pure people, that will serve me in righteousness" (D&C 100:16). Upon the pure people, or Zion, the Lord bestows marvelous blessings:

> For, behold, I say unto you that Zion shall flourish, and the glory of the Lord shall be upon her; And she shall be an ensign unto the people, and there shall come unto her out of every nation under heaven. And the day shall come when the nations of the earth shall tremble because of her, and shall fear because of her terrible ones. The Lord hath spoken it. Amen. (D&C 64:41–43)

The Saints are to cultivate, through faith and sacrifice, the nature and qualities of a Zion people by following "the principles of the law of the celestial kingdom" (D&C 105:5). Only those who have overcome sin through the Atonement of the Savior can be citizens of the city of Zion and heirs to the riches of eternity: "But no man is possessor of all things except he be purified and cleansed from all sin" (D&C 50:28). Similarly, Zion consists of a unified people like the people of Enoch: "And the Lord called his people ZION, because they were of one heart and one mind, and dwelt in righteousness; and there was no poor among them" (Moses 7:18). What are the implications of being such a people? "And Enoch and all his people walked with God, and he dwelt in the midst of Zion; and it came to pass that Zion was not, for God received it up into his own bosom; and from thence went forth the saying, ZION IS FLED" (Moses 7:69).

The Saints of the Restoration—for all their travail and struggles, triumphs and accomplishments—fell short of the commission to be a Zion people because "they were slow to hearken unto the voice of the Lord their God (D&C 101:7). Nevertheless, the Lord was "filled with compassion towards them" and promised not to "utterly cast them off; and in the day of wrath [He] will remember mercy" (D&C 101:9).

The term Zion draws the mind heavenward toward God, the spirit inward toward a state of worthiness and gratitude, the heart outward in service toward others, and the feet onward toward a "place of refuge, and for a covert from storm and rain" (Isa. 4:6). Zion is a place, an institution, a state of mind, a noble destination, a people, a vision of perfection, an abode of God, an encapsulating summary of everything that is "honest, true, chaste, benevolent, virtuous . . . lovely, or of good report or praiseworthy" (A of F 1:13).

Zion is not a utopia beyond mortal access: it is a reality that has already been manifested at times upon the earth among mortals who have exhibited an exemplary level of peace, unity, and spiritual attainment and thus evoked the highest blessings of the Father. The dispensation of the fulness of times provides the unique framework for the unfolding of a Zion people and a Zion city in the latter days. It is the will of the Lord that such an establishment be forthcoming. It is a glorious destiny proffered the Saints of God to be enlisted in such a work.

ZORAMITES

The Zoramites (see D&C 3:17) were descendants of Zoram, servant of Laban (the keeper of the brass plates obtained by Nephi). Zoram was persuaded to join the circle of Lehi and journey to the Promised Land, where he married the oldest daughter of Ishmael (1 Ne. 16:7). The Zoramites constituted one of the divisions of the Nephite people:

> Now the people which were not Lamanites were Nephites; nevertheless, they were called Nephites, Jacobites, Josephites, Zoramites, Lamanites, Lemuelites, and Ishmaelites.
>
> But I, Jacob, shall not hereafter distinguish them by these names, but I shall call them Lamanites that seek to destroy the people of Nephi, and those who are friendly to Nephi I shall call Nephites, or the people of Nephi, according to the reigns of the kings. (Jacob 1:13–14; compare 4 Ne. 1:36–37; Morm. 1:8)

CHRONOLOGY OF THE RESTORATION AND THE DOCTRINE AND COVENANTS

Year	Date	Event
1805	December 23	Birth of Joseph Smith Jr. (hereafter Joseph Smith) in Sharon, Windsor County, Vermont.
1816	[unknown]	Joseph Smith moves with his family to Palmyra, New York.
ca. 1818–1819	[unknown]	Joseph Smith moves with his family to a log home near Palmyra, New York.
1820	early spring	First Vision occurs in the Sacred Grove near the Smith home.
1823	September 21–22	Initial visit to Joseph Smith by the angel Moroni; subsequent visits occur in 1824, 1825, and 1826. Section 2, concerning the coming of Elijah, is received the evening of September 21.
1827	January 18	Joseph Smith and Emma Hale married by a justice of the peace in South Bainbridge, New York.
1827	September 22	Joseph Smith obtains the gold plates from the angel Moroni.
1827	December	Because of persecution, Joseph Smith moves to Harmony, Pennsylvania, and soon begins to translate the Book of Mormon.
1828	February	Martin Harris shows scholars Charles Anthon and Samuel T. Mitchill in New York City a copy of some of the characters from the gold plates.
1828	June–July	Martin Harris loses the translation of the first 116 pages of the Book of Mormon; Joseph Smith receives severe censure from the Lord. Section 3 is received in July at Harmony, Pennsylvania.
1828	Summer	Section 10, concerning the lost 116 pages, is received at Harmony, Pennsylvania.

Year	Date	Event
1829	February	Section 4, great missionary revelation, is received at Harmony, Pennsylvania, on behalf of Joseph Smith Sr.
1829	March	Section 5 is received on behalf of Martin Harris at Harmony, Pennsylvania.
1829	April	Sections 6–9 are received at Harmony, Pennsylvania. Sections 6, 8, and 9 to Oliver Cowdery concern personal revelation.
1829	April 5	Oliver Cowdery arrives in Harmony to meet the Prophet Joseph Smith.
1829	April 7	Translation of the Book of Mormon resumes.
1829	May 15	Restoration of the Aaronic Priesthood under the hands of John the Baptist along the banks of the Susquehanna River, near Harmony, Pennsylvania (section 13). Joseph Smith and Oliver Cowdery baptize one another. Sections 11, 12 received in May.
1829	Late May (perhaps June)	Restoration of the Melchizedek Priesthood under the hands of Peter, James, and John (see D&C 27:12).
1829	June	Sections 14–18 received in Fayette, New York. Section 17 concerns the three witnesses of the Book of Mormon. Section 18 contains the passage concerning the joy of bringing souls to Christ (verses 13–16).
1829	June	Translation of the Book of Mormon completed.
1829	June	The three witnesses—Oliver Cowdery, David Whitmer, and Martin Harris—see the plates and the angel Moroni; the Eight Witnesses—four Whitmers (Christian, Jacob, Peter Jr., and John), three Smiths (Joseph Sr., Hyrum, and Samuel H.), plus Hiram Page—see and handle the plates.
1830	March	Section 19, containing precious statements of the Lord concerning His suffering during the Atonement, received on behalf of Martin Harris.
1830	March 26	First copies of the published Book of Mormon released at the Egbert B. Grandin bookstore in Palmyra.

Year	Date	Event
1830	April 6	The Church is formally organized at the home of Peter Whitmer Sr. in Fayette, New York (see D&C 20:1). Section 21, calling Joseph Smith to be "a seer, a translator, a prophet, and apostle of Jesus Christ, and elder of the church" (verse 1) is received on April 6 in Fayette. Section 20, about the operation of the priesthood, is given in April in or near Fayette.
1830	April	Sections 22 and 23 received in Manchester, New York.
1830	April 11	Five days after the organization of the Church in Fayette, New York, Oliver Cowdery preaches "the first public discourse" (HC 1:81). This is in harmony with a revelation to Joseph Smith on April 6, that Oliver Cowdery is to be "the first preacher of this church" (D&C 21:12).
1830	June	Inspired translation of the Bible by the Prophet Joseph Smith commences.
1830	June 9	First conference of the Church convened in Fayette, New York.
1830	July	Sections 24–26 received at Harmony, Pennsylvania. Section 25 is given for Emma Smith, "an elect lady" (verse 3), who is to comfort her husband and prepare a selection of hymns.
1830	August	Section 27, concerning the sacrament emblems and the events of the Restoration (such as the restoration of the Melchizedek Priesthood), received at Harmony, Pennsylvania.
1830	September	Joseph Smith moves from Harmony, Pennsylvania, to Fayette, New York.
1830	September	Sections 28–31 received at Fayette, New York. Missionary work among the Lamanites to commence (see D&C 28:8; 30:5–6).
1830	October	Missionaries sent among Lamanites on the frontier west of Missouri. Sections 32, 33 received at Fayette, New York.
1830	December	Sections 35–37 received at Fayette, New York; the Lord directs the Saints to gather to Ohio.
1831	January	Sections 38–40 received in Fayette, New York.
1831	early February	Joseph Smith arrives in Kirtland, Ohio.

Year	Date	Event
1831	February	Sections 41–44 received in Kirtland, Ohio. Section 42 constitutes "the law of the church."
1831	March	Sections 45–49 received. Section 46 outlines gifts of the Spirit.
1831	May	Section 50, received in Kirtland, Ohio, indicates that the gospel is to be taught by the Spirit to edify both teachers and learners.
1831	May	Section 51 is received in Thompson, Ohio.
1831	June	Sections 52–56 received in Kirtland, Ohio. First ordinations to office of high priest made at this time (section 52, given June 7).
1831	July 20	In Independence, Missouri, the Prophet Joseph receives section 57, identifying that city as the center place of Zion.
1831	August 1	Section 58 received in Jackson County, Missouri.
1831	August 2	Jackson County, Missouri, dedicated as the land of Zion.
1831	August 3	The Prophet Joseph dedicates the temple site in Independence.
1831	August 4	First conference of the Church held in "Zion" (Missouri) at the home of Joshua Lewis, in Kaw Township.
1831	August 7	Section 59 received in Jackson County, Missouri, concerning the Sabbath Day and the law of the fast.
1831	August 8	Section 60 received in Jackson County, Missouri.
1831	August 12	Section 61 received near the Missouri River in Missouri.
1831	August 13	Section 62 received near the Missouri River in Missouri. Elders are assured their testimonies are "recorded in heaven for the angels to look upon" (verse 3).
1831	late August	Section 63 received in Kirtland, Ohio, concerning the gathering of the Saints.
1831	September 11	Section 64 received in Kirtland, Ohio, with the counsel to "be not weary in well-doing, for ye are laying the foundation of a great work. And out of small things proceedeth that which is great" (verse 33).

Year	Date	Event
1831	October	Section 65, in the form of a prayer, given in Hiram, Ohio.
1831	October 25	Section 66 received in Orange, Ohio.
1831	November	Sections 67–69 received in Hiram, Ohio. Section 68 promises that "whatsoever they [the elders] shall speak when moved upon by the Holy Ghost shall be scripture, shall be the . . . word of the Lord . . . and the power of God unto salvation" (verse 4).
1831	November 1	Section 1—the Lord's Preface—received in Hiram, Ohio.
1831	November 3	Section 133 given in Hiram, Ohio, serving originally as the appendix to the Doctrine and Covenants.
1831	November 12	Section 70 received in Kirtland, Ohio, concerning plans to publish "The Book of Commandments" (the early version of the Doctrine and Covenants).
1831	December 1	Section 71 received in Hiram, Ohio, directing the Prophet Joseph Smith to set aside the work of translating the Bible and go with Sidney Rigdon to preach in the surrounding areas to offset the influence of anti-Mormon literature.
1831	December 4	Section 72 received in Kirtland, Ohio, calling Newel K. Whitney as bishop.
1832	January	Sections 73, 74 received at Hiram, Ohio.
1832	January 25	Section 75 received in Amherst, Ohio, concerning sustaining Joseph Smith as the President of the High Priesthood.
1832	February 16	Section 76, received in Hiram, Ohio, recounts the visions of glory as experienced by Joseph Smith and Sidney Rigdon.
1832	March	Sections 77–81 received in Hiram, Ohio.
1832	March 8	First Presidency organized, with Joseph Smith as President and Sidney Rigdon and Jesse Gause (soon to be replaced by Frederick G. Williams) as counselors.
1832	March 24	Joseph dragged from the John Johnson home in Hiram, Ohio, by a mob and is brutally beaten, tarred, and feathered. Next day (Sunday) he gives a sermon on forgiveness.

Year	Date	Event
1832	April 14	Brigham Young, "the Lion of the Lord" (HC 7:435), baptized after two years of intensive study and prayer centered on the Book of Mormon.
1832	April 26	Section 82 received in Jackson County, Missouri.
1832	April 30	Section 83 received in Jackson County, Missouri.
1832	August	Section 99 received in Hiram, Ohio.
1832	September 22–23	Section 84, one of the great revelations on the priesthood, received at Kirtland, Ohio.
1832	November 27	Section 85 received at Kirtland, Ohio.
1832	December 6	Section 86, including an explanation of the parable of the wheat and the tares, received at Kirtland, Ohio.
1832	December 25	Section 87, the prophecy on the Civil, given through the Prophet Joseph Smith at Kirtland, Ohio.
1832	December 27–28, 1832, and January 3, 1833	Prophet Joseph directed to build a temple in Kirtland, Ohio (D&C 88:119–120). Section 88 designated by the Prophet as the "olive leaf . . . plucked from the Tree of Paradise, the Lord's message of peace to us."
1833	January	School of the Prophets begins.
1833	January 23	Joseph the Prophet administers the ordinance of the washing of feet for the first time in this dispensation (D&C 88:74–75) to members of the School of the Prophets in the nearly completed Kirtland Temple.
1833	February 27	Section 89, the Word of Wisdom, received at Kirtland, Ohio.
1833	March 8	Section 90, a further step in the organization of the First Presidency, received in Kirtland, Ohio.
1833	March 9	Section 91, concerning the Apocrypha, received at Kirtland, Ohio.
1833	March 15	Section 92 received in Kirtland, Ohio.
1833	May 6	Sections 93, 94 received at Kirtland, Ohio. Section 94 concerns the Savior and the nature of glory and intelligence
1833	June 1	Section 95 received at Kirtland, Ohio.

Year	Date	Event
1833	June 4	Section 96 received at Kirtland, Ohio.
1833	July 2	Initial work on the inspired translation of the Bible completed.
1833	July 20	Mob destroys the W. W. Phelps press in Independence, on which the "Book of Commandments" is being printed. A few copies of the printed pages are recovered.
1833	July 23	Cornerstones of the Kirtland Temple laid.
1833	August 2	Section 97 received at Kirtland, Ohio.
1833	August 6	Section 98, concerning the persecution in Missouri, received at Kirtland, Ohio.
1833	October 12	A great missionary revelation (section 100) received while Joseph Smith and Sidney Rigdon are proselyting in New York State and Canada (see HC 1:419–421: "For it shall be given you in the very hour, yea, in the very moment, what ye shall say" (verse 6).
1833	December 16	Section 101, in response to the acute suffering of the Saints in Missouri, received at Kirtland, Ohio.
1833	December 18	Joseph Smith Sr. ordained Patriarch to the Church.
1834	February 17	First high council of the Church organized in Kirtland, Ohio; minutes of this event constitute section 102.
1834	February 24	Section 103, concerning establishment of Zion and organization of Zion's Camp, received in Kirtland, Ohio.
1834	April 23	Section 104, concerning the United Order, received at Kirtland, Ohio.
1834	May 3, 1834	Name of the Church changed from the Church of Christ to The Church of Latter Day Saints (compare April 26, 1838).
1834	May–July	Zion's Camp organized and sent to Missouri to aid the beleaguered Saints.
1834	June 22	Section 105 received at Fishing River, Missouri, during Zion's Camp excursion.
1834	November 25	Section 106 received at Kirtland, Ohio.

Year	Date	Event
1834	December 5	Prophet Joseph Smith ordains Oliver Cowdery an Assistant President of the Church.
1835	February 14–15	Quorum of the Twelve Apostles is organized and all but three members, who were away on missions, ordained.
1835	February 28	Quorum of the Seventy organized.
1835	March 28	Section 107, concerning the priesthood, received at Kirtland, Ohio (some passages received as early as November 1831).
1835	July	Egyptian papyri are obtained (containing material from the hand of Abraham).
1835	August 17	Section 134, declaration of beliefs concerning governments and laws (drafted by Oliver Cowdery), adopted at a general assembly of the Church in Kirtland, Ohio.
1835	September	First edition of the Doctrine and Covenants printed.
1835	November	Hymnal prepared by Emma Smith published.
1835	December 26	Section 108 received in Kirtland, Ohio.
1835	January 21	Section 137, Joseph Smith's vision of the celestial realm, including doctrine of salvation for the dead, received in the Kirtland Temple.
1836	March 27	Joseph Smith dedicates Kirtland Temple (see D&C 109 for the dedicatory prayer).
1836	April 3	Jesus, Moses, Elias, and Elijah appear to Joseph Smith and Oliver Cowdery in the Kirtland Temple; important priesthood keys restored (see section 110).
1836	August 6	Section 111, concerning relieving indebtedness of the Church, received in Salem, Massachusetts.
1837	June	First missionaries to be sent beyond U.S. dispatched to Canada and England.
1837	July 23	Heber C. Kimball, Orson Hyde, and other missionaries called to Great Britain give first sermons in that land and begin gathering receptive and humble from among the people (HC 2:498–499). Joseph Smith also receives section 112 on behalf of Thomas B. Marsh, President of the Quorum of Twelve Apostles.

Year	Date	Event
1837	July 30	George D. Watt becomes first convert baptized in England.
1838	January 12	Prophet Joseph Smith leaves for Far West, Missouri, due to mob violence and persecution in Kirtland.
1838	March 14	Church headquarters established in Far West.
1838	March	Section 113, concerning questions about the writings of Isaiah, given through Joseph Smith at or near Far West, Missouri.
1838	April 17	Section 114 received at Far West, Missouri.
1838	April 26	Section 115, received at Far West, Missouri, changes name of Church permanently to The Church of Jesus Christ of Latter-day Saints.
1838	April 27	Joseph Smith commences writing history of the Church.
1838	May 19	Section 116, concerning Adam-ondi-Ahman, received at Spring Hill, Daviess County, Missouri.
1838	July 6	"Kirtland Camp" of some 529 Saints commences 870-mile trek from Kirtland to Far West and on to Adam-ondi-Ahman, Missouri. Organized and directed by seventies in response to commandment of the Lord to remove to Zion (D&C 58:56).
1838	July 8	Sections 117–120 received at Far West, Missouri. Saints are to pay "one-tenth of all their interest annually" (D&C 119:4).
1838	October 28	Missouri governor Lilburn W. Boggs issues extermination order against the Mormons.
1838–1839	Winter–Spring	Saints flee Missouri and seek refuge in Illinois.
1838	October 30	Mob of some 240 armed men assaults 30 or so families residing at, or passing through, village of Haun's Mill, killing at least 17 (including two young boys) and wounding 13 (HC 3:182–188).
1838	November 30–December 1	Joseph Smith and other associates imprisoned in Liberty Jail, Missouri.

Year	Date	Event
1839	March 20	Joseph writes to the Saints from Liberty Jail; portions of epistle become sections 121–123. Section 121 addresses principles upon which the priesthood is to operate. The Lord comforts Joseph Smith in his tribulations in section 122: "The Son of Man hath descended below them all. Art thou greater than he?" (verse 8).
1839	mid-April	Joseph Smith is allowed by his guards to escape from custody.
1839	April 20	"The last of the Saints left Far West" (HC 3:326). This journal entry of the Prophet Joseph Smith (HC 3:326) closes that part of the Missouri chapter wherein the Saints were prevented from carrying out the Lord's commandment to build a community and temple at Far West (see D&C 115:11–17).
1839	April 22	Joseph Smith rejoins his family in Quincy, Illinois.
1839	May 10	Joseph Smith and his family move into a log home in Commerce, Illinois (later called Nauvoo).
1839	July 22	"A day of God's power" (CHFT, p. 218). Malaria-bearing mosquitoes from swamplands infect Saints at new gathering place of Nauvoo along the banks of the Mississippi River. Many contract the disease, including the Prophet, but he heals many through administration of priesthood blessings.
1839	November 29	Joseph Smith visits President Martin Van Buren in Washington, D.C., to seek redress on behalf of the embattled Saints.
1840	August 15	Doctrine of baptism for the dead announced by the Prophet Joseph Smith during a funeral in Nauvoo. The first baptism for the dead in this dispensation performed that day in the Mississippi River (see CHFT, p. 251).
1840	September	First Presidency announces time has come to build a temple in Nauvoo.
1841	January 19	Lord reveals baptism for the dead to be performed only in a temple (D&C 124:30; given at Nauvoo, Illinois). Saints commanded to build a temple in Nauvoo including baptismal font. Section 124, received this day, reveals organization of the Church to that point. Hyrum Smith called as Patriarch to the Church (verses 91–96).

Year	Date	Event
1841	January 30	Joseph Smith recorded: "At a special conference of the Church of Jesus Christ of Latter-day Saints, held at Nauvoo pursuant to public notice, I was unanimously elected sole Trustee-in-Trust for the Church" (HC 4:286).
1841	March	Section 125 received at Nauvoo, Illinois.
1841	April 6	Cornerstones laid for the Nauvoo Temple.
1841	July 9	Section 126 received at Nauvoo, Illinois. Brigham Young to work closer to home and care for his family.
1841	October 24	Orson Hyde dedicates the Holy Land from the Mount of Olives (see HC 4:456).
1841	November 8	Baptismal font of Nauvoo Temple dedicated by Brigham Young.
1841	November 21	First baptisms for the dead performed in dedicated font of Nauvoo Temple, which is still not completed.
1841	November 28	Prophet Joseph Smith spends day in dialogue with the Twelve at home of Brigham Young. He "told the brethren that the Book of Mormon was the most correct of any book on earth, and the keystone of our religion, and a man would get nearer to God by abiding by its precepts, than by any other book" (HC 4:461).
1842	March 1	Prophet Joseph Smith publishes Wentworth Letter (containing the Articles of Faith) in Times and Seasons.
1842	March, May	Book of Abraham published in Times and Seasons.
1842	March 17	Joseph Smith organizes Female Relief Society of Nauvoo with Emma Smith as president.
1842	May 4	Prophet Joseph Smith administers first endowment ordinances in upper room of Red Brick Store in Nauvoo.
1842	May 19	Joseph Smith elected mayor of Nauvoo.
1842	September	Sections 127 (September 1) and 128 (September 6) comprise two epistles sent to the Church by Joseph Smith concerning the doctrine of baptism for the dead.

Year	Date	Event
1842	December 20	Prophet Joseph Smith records in his journal: "Elder Lorenzo D. Barnes died this morning at a quarter past three o'clock, at Bradford England. He is the first Elder who has fallen in a foreign land in these last days" (HC 5:207).
1843	February 9	Section 129, instructions concerning ministering angels and spirits, given by Joseph Smith at Nauvoo, Illinois.
1843	April 2	Section 130, instructions and observations on various doctrines and principles, given by the Prophet Joseph Smith at Ramus, Illinois. Included is the dictum: "There is a law, irrevocably decreed in heaven before the foundations of this world, upon which all blessings are predicated— And when we obtain any blessing from God, it is by obedience to that law upon which it is predicated" (verses 20–21).
1843	May 16–17	Section 131, observations on several important doctrinal matters (including celestial marriage), given by the Prophet Joseph Smith at Ramus, Illinois.
1843	July 12	Prophet Joseph Smith dictates to his scribe, William Clayton, revelation (section 132) on new and everlasting covenant (including the covenant of eternal marriage) likely first revealed to the Prophet in 1831 while working on revision of Old Testament (see HC 5:xxix–xlvi; 500–507).
1844	January 29	Joseph Smith announces candidacy for presidency of the U.S.
1844	March	Joseph Smith meets with the Twelve Apostles and confirms process of succession; Twelve have keys, authority, and ordinances to assume leadership at death of the Prophet.
1844	May 12	Prophet Joseph Smith preaches sermon in Nauvoo and states: "Every man who has a calling to minister to the inhabitants of the world was ordained to that very purpose in the Grand Counsel of heaven before the world was. I suppose that I was ordained to this very office in that Grand Council" (HC 6:364–365).
1844	June 27	Joseph and Hyrum martyred at the jail in Carthage, Illinois. At Nauvoo, Illinois, John Taylor writes inspired statement concerning this event, now included as section 135.
1844	June 29	Joseph and Hyrum buried at Nauvoo, Illinois.

Year	Date	Event
1847	January 14	D&C Section 136 given through President Brigham Young at Winter Quarters near Council Bluffs, Iowa, as "the word and will of the Lord concerning the Camp of Israel in their journeyings to the West" (verse 1).
1847	July 24	Just over three years after the Martyrdom, Brigham Young and company of pioneers reach the Salt Lake Valley, where he says, "It is enough. This is the right place. Drive on" (CHFT, p. 333).
1890	September 24	Manifesto on the suspension of the practice of plural marriage (Official Declaration—1) given by President Wilford Woodruff; sustained by the Church on October 6, 1890.
1918	October 3	Section 138, vision to President Joseph F. Smith concerning the work of salvation in the spirit world, received in Salt Lake City, Utah; accepted on October 31, 1918, by counselors in First Presidency, Council of the Twelve, and Patriarch to the Church.
1978	June 8	Official Declaration—2, that the priesthood, including all temple blessings, is available to all worthy priesthood brethren, announced in Salt Lake City by President Spencer W. Kimball; sustained by the Church on September 30, 1978.

CONTEMPORARIES OF JOSEPH SMITH
REFERENCED IN THE DOCTRINE AND COVENANTS
AND THE RECORD OF THEIR FAITHFULNESS IN THE CHURCH

Name	Infant	Weak Conversion or little info.	Moderately Supportive	Strong and valiant	Fell away then returned	Fell away and did not return	Fell away and fought the Church
1. Major N. Ashley						X	
2. Almon Babbitt					X		
3. Jesse Baker				X			
4. Wheeler Baldwin						X	
5. Heman Basset						X	
6. John C. Bennett							X
7. Ezra T. Benson				X			
8. Samuel Bent				X			
9. Titus Billings				X			
10. Ezra Booth							X
11. John F. Boynton						X	
12. Seymour Brunson				X			
13. Stephen Burnett						X	
14. Philip Burroughs		X					
15. Josiah Butterfield						X	
16. Reynolds Cahoon				X			
17. Gideon Carter				X			
18. Jared Carter						X	
19. John S. Carter				X			
20. Simeon Carter				X			
21. William Carter		X					
22. Joseph Coe						X	
23. Zebedee Coltrin				X			
24. Leman Copley						X	
25. John Corrill						X	
26. James Covill		X					
27. Oliver Cowdery					X		
28. Warren A. Cowdery						X	
29. Alpheus Cutler						X	
30. Amos Davies			X				
31. Asa Dodds		X					
32. David Dort				X			
33. Ruggles Eames						X	
34. James Foster			X				
35. Robert D. Foster							X
36. Edson Fuller						X	
37. David Fullmer			X				
38. Isaac Galland						X	

Name	Infant	Weak Conversion or little info.	Moderately Supportive	Strong and valiant	Fell away then returned	Fell away and did not return	Fell away and fought the Church
39. Jesse Gause						X	
40. Algernon Sidney Gilbert				X			
41. John Gould				X			
42. Oliver Granger				X			
43. Selah J. Griffin						X	
44. Thomas Grover				X			
45. Levi W. Hancock				X			
46. Solomon Hancock				X			
47. Emer Harris				X			
48. George W. Harris			X				
49. Martin Harris					X		
50. Peter Haws						X	
51. Henry Herriman				X			
52. John A. Hicks							X
53. Elias Higbee				X			
54. Solomon Humphrey				X			
55. William Huntington				X			
56. Orson Hyde					X		
57. George James						X	
58. Vienna Jaques				X			
59. Aaron Johnson				X			
60. John Johnson						X	
61. Luke S. Johnson					X		
62. Lyman E. Johnson						X	
63. Heber C. Kimball				X			
64. Joseph Knight Sr.				X			
65. Newel Knight				X			
66. Vinson Knight				X			
67. William Law							X
68. Amasa Lyman						X	
69. William Marks						X	
70. Thomas B. Marsh					X		
71. William E. McLellin							X
72. Daniel Miles				X			
73. George Miller						X	
74. Isaac Morley				X			
75. John Murdock				X			
76. Noah Packard				X			
77. Hiram Page						X	
78. John E. Page						X	
79. Edward Partridge				X			
80. David W. Patten				X			
81. Ziba Peterson						X	
82. William W. Phelps					X		
83. Orson Pratt					X		

Name	Infant	Weak Conversion or little info.	Moderately Supportive	Strong and valiant	Fell away then returned	Fell away and did not return	Fell away and fought the Church
84. Parley P. Pratt				X			
85. Zera Pulsipher				X			
86. Charles C. Rich				X			
87. Willard Richards				X			
88. Sidney Rigdon						X	
89. Burr Riggs						X	
90. Samuel Rolfe				X			
91. Shadrach Roundy				X			
92. Simonds Ryder							X
93. Jacob Scott						X	
94. Lyman Sherman				X			
95. Henry G. Sherwood						X	
96. Alvin Smith				X			
97. Don C. Smith				X			
98. Eden Smith					X		
99. Emma Smith				X			
100. George A. Smith				X			
101. Hyrum Smith				X			
102. John Smith				X			
103. Joseph Smith III	X						
104. Joseph F. Smith	X						
105. Joseph Smith Sr.				X			
106. Lucy Mack Smith				X			
107. Samuel H. Smith				X			
108. Sylvester Smith						X	
109. William Smith						X	
110. John Snider				X			
111. Erastus Snow				X			
112. Lorenzo Snow				X			
113. Daniel Stanton				X			
114. Northrop Sweet						X	
115. John Taylor				X			
116. Ezra Thayre						X	
117. Robert B. Thompson				X			
118. Joseph Wakefield							X
119. Micah B. Welton				X			
120. Harvey Whitlock						X	
121. David Whitmer						X	
122. John Whitmer						X	
123. Peter Whitmer Jr.				X			
124. Peter Whitmer Sr.						X	
125. Newel K. Whitney				X			
126. Lyman Wight						X	
127. Frederick G. Williams					X		
128. Samuel Williams				X			

Name	Infant	Weak Conversion or little info.	Moderately Supportive	Strong and valiant	Fell away then returned	Fell away and did not return	Fell away and fought the Church
129. Calves Wilson		X					
130. Dunbar Wilson				X			
131. Wilford Woodruff				X			
132. Brigham Young				X			
133. Joseph Young				X			
Totals	2 (1.5%)	5 (3.75%)	4 (3%)	64 (48.1%)	10 (7.5%)	40 (30%)	8 (6%)
Faithful vs. Unfaithful Adults	(N/A)	83 (63.3% of adults)				48 (36.7% of adults)*	

*Thus around one-third of these adults rebelled and were separated from the mainstream of the restored Church. Does this sound familiar? (See D&C 29:36.)

Art Credits

Page 1   *Moses and Aaron in the Court of Pharaoh* © Robert T. Barrett. For more information visit www.robertbarrett.com.

Page 3   *Christ with Adam at Adam-ondi-Ahman* © Clark Kelley Price.

Page 4   *Joseph Smith in Front of Nauvoo Temple* © Dale Kilbourn.

Page 6   *John C. Bennett*. Courtesy of the Church Archives, The Church of Jesus Christ of Latter-day Saints.

Page 7   *Ezra T. Benson*. Courtesy of the Church Archives, The Church of Jesus Christ of Latter-day Saints.

Page 8   *Titus Billings*. Courtesy of the Church Archives, The Church of Jesus Christ of Latter-day Saints.

Page 9   *Lilburn W. Boggs*. Courtesy of the Church Archives, The Church of Jesus Christ of Latter-day Saints.

Page 10   *John F. Boynton*. Courtesy of the Church Archives, The Church of Jesus Christ of Latter-day Saints.

Page 12   *Reynolds Calhoun*. Courtesy of the Church Archives, The Church of Jesus Christ of Latter-day Saints.

Page 15   *Zebedee Coltrin*. Courtesy of the Church Archives, The Church of Jesus Christ of Latter-day Saints.

Page 17   *James Covill*. Courtesy of the Church Archives, The Church of Jesus Christ of Latter-day Saints.

Page 18   *Joseph Smith Baptizes Oliver Cowdery* by Del Parson © Intellectual Reserve, Inc.

Page 21   *Alpheus Cutler*. Courtesy of the Church Archives, The Church of Jesus Christ of Latter-day Saints.

Page 24   *Eight Witnesses Shown the Gold Plates* © Paul Mann.

Page 26   *City of Zion* by Del Parson © Intellectual Reserve, Inc.

Page 27   *Jacob Blessing Ephraim and Manasseh* © D. Keith Larsen.

Page 28   *Adam and Eve in the Garden* by Lowell Bruce Bennett © Intellectual Reserve, Inc.

Page 29   *The Prophet Ezekiel* by Lyle Beddes © Intellectual Reserve, Inc.